Shelter from the Machine

Shelter from the Machine

*Homesteaders in the
Age of Capitalism*

JASON G. STRANGE

UNIVERSITY OF
ILLINOIS PRESS
Urbana, Chicago, and Springfield

Library of Congress Cataloging-in-Publication Data
Names: Strange, Jason G., author.
Title: Shelter from the machine : Homesteaders in the
    age of capitalism / Jason G. Strange.
Description: Urbana : University of Illinois Press,
    [2020] | Includes bibliographical references and
    index.
Identifiers: LCCN 2019032949 (print) | LCCN
    2019032950 (ebook) | ISBN 9780252043031
    (cloth) | ISBN 9780252084898 (paperback) | ISBN
    9780252051890 (ebook)
Subjects: LCSH: Self-reliant living—Appalachian
    Region, Southern. | Self-reliant living—Kentucky.
    | Frontier and pioneer life—Appalachian Region,
    Southern. | Frontier and pioneer life—Kentucky.
    | Subsistence economy—Appalachian Region,
    Southern. | Subsistence economy—Kentucky. |
    Sociology, Rural—Appalachian Region, Southern. |
    Sociology, Rural—Kentucky. | Appalachian Region,
    Southern—Social conditions—21st century. |
    Kentucky—Social conditions—21st century. |
    United States—Rural conditions.
Classification: LCC HN79.A127 S77 2020 (print) | LCC
    HN79.A127 (ebook) | DDC 307.7209756/9—dc23
LC record available at https://lccn.loc.gov/2019032949
LC ebook record available at https://lccn.loc.gov/2019032950

To my parents, who gave the gift of books

Contents

Acknowledgments

The one person guaranteed to learn a ton from a book is the one who writes it. Partly that's because of writing's unique power to support learning and self-transformation—but it's also because the writing process requires so much feedback and support from other people. Acknowledgments abound with heartfelt thanks, and now I know why: it is both humbling and exhilarating when others read your words and suggest ways to make them more accurate, perceptive, and graceful.

Special thanks to those who provided wisdom and guidance the whole way through, or a hand up at crucial moments: James Engelhardt, George Strange, Julya Westfall, Chad Berry, and Dave Zurick. And to those who gifted my drafts with the benefit of their insight and skill: Nancy Sowers, Chris Green, Beth Feagan, Nancy Gift, Broughton Anderson, Mai Nguyen, Michelle Flannery, Amy Harmon, and Kent Gilbert. Steve Fisher and an anonymous reviewer gave the manuscript incredibly generous and helpful reads. The staff at the University of Illinois Press served as gentle, expert guides in a long and complicated process. Finn was an upbeat companion as I wrote and edited, often in different parts of the country in our VW van, and was usually the first to hear a newly finished chapter and offer his dad an encouraging pat on the back.

As the culmination of years of writing and research and thinking and living, this book could not exist without that web of mutual support that makes us human—friends and family, teachers and mentors. For me, that web includes, in addition to those already named, Debbie Barack, Isaac Bingham, Michael Burawoy, Alice Driver, Patrick and Mary Finn, Alejandro Guarin and Elisabeth Norcliffe, Tim Hensley and Jane Post, Michael Johns, Micah and Zuojay Johnson, Rebecca Lave and Sam DeSollar, Abe and Amanda Lentz, Seth Lunine, Meta Mendel-Reyes, Chris Niedt, Orowi Oliver and Peter Rigden, Jesse and Gina Otterson, Sue Roberts, Jean Perry, Naomi Schulz, Josh Strange, Michael Watts, Althea Webb, Tina West, and Craig Williams. I'm sure I'm forgetting someone important and dear, but only for a tired moment!

Berea College students in two fieldwork classes conducted and transcribed more than twenty archive-quality interviews with both country and bohemian homesteaders, which form part of the empirical foundation of this work. Thanks and props to Maryam Ahmed, Huda Al-Sammarraie, Lucas Bates, Duncan Blount, Dalton Brennan, Courtney Conyers, Kahndo Dolma, Mirline Duphresne, Jessica Elston, Anna Harrod, Dondlyn Jackson, Lakeya Jackson, Travis Jones, Erika Mamani, Barry Manley, Ruthnie Mathurin, Keyahdah Muhammad, Bradley Niederriter, Kody Noonan, Katrina Owens, Jazzmine Ramey, Darian Shakelford, Josiah Thomas, Shelby Wheeler, and Shawn Williams. Also, a shout-out to Terry Allebaugh for the wonderful series of interviews he conducted in Disputanta, Kentucky, in the 1970s.

Generous funding is crucial for research and scholarship, and I gratefully acknowledge the support of a Graduate Research Fellowship and a Doctoral Dissertation Research Improvement Grant, both from the National Science Foundation; the University of California's Labor and Employment Research Fund Dissertation Fellowship; UC Berkeley's Chancellor's Dissertation Year Fellowship; and, in so many ways, Berea College.

Last but certainly not least, deep gratitude to all the homesteaders who shared the stories of their fascinating lives. I had the honor and pleasure of trying to capture some of that wealth in words—but I didn't create it. This book is truly theirs.

Introduction
Heaven in a Flower

Even though this book is set in eastern Kentucky, I wrote much of it on my family's three acres in a remote part of northern California. Those three acres represent what I call a homestead—a piece of land on which people grow food and build a home and otherwise provide for some of their own needs—and it's beautiful. The Trinity River flows across the foot of the property, clear and cold and swift from the mountains. Bears leave their wide pawprints pressed into the sandy riverbank, beneath ten-foot-high thickets of Himalayan blackberry. Above the river's edge are fields full of crops—summer squash and heirloom tomatoes, red potatoes and sweet corn. There's a jungle-patch of brown turkey figs, and pomegranate trees covered in flowers shaped like scarlet ballerinas. There are things I can't grow at home in Kentucky, like apricots and peaches and Asian pears. My nine-year-old nephew wanders the farm like Mowgli, hair down his back, barefoot and shirtless, feeding himself on blueberries and swimming in the river. My mother stocks the pantry with jars of jam, salsa, and canned salmon from the smokehouse. WOOFers—young people who work on farms in exchange for room and board—travel from Poland and Chile and Quebec to learn about homesteading.

But there are problems. In one corner, a straw-bale house sits empty and abandoned. The bales were laid too close to the ground, and fungus threaded itself through the walls. Thousands of sweet cherries withered on the branch just as they ripened, victims of a new invasive insect. On shelves in the pantry, dozens of last autumn's butternut squashes molder, rat-chewed and wasted. The jars of smoked salmon are almost used up; a couple of years ago, an inexperienced visitor burned down the smoke-house. Yesterday, just as the temperature hit 103°, the controller on the irrigation pump shorted out, and the plants droop in the fields. My family works late, scrambling to bring in money to cover the mortgage. Then they get up early, scrambling again to keep the cherries sprayed and the chickens watered and the rats trapped. Their homestead is by no means a failure; it's a work of art, a living sculpture. At the same time, it's like a broken-winged bird that can't quite get off the ground. Is the labor worth it? Does it make economic sense? Why do they persist?

Questions about homesteading have been with me a long time. When I was nine, my parents bought fifty acres of wooded hills at the end of a gravel road near our hometown of Berea, in Appalachian Kentucky. They dreamed of building their own home, of gardening, of living in peace and beauty outside the system. They weren't alone. Together with the neighbors, we raised pigs and split firewood and sawed out lumber. We drove country roads to work parties and pottery firings and Harvest Moon celebrations where back-to-the-landers danced all night beside the bonfire. We played volleyball at potlucks, in pastures balanced on hillsides, where an errant ball would scatter the chickens and send a bare-chested hippie leaping down the mountain in pursuit, braid dancing behind him like a horsetail.

When I was sixteen, my mother moved us to the Yurok Reservation in northern California, on the banks of the Klamath River—forty miles downstream from where she lives now. She was a doctoral student in linguistics, doing fieldwork on the Yurok language and falling in love with a Yurok man. This was a continent away from eastern Kentucky, and yet it felt strangely familiar; again, I saw people engaged in serious self-provisioning activities. A traditional fisherman, my stepfather netted salmon, steelhead, and sturgeon in the river, gaffed lamprey eels at the river mouth, and collected mussels, clams, and candlefish on the beach. He gathered acorns for soup in inland oak groves, and yerba buena leaves for tea from grassy slopes overlooking the gray swells of the Pacific. He kept a smokehouse full of meat, split and stacked cords of firewood, and some summers—when the mood struck him—he grew vegetables on the hill beside his house. If his boat or truck needed work, he would often barter, trading jars of salmon for carburetors and spark plugs.

Over the following years, I encountered homesteading all across the United States. Like the Appalachian Mountains and the coastal ranges of California, the Ozarks in Arkansas are full of homesteaders, such as the family I met who lived in a house built into a cave mouth. Two twelve-volt truck batteries supplied their electricity; when one ran low, they swapped it for the other, freshly charged from being driven around in the truck. The blueberry barrens of Maine are dotted with owner-built homes and late-summer gardens. I've spent a week on a large Mennonite collective in Tennessee, where it's hard to tell you're not in the 1800s, and seen crops sprouting on the abandoned lots of hollowed-out Detroit neighborhoods. In the piedmont of North Carolina, between the ridges of the Rocky Mountains, baking in the New Mexican scrub—pretty much everywhere that land is not insanely expensive or forbiddingly arid, you'll find people growing zucchinis and building cabins, planting mulberries and milking goats, boiling off maple sap and digging ponds.

I kept wondering: why are so many people still engaged in subsistence? (That's the word scholars use when a family makes or grows or builds things for their own use.) With the rise of farmers' markets and slow food and Michael Pollan, there is increasing interest in the back-to-the-land movement, but for years I didn't see many books or articles or TV segments about the unexpected persistence of subsistence here in the modern United States. As a graduate student, I spent a semester in southern Mexico. With more than a dozen indigenous groups, scattered across an exotic landscape of cloud forest and desert canyons, the place crawls with academics; there are neighborhoods in Oaxaca where you can't light off a bottle rocket at a street festival without hitting an anthropologist. At the same time, here in the United States, homesteaders mostly carry on without such attention from researchers. They're part of a vast social movement, but one happening almost without notice.

I wondered also about a second question. In many places, homesteaders come mainly in two groups, which refer to each other, not always kindly, as "hicks" and "hippies." Why do they reliably form these two factions? They could, after all, form one big group. Or they could be subdivided infinitesimally, like church denominations, into many little groups. Is it just that "hicks" are from the country and "hippies" from the city? Nope. It's not that simple. This second question is intimately connected to the first: to figure out why people homestead, we have to know who they are.

In some areas, of course, there are other groups. In northern California, the First Peoples—Karuk, Yurok, Hoopa, and other tribes—constitute another subsistence-pursuing group, as do the Mennonites I visited in Tennessee and the African Americans in Detroit. But the hick-hippie distinction is ubiquitous.[1] I have encountered it all across the United States, in every location in which there is any hint of ongoing homesteading, from Vermont to northern California to the hill country of Texas where, a friend told me with a chuckle, "You're either buried with your crystals or your shotgun." In New England, it's cross-country skis versus snowmobiles. Hiking in the Big South Fork wilderness, in Tennessee, I came across this difference literally inscribed into the landscape: on the left was the John Muir Trail, for backpackers, and on the right, not five feet away, was a rutted dirt track, for four wheelers.

This second question—why two groups?—has an urgency. As we shall see, homesteaders are divided by a kind of cultural chasm, a fault line that cleaves not just rural farmsteads, but US society as a whole. It was apparent recently when I took a group of Berea College students to a Trump rally in Cincinnati: on one side of the street, liberal protestors chanted "This is what democracy looks like!" and on the other—held back by a phalanx of police and Secret Service agents—conservatives in red baseball caps tried to drown them out with "USA! USA! USA!" The air was tight with anger and defiance. I kept my students together in a pod, so we could scoot if violence erupted. We had to shout in each other's ears to be heard. On the walk back to the vans, a black student, distraught, squeezed his fists and blinked back tears. "I can't believe it," he said, giving voice to one view of this painful division. "Those are the people who lynched my ancestors."

* * *

One of my favorite classes to teach at Berea College is a freshman course called *Foundations of Peace and Social Justice.* Given that the biggest injustices in the world have to do with wealth and poverty, the first half of the semester is a tour of global history. The goal is to help students understand how we ended up with such a lopsided planet, where power and riches have been concentrated in certain places and stripped from others. On the first day of class, I'll pull a banana out of my backpack, peel it slowly, and start munching. Once the students look sufficiently puzzled, I'll ask, "Am I committing—right now, eating this banana—an act of injustice?"

The banana seems like such a small, simple object—just a few ounces of pulpy, yellow fruit. But it's not. If we could perceive the fullness of time and space, we would see that the banana is more flow than thing. To fully explain how that banana came to be, we would have to leave the thing itself behind, and follow the flow far upstream: to wild banana trees in south Asia, pollinated by giant, gargoyle-eyed fruit bats; to 160 million years ago, when flowering plants first evolved; further still, to the point when the tree of life converges to a single root, three or four billion years ago, where we find that the banana is our sibling—that, ultimately, we share one mother. Tracing that stream to its headwaters, we discover nothing less than the universe itself. Indeed, the heavier elements that make up the banana—the atoms of carbon and nitrogen and potassium—were, like Thor's hammer, "forged in the heart of a dying star."[2]

Even to answer my more human-centric question about fruit and injustice, we have to travel far afield: to a plantation in Guatemala, more than a thousand miles away, where workers labor for a pittance. We have to deal with the history of European colonization, with racism, with CIA-led coups and wage slavery. The banana has been grown and harvested in conditions so suffused with violence and exploitation that the answer turns out to be *yes*—I probably am committing an act of injustice when I eat it. I am, at the very least, an accessory. But to see that, we had to follow the flow away from the object itself.

In this book, I don't eat a banana. I have a different starting point in mind. To trace similar questions about wealth and poverty and injustice, we'll begin with visits to a couple of contemporary homesteads in a beautiful part of Appalachian Kentucky called Bear Lick Valley. But, as the example of the banana illustrates, to truly explain something, you have to travel. It is no different with the main questions here: why are people in eastern Kentucky still homesteading, and why do they form two groups? Like most good questions, these are deeper than they seem at first glance; the quiet vegetable gardens and rustic-seeming cabins hidden deep in the countryside of Appalachia, it turns out, are expressions of fundamental social processes that shape and weave together many different times and places.

The search for answers will send us far back in time—first, to the moment more than two centuries ago when poor white settlers, fleeing oppression, flooded the frontier of Kanta-ke, only to find new oppression awaiting. Then we'll visit the period around World War II, when a modernizing economic boom brought an end to homesteading as the basic way of life in Bear Lick Valley—but was followed by the outburst of social dissent in the 1960s that led to a new round of homesteading, as people headed to the mountains in search of better ways of living.

Ultimately, to really answer these two questions, we must learn about the disconcerting inner workings of this class-based civilization we have inherited. In the middle three chapters, we journey not only in time but in space, to examine the far-flung machinery of a capitalist society. We travel to classrooms where young people learn, above all, to loathe certain kinds of learning; to a factory where Kentuckians work until their souls ache and their bodies are broken; even to Manhattan to the corporate studios of Fox News, where division and discord are mass produced. And we will find that, in too many ways, the bloody colonization that birthed Kentucky long ago, while less violent than it once was, never truly ended.

At the end of our exploration, as explorers do, we arrive back where we started, with the owner-built homes and chicken coops and campfires of Bear Lick Valley. There we'll find that homesteading is a serious form of activism and resistance, that both groups of homesteaders are working hard, with skill and creativity and dedication, to build lives that make sense within a society that often does not. But they do so as people indelibly marked by the system they dream of escaping.

*   *   *

My nine-year-old son loves to play a game we call "lawyer mode." To play, you pretend anything the other person says was meant to be literally and precisely true. "Hurry up, Finn!" I'll say, "It's time to go! Everything's loaded in the van." And he'll hold up his index finger and declare, "Well, not *every*thing. You didn't load the cats. Or the garden. Or the solar system. You didn't even load Uranus!"

All too often, this is the game that academics play when we write for each other. We dissect infinite shades of meaning within words—interpolate, poststructural—that we just recently made up. Call each other out for minor omissions and missing citations. Hunt for trivial errors. Fixate on minutiae. Even though this produces a lot of papers, it's not just an academic game, for when we write in lawyer mode, we slam the doors of scholarship in everyone else's faces.

The effects of this humorless, nitpicking approach to writing are visible in many ways. Much of my job as a teacher is to help young people feel the power—and pleasure—of the written word, to introduce them to the vital necessity of science and scholarship. This is an uphill battle: there are powerful strands of anti-intellectualism that run through the United States, which is one of the themes of this book. Many of my students don't enjoy reading; many hate it. I cannot ask them to read the vast majority of academic writing, because it will only confirm what they already think they know: reading is a waste of time. Or consider this: social scholars have written thousands of articles critiquing *neoliberalism*, which is the academic word for the elite-led class war that took off in the 1970s under the guise of "free markets" and has raged across the planet ever since. These critiques are important; neoliberalism affects everyone, and usually not for the better. But I could walk the streets of my hometown in Kentucky all day, asking people about neoliberalism, and no one would have ever heard the word. I could even stand outside our lovely public library, where book lovers congregate, and the majority of them wouldn't have heard the term either. You can build the most devastating critique of neoliberalism—but if only a handful of people encounter it, it has little power in the world.

Of course, obscure writing isn't the only thing that stands between people and the power of scholarship. But why throw up another barrier in a landscape already crisscrossed with trenches and razor wire?

Lawyer mode has its place. Sometimes a fallacy can be detected only through nitpicking. Sometimes a question does actually turn on minute detail. Sometimes subtle shades of meaning are crucial, or a word has to be coined to capture a new concept. But, particularly among social scholars, lawyer mode has another, less defensible purpose: not to painstakingly uncover truth, but as a means of achieving intellectual status. Marvel at the fiendish complexity of my thought—you can't begin to understand it without years of study! You can't read it without suffering! Many of the canonical texts of left-wing scholarship I waded through during my graduate work at UC Berkeley are marked by both extreme erudition and extreme opacity. That's part of why they're canonical: they must be read over and over for anyone to have a chance of deciphering what they mean.

Proving the merit of scholarship lies in precisely the opposite direction: in writing to wider audiences, not narrower ones. Instead of trying to please a panel of stern and statured professors, how about a classroom full of third graders? They make fantastic detectors of bull and posturing. As a friend of mine once quipped, "How do you find out if you're getting fat? Ask a child to draw a picture of you." In this case, how do you find out if you're getting fatuous? See if you can describe your scholarship so that a child can follow. "If you can't explain it to a six-year-old," the physicist Richard Feynman is supposed to have said, "you don't really understand it." But there's a related challenge that's just as important: can you explain your ideas so a child *wants* to hear them? Because if not, after a minute or two, you're just talking to yourself. And that's too bad, because scholarship is too important to be wasted on scholars.

As much as possible, this book is written in anti-lawyer mode. For better or worse, it's not aimed at six-year-olds—but if a college freshman couldn't read it with a measure of pleasure and profit, I have fallen short. I have taken a cue from many of the brilliant popular science writers we are blessed with—authors like Elizabeth Kolbert, Gary Paul Nabhan, and David Quammen—who take complex and important scientific theories and tell them as stories. To make it feel more story-like, I have largely hidden the research "apparatus"—the hundred hours of interviews, the decade of participant observation, the million words of transcriptions and notes, and the ethnography field courses I taught at Berea College. I have also combined real people into composite characters with made-up names. Partly this is in the interest of narrative compactness, but it also allowed me to write more honestly: when I tried using real names and actual identities, it was, ironically, harder to tell the truth. Certain aspects of peoples' lives are just not meant to be made public by someone else, whether their sexuality, friction with neighbors, or drug use. (Which reminds me: there is occasional adult language.) Even a carefully written portrait is necessarily something of a caricature, selective and narrow in comparison with the richness of that person's actual being and experience.

I have done something similar with place: Berea and Berea College are real, but there is no Bear Lick Valley, or not quite; it's a combination of several adjacent locations to the south and east of Berea. Again, this is partly to protect the privacy of informants, but also because it's unwieldy to force the reader to track a dozen different sites in three different counties. It becomes an overwhelming proliferation of locations and place names, like in *Game of Thrones*. But everything in these pages is something that really happened, in places that match their description, and all the quotes came out of an informant's mouth and directly into a voice recorder or field journal.

Because of the anti-intellectualism common in America, we have a population imminently susceptible to propaganda. We have successful politicians whose platforms and stump speeches are simply strings of false claims. These don't even have to be subtle dodges or slight twistings of truth—they get away with flat-out, bold, in-your-face lies. Part of the reason these lies grab people's minds is that they are like miniature Hollywood movies, with plots and perils, with good guys and bad guys. In other words, they're stories. As scholars, we often try to push back against these stories like lawyers in a courtroom, with facts and statistics and painstaking analysis. But we can't fight this stuff with data alone. To fight ugly, fake stories, we have to tell stories that are beautiful, and true.

PART I

The Story of Homesteading over Time

1 You Can See Other People's Poop

It's a sunny Saturday afternoon in early June, and I'm heading to an all-night pig roast at Nathan Hamilton's homestead. I start from Berea, the little college town where I live and work, driving east on the winding two-lane road that runs through Bear Lick Valley. The valley is twenty miles long and cuts through three different counties; its bottom, carved by Bear Lick Creek, is a rolling grassland of cornfields and cow pastures, overcome a bit more each year by a rectilinear tide of crewcut lawns and vinyl-clad ranch houses. On both sides of the valley, steep wooded slopes rise five hundred feet into ridges and knobs, the trees dark and lush. A white limestone cliff-line rings the ridgetops and peeks through the forest like a grin. When fogs cloak the valley floor in the morning, the mountains look unreal, like a watercolor painting of themselves. Like someplace far away and long ago.

I drive past clusters of pickup trucks at the country store. Past the gravel lot where a dozen families spread worn merchandise in an impromptu open-air flea market. Past mobile homes with their homemade front porches and barking dogs. Chicory and tiger lilies crowd the roadside like children at a parade. After twenty minutes, I take a left onto a single-lane road that leads to a holler known as Redbud Branch. It's a four-wheel-drive route in the best of weather, so I park my Honda Civic on the edge of the gravel, up against thick bouquets of poison ivy. A hundred feet ahead, the narrow road drops over the bank and into Redbud Creek—road

A Bear Lick side holler

and stream become one. I slip off my shoes and hike upstream through the cold current, the shallow water flowing over ledges of flat black slate. Golden nodules of crystalline pyrite poke up like fried eggs from the ebony stream bottom. In the deeper pools, crawdads backpedal from my splashing feet.

After walking up the creek for a mile through a quiet tunnel of forest, I emerge into open space: a meadow nestled deep between the mountains, with fresh-cut hay stacked ten feet high on poles set alongside the dusty road. The way branches along with the creek, heading off into different side hollers, where a half-dozen homesteads are scattered and hidden throughout the woods.

Following the main creek for another half mile, I arrive just as the first breeze of evening cools my brow. Nathan's place is an extraordinary example of a contemporary homestead, even for rural Appalachia. A large cabin sits on a hillside among the trees, with board-and-batten siding, a tin roof, and a wrap-around porch. The foundation is dry-stacked stone from the creek. On the slope behind the house stands a little ivy-covered outhouse with a crescent moon cut into the rough-sawn door. We are far from the grid: the cabin has no electricity, no television, no phone, no municipal water. It's not a "push-button home," as Nathan would say. He lives alone at present—he has a grown son from an early relationship—and cooks on a wood-fired stove, lights with kerosene lamps, and pumps well water with a foot pedal under the sink. Built from lumber that he and his uncles and brothers logged and milled with a portable band saw, the house looks like a photo from a hundred years ago—except for the bright red and yellow cylinder of an Igloo water cooler set on the edge of the porch, which turns out to be full of cold sassafras tea. On the flat ground by the creek, a half-acre garden, plowed and disked in the slightly wandering lines drawn by a team of horses, is green with spinach and beans and potatoes and squash. Beside the garden is a pond full of fat catfish, and a barn where Nathan keeps a milk cow, some goats and chickens, and a sibling pair of workhorses.

Nathan was born in a cabin much like this, without electricity or running water, on top of a nearby mountain. "I was born up there at Grandpa and Grandma's house," he told me once, when I asked about his early life. "We

A non-push-button kitchen

stayed there until I got healthy enough, strong enough to travel, and then went home. They packed me home on a horse, right on a saddle, and it was the *awfullest* blizzard I reckon that's *ever* been in this country, I mean zero and below zero temperatures, and a huge snow."[1] Nathan grew up working the garden, feeding the animals, helping his father craft rocking chairs for sale, and gathering ginseng, goldenseal, and mayapple. But mostly, he said, he ran wild in the woods. By his tenth year, he spent days alone in the forest, coon hunting with his hound dogs and his pony. He never set foot in a schoolhouse. He has never been to a doctor. He has no social security card, driver's license, or formal institutional existence whatsoever.

This sounds like a story from long ago. But Nathan was born in the blizzard of 1978. As I write, he is thirty-nine years old, strong and energetic but no longer lean, a handsome man with dark hair and a big dark beard and a ready laugh. He has a thick country accent that, unlike the television stereotype, strikes a mainstream American ear—like many British accents—as dignified.[2] He is one of the sharpest people I have ever known, and often unleashes better sentences on the fly, verbally, than I can build painstakingly on paper. His diction is his own, full of words like "dramastically," a melding of dramatic and drastic, which you won't hear anywhere else.

I hiked into the holler both to be with friends and in search of answers to a question: why do people live like this? Why do people still turn to the land? Looked at a certain way, it seems a dumb question. Listen to the music of the creek! Breathe the scent of wildflowers! Why would anyone *not* live like this? But in many ways, it's a hard life, and not one most of us show any serious interest in pursuing. In the winter, families in Redbud Branch often can't get in or out, sometimes for weeks. Nathan's postcard-ready garden and cabin and barn are the fruit of hard labor. There's no Netflix. No microwave. No pad thai delivered to your apartment door. Many things that make life in a town or city seem worthwhile are absent here.

*   *   *

When I get to Nathan's cabin, it's quiet, though people have started to arrive. On the grass verge between road and creek, a few four-wheelers are parked beside a wooden horse-drawn buggy that sports modern rubber

Old-fashioned torque

tires. Several generations of the family have gathered to prepare for to-morrow, and the pig has already been split and laid on the grill, covered tightly with a lid shaped from roofing metal. Nathan and a half-dozen uncles and brothers sit on chunks of firewood in a circle around a nearby campfire. They're wearing leather work boots, jeans, long-sleeve flannel shirts, and suspenders. Most grow their beards long and shade themselves with Amish straw hats. Talking and tending the meat, they'll stay up through the night. There's no drinking and very little swearing. Nathan used to drink, but it "cut me down hard," he said, and he swore it off.

Tomorrow, on foot and horseback and piled four and five on ATVs, two hundred people will roll into the holler. A line of hay wagons beside the garden will brim with potluck dishes—pies and casseroles and potato salads and more pies. A mare will lumber placidly up the endless hill of a treadmill; horse-powered treadmills were a nineteenth-century source of torque. In this case, that torque will be used to churn ice cream. Two stallions will get in a fight, an incredible mass of animal, rearing and snapping at each other's necks, dogs snarling at their hocks. Waving hats and bellowing, the men will charge in, but the fight ends only when one stallion tumbles over the bank and flees clattering down the creek bed.

For now, the sun is setting and everything is calm. The men pass stories back and forth across the fire. They talk farming: spray bleach or vinegar on a field, it'll kill the weeds. They talk trades; they love to trade. Nathan no sooner gets one truck than he's ready to swap for another. They appraise a gooseneck trailer parked by the creek, put prices on it. "I'd like that one," says Nathan's brother Abe, "it's got no wood to rot out." They talk about breaking horses and mules. A local man, Everett Combs, was renowned for how well-trained his mules were. "Once," another brother says—pronouncing it *wunst*—"I was driving down Big Hill, and there come the mules and the wagon, and no driver. Then, presently, around the corner, comes Everett on the tractor." That gets a laugh. Uncle James recalls the time Everett overdrank and passed out in his wagon—and the steady mules guided him home over miles of country roads.

Since we're talking about animals, Nathan has a concern to air. He pulls his beard and ventures, "Fellers, I think my dogs are bitin' my cow."

His uncle Hiram has an easy answer for that: "Castrate 'em." He volunteers to tackle the job. "I'll castrate just about any kind of critter," he says, "if it's aggravatin' me." He bought a boar once, but the "maleness stinks up the meat." Boar taint, they call it. "Not even a billy goat is like that!" So they tied his forelegs to the front end of the truck and pulled him out and his "balls just hung right there off the tailgate." Easy clipping. Then they fattened him up on corn, and the meat, he says, was tender and delicious.

In the dusky light, a four-wheeler growls along the dirt road and into the yard. One of Nathan's teenage nephews is driving, an elderly woman perched on the seat behind him. Ruth Hamilton, Nathan's grandmother and the family matriarch, has spent the afternoon at her cabin, a couple of hollers over, baking vinegar pies for the gathering. Clad in a long brown dress and bonnet, thin face alert like a raptor, Ruth walks up to the fire to greet her children. The talk was already trending spiritual before Ruth showed up—but life, for her, is nothing more nor less than a celebration of the Lord. She is a holy woman, ecstatic and forceful in her faith.

I am a little concerned: raised by two southern whites recoiling from conservative Christianity, I experienced exactly zero church services in the first twenty years of my life; the handful since, I have attended in a sociological mode. What if Ruth asks if I've embraced the Lord our Savior? Or suggests that I lead a prayer? I can't imagine not being honest about my lack of religious belief—but how would they respond?

Ruth takes a seat by the fire and salts the conversation with well-timed interjections of "Praise the Lord!" Her hallelujahs soon have them in an overtly religious mood, which puts Hiram in mind to tell a story. "You know, I can't read much," he begins; like Nathan, Hiram has never been in a schoolhouse. "But that Bible, sometimes, it's just as clear as water." He was reading in Revelation a few weeks back, he says, serious now, "reading about the Beast." No more laughing; this isn't a story about pinching the balls off some punk tomcat. He walks us through the scripture. The Beast came out of the ocean. From the bottomless pits. In its nostrils were fire and black smoke. It's deadly, full of power, and even kings kneel helpless before it.

"I kept wondering, kept asking myself, what *is* the Beast?" He pauses, rearranging the embers with a stick. Gives us time to feel his question. "Then, finally, it came to me," he says. "The beast is crude oil." What else rises from the ocean depths with smoke and flame? What else has such power to control and destroy? What else holds the people so tightly in its grip? We all drive, Hiram points out. We all buy gas. "We all," he concludes, "carry the mark of the Beast."

Once that knowledge came to him, he parked his truck, hitched the horses to his buggy, and hasn't driven since.

The sun sets, and night folds 'round. Ruth calls for a prayer. Everyone stands up from their seat around the fire and faces out into the dark forest. I expect Ruth to lead, but each pray to themselves. Even as an atheist, I can feel that sense of supplication before larger forces. Of voices raised within the mystery. I feel our ephemerality; we are here and then gone, like a raindrop born in cloud and sundered on the earth. Beside me, I hear Nathan singing a quiet hymn. "Without Jesus' blood washing me of my sins," he whispers, "I'd be gone tomorrow."

*   *   *

My arms are covered to the elbow in mud and prickly bits of straw. The mud tugs pleasantly on my skin as it dries. It's late June now, and sweltering; Bear Lick Valley is living up to its official designation as part of the humid subtropics. Beside me, Virginia Webb grabs a double fistful of wet straw and clay from a wheelbarrow and crams it into a gap in the wall in front of us. The wall is made of straw bales, stacked in staggered rows like giant bricks. We're rushing to fill all the joints, so that when the first coat of earthen plaster is applied to this section of wall—hopefully later this afternoon—it won't disappear uselessly into crevices and fissures.

Virginia is in her mid-forties, with a firm, full body strengthened by labor. Her black hair is pulled out of the way in a French braid. She works as a potter, renting a little craft shop in Berea with several other artisans. About thirty people have gathered on this Saturday for a work party to help finish her straw-bale house, which she began three years ago with her partner Lisa, an elementary-school teacher from Philadelphia. They painstakingly built a timber frame and a roof, and then Lisa—burned out from working in the evenings, tired of being a lesbian in rural Kentucky, missing the lights of the city—bailed back to Philly. Virginia and her teenage daughter, Rachel, lived for a year inside the unfinished structure, out of the rain but in the open air, sleeping in a tent to keep out the mosquitos in July, and the frost in December. Taking a pause from building, resting, recalibrating their lives. "I wasn't sure what to do," Virginia told me with a sigh, "after Rachel started college. It's a much bigger project, when you're alone. I really thought about moving to town."

She decided to push on, and the house looks nearly finished now. The bales are stacked and the windows and doors are framed—but the exterior walls are only halfway plastered. Like many straw-bale houses, it's both home and artwork. From a distance, it looks like a cuter, smaller version of a normal house: a rectangle with a gabled roof of tin, perched on the side of a hill overlooking Virginia's garden and, a couple hundred feet below, the green floor of Bear Lick Valley. But when you get closer, you notice subtle curves and undulations in the walls. A bas relief phoenix flies up one side of the house, sculpted from clay, and at the top of one wall, wine bottles are laid within a cob mortar, to let multihued light filter inside.

Straw bales make beautiful, functional homes. When the foundation is done correctly, they're as rot-resistant as a framed house. They stack quickly, like giant Legos—walls often go up in a day—and they are superbly insulated. But, without much help from machines, the plastering is fiendishly labor intensive. Virginia has dug the clay for the plaster on site, and painstakingly worked it through a screen to remove stones. There's a great turnout for the work party today, but we will only get through part of the plastering that remains to be done.

In addition to being a homebuilder, Virginia is such a skilled gardener that when I buy groceries at Berea's Wal-Mart, I feel her sitting, as it were, upon my shoulder, shaking her head in disgust as I pay for things I ought to have grown. But it makes for a busy life. Today has been typical: in the middle of preparing to host a work party, she says with an edge of exasperation, a package arrived in the morning mail, one that had to be dealt with quickly. Virginia is also a beekeeper, and the package contained a live queen, sequestered in a tiny box with a small retinue of helper bees. I've watched her check the hives before. Wearing the usual netted cowl over her head, but with her hands bare, she handled the honeycomb with a watchmaker's precise touch, leaving the bees calm. Striped yellow and brown, they crawled over her fingers like rings hammered from living gold.

"Last week," she tells me, gathering another clump of straw-clay mix, "I decided that one of the hives needed re-queening."

"I'm not sure what that means," I reply.

"The old queen wasn't producing eggs in a strong, healthy pattern," she explains. Her love of bees smooths the stress from her voice. "Ultimately, this means the demise of the hive." Plus, she spied a bit of spider-webby stuff clinging to one of the honeycombs, which meant wax moths were infiltrating—another sign of a weak hive. In a strong one, worker bees destroy wax moth eggs before they hatch. "So I had to pinch the old queen to death."

"You *pinched* it?" I ask. "Isn't that kinda brutal?"

"I know it sounds rough," she replies, wiping sweat from her temple with a clean bit of shirtsleeve, "but leaving the queen's body in the hive allows the workers to mourn, which helps prepare them for the new queen."

It was a purely logical regicide. Even so, you can't just plop an alien queen into a hive—the worker bees won't recognize her smell, and they'll kill her. This morning, when Virginia placed the new mail-order queen into the hive, she was trapped inside a little plastic box that looks like a mini walkie-talkie. The "antenna" is a sugar-filled tube that the worker bees have to chew through. It takes them a day or two to do this—and in the meantime, the new queen's pheromones are suffusing the hive. By the time she's freed, Virginia tells me, "the hive is ready to embrace her."

I have just been taught, I realize, as I reach for more clay, how to hack a beehive.

*   *   *

Around 1:30, when everyone's bending under the heat, we break for a potluck meal. I stand off to the side, to let others fill their plates and to observe. It seems that once I left Nathan Hamilton's pig roast, I slipped through a wormhole into a mirror-image universe: I am on a vibrant homestead much like Nathan's, but everything is slightly different. Tilted a few degrees to the left. The food, for example. At Nathan's, there was lots of meat; in addition to the pig itself, they grilled a pile of burgers and two turkeys. The closest you'll get to "burger" here at Virginia's is "bulgur." The potato salad is tossed in olive oil, not slathered with mayo. There are no lemon merengue pies or Jell-O salads; the apple pie has a whole-wheat crust made without Crisco. There are ingredients I didn't see at Nathan's: not just bulgur, but alfalfa sprouts and hummus, sliced avocados and tofu.

The differences are everywhere. Nathan plows his garden and leaves the soil bare so he can cultivate between rows. Virginia does not plow or till, and covers the soil with a heavy layer of mulch. She doesn't plant in linear rows—the beds are long, raised mounds curving across the hillside, with all sorts of species "companion planted" in a profuse jumble. Nathan isn't above an occasional sprinkle of Sevin Dust to keep the vine borers from killing his squash; Virginia wouldn't dream of it. Nathan is off the grid, without electricity; Virginia is, too, but beside her garden, she has set photovoltaic panels onto a steel post, producing enough current to run her laptop, a few lights, a fan, and a small pottery wheel. Virginia has bees and ducks and chickens, but no cows or horses. Is that the point of overlap—that they both have chickens? They both also have outhouses, but in Virginia's the poop goes in a bucket for composting, while at Nathan's it drops permanently into a hole in the ground. Virginia's home is passive solar, which means that windows are clustered in the south wall, so that rays from the winter sun warm the interior. Nathan's is not. Four wheelers are common there and rare here; skinny dipping is common here and rare there. The can of Skoal that gets passed around there—that's a joint, here. I could go on. Conversational topics. Parenting styles. Fears. Nearly every object and action are suffused with cultural difference. The hick-hippie distinction, while hard to explain, is not hard to see.

After the meal, I help mix the clay-straw slip that Virginia is using to fill voids in the wall. A big plastic tarp has been draped over a rectangle of leftover straw bales, forming a square pit on the ground. You shovel in a bunch of pre-sifted clay, toss in a couple armloads of straw, pour in a gallon or two of water from a bucket, and then mix. There's just enough room in the pit for two adults to work side by side, occasionally leaning on each other's shoulders, stomping and stirring the mess with bare feet like old-time Italian grape crushers. Now I'm muddy to my knees instead of my elbows. Within a few minutes, I'm pretty sure all the dead skin on my feet has been debrided, and maybe some of the live skin as well.

Cody Shulyer is breathing hard next to me in the pit, tall and strongly built, his long sandy hair escaping its braid and clinging in spirals to the sweat on his forehead. He's warm and upbeat even as he shares his well-honed view of society's myriad malfunctions. I'm used to seeing him with a big mountain-man beard, but he's clean-shaven now. "A couple of weeks ago," he says, "I found a tick the size of a marble in there—tucked under my jawline—and . . . yeah. That's it for the beards for a *while*."

Cody has milled lumber with Nathan and worked with several of the Hamilton men on a carpentry crew, so I tell him about spending the night at the pig roast, and about Hiram's story regarding crude oil. "That's not bad," he says with a chuckle. "He's got a point there. But a two-thousand-year-old set of tribal myths might not be the best place to go to figure out energy policy." Environmental decline is a topic he has pondered, however, and for a while we talk about various looming crises, from peak oil to global warming to ehrlichiosis.

Once we've mixed a batch of slip, we shovel it into a wheelbarrow—taking care not to cut the tarp with the edge of the shovel. "You know, Hollywood keeps making these movies about the end of the world," Cody says, tossing a shovelful into the barrow, "where aliens land from space, or where a computer wakes up one day and goes all Skynet on us. Like it's science fiction. Like it's make-believe. But the scary thing?" He leans on his shovel handle. "It's already *happened*."

I bend my knees and heave a load toward the wheelbarrow; wet clay is absurdly heavy and sticks to the shovel blade. "I'm not sure what you mean," I tell him between breaths.

"We've *already* been taken over by artificial intelligences," he says. "They're called corporations. We built them—but they aren't human. They're made up of humans—but humans don't run them. Think about it. A corporation is a machine designed for one thing: maximizing shareholder value. It's an algorithm. And there's only one outcome that feeds back into the algorithm: stock price. If some behavior maximizes stock price, the corporation does it. If not, the corporation doesn't do it." He lifts his shovel and throws fresh, unmixed clay into the pit to start another batch. "It's taking in information and computing behavioral outputs. That's an artificial intelligence. An AI. And we just sat back, watching TV, shopping, not paying attention, and let these AIs grow and spread. At this point, they write the laws, they shape the news we're fed, they're pretty much in control—*and most of us don't even know it.*"

He slams his shovel into the clay. "And if destroying the whole fucking planet maximizes shareholder value? That's what the AIs will do."

*   *   *

While homesteading is not rare in the contemporary United States, most of us are far removed from it. We live thoroughly modern lives, distanced by countless technological and scientific revolutions from the world as it was mere centuries ago. We reside in gigantic cities, many of us doing work—programming phones, splicing DNA—that didn't even exist fifty years ago. The industrial materials we rely upon are churned out in torrents; our lives flow upon streams of silicon, rivers of petroleum, deltas of vinyl. I am typing these words on a laptop computer smaller than an apple pie, and they will travel in microseconds to a tiny spinning sheet of Mylar on the other end of the continent, coursing through wires spun from glass more transparent than mountain air. Behemoths of steel and carbon chalk the sky overhead, as familiar as the clouds themselves. Moreover, some optimistic versions of the future are founded on visions of ever more technological change, with fusion power and colonies on Mars, with pervasive computing and digital servants that not only pour our coffee and drive our cars, but write our correspondence, handmaiden our courting, and substitute for our memory.

Seen in this light, contemporary homesteading is an anomaly. Why are there still all these people out in the woods acting like peasants? This doesn't look like a world in which small-scale subsistence production has a place; it's not in the economic forecast. Yet here in one of the most technically advanced nations on earth, in the heart of industrial and postindustrial capitalism, hundreds of thousands of people, perhaps millions, are devising their own shelter and eating food they grew in the sweat of their brows—striving, it seems, to swim backward against the currents of progress.

In addition to being anomalous, contemporary homesteads are exotic. Compared with mainstream, modern American settings—suburbs with their fescue deserts, classrooms gridded with desks, the interchangeable plastic counters of fast-food joints—homesteads are eccentric places where people do eccentric things, like dip their naked hands into beehives, build walls of mud and straw, and bathe in the rain. I have taken Berea College students to spend weekends on these homesteads, and many of them respond in the same way they would to international travel: they find the experience profoundly enlightening, and a little frightening.

"I had no idea people lived like this," wrote one. "I was totally freaked out and still a bit shocked when we were going on a tour of the place because I had never seen anything like this before." "They live only about twenty minutes outside of town," wrote another, "but it seems like you are entering a different dimension." One student, who grew up in war-torn Iraq, found it hard to relax. "This was my first time actually sleeping in a tent," she wrote. "I was kind of scared and I rethought taking the class when I found out that we were going to have to camp.

But then I asked myself, what's the worst thing that can happen? Being stung by some insects maybe? That's a lame excuse for not sleeping in a tent! I survived wars and random street gunshots many times for many years!"

The food is different—delicious, wholesome, but also unusual and thus worrisome. The outhouse is an adventure: "you can see other people's poop!" On one excursion, I offered extra credit to students who would sleep in the open rather than in a tent. It was late spring, cold at night, and there were few insects out—just the lambent glow of the Milky Way splashed across the firmament. Still, they thought I was joking. "What about bears?" In short, these homesteads are nearly as foreign to many young people as the sands of the Atacama Desert or the stone alleys of Zanzibar. As one student summed it up, visiting her first homestead "affected my life in a permanent way."

If you are experienced with homesteading, or other intensive outdoor activities like backpacking or hunting, it is easy to chuckle at the discomfort the students felt. But these are simply the normal reactions of people who have spent their entire lives either indoors, or in the tamed and groomed spaces of backyards, campuses, and shopping centers. Which is to say, much of the population of the modern United States.

* * *

Like many exotic things, homesteading is treated with ambivalence. On one side of this ambivalence is a great deal of interest and excitement. Seed catalog sales are booming.[3] Urban farms and community gardens are spreading all over like, well, weeds. Elementary schools freak the students out by growing actual living strawberries and tomatoes—still attached to the plant! Farmers' markets thrive. Suburban parents build chicken tractors in their backyards, read Joel Salatin, and drive on Saturday mornings to buy raw milk at semi-clandestine rendezvous. The *New York Times* features stories on the tiny-house movement and "cabin porn."[4] There's something deeply American about homesteading: the mythos of the rugged pioneer family, capable, independent, and unyoked, free of paperwork and debt. All they ever needed to buy, go the tales, were bags of nails and cans of coffee.

On the other side of this ambivalence lies ridicule and cynicism. Contemporary homesteading is often dismissed by lay people and scholars alike—when it's noticed at all—with clichéd pictures and explanations. This dismissal has several components. First, unless you have first-hand experience, it is easy to think only a dwindling handful of people are involved, that homesteading is just a fringe movement, like base jumpers or Scientologists. Homesteading can appear to be a fringe movement geographically as well. In this view, it is only found in certain out-of-the-way places—a few old-timers in the remote hollers of Appalachia, some aging communards on the back roads of Humboldt County.

The ridicule extends to the two main categories of people who engage in homesteading, "hicks" and "hippies." Those words carry a raft of dismissive stereotypes; they are often insulting and I will use them sparingly. Hicks—let's call them *country homesteaders*—are sometimes seen as quaint rural folk, clinging to the vestiges of a lifestyle that used to make sense but is now anachronistic. In the mocking words of one group of left-wing economists, they are "oddball 'mountain men'" who are "trying (mostly in vain) to live according to . . . antiquated precepts." Hippies—let's say *bohemian homesteaders*—were supposedly privileged rebels from the late sixties and early seventies who dreamed naïvely of bucolic utopias. "In the 1960s," according to a typical journalistic belittling, "when it was cool to own beads and sandals, but little else, an entire generation of hippies was spared a lifetime of hanging out in coffee houses when a gnarled finger poked out from a cloud of marijuana smoke (one can only guess) and pointed the way: 'Hey man, back to the land.'"[5]

Like many stereotypes, these are not entirely incorrect. But they blunt our curiosity about an unusual and unexpected phenomenon, replacing what ought to be questions with assumptions. They leave us with a limited understanding of this unusual social movement. For example, consider this simple question: how many homesteaders are there? The answer: we don't know. No researchers gather the relevant data. No census tracks the activities that typically comprise homesteading. This absence of data is partly a product of the assumption that homesteading is pursued by an insignificant number of people. The lack of data then reinforces that same assumption; because we don't know how many homesteaders there are, it's easy to assume there aren't many. But, as the saying goes, lack of evidence is not evidence of lack.

*   *   *

The first and most basic question we must ask about homesteading is, "what is it?" Without an answer to this question—without, in other words, a definition of homesteading—it would be impossible to figure out why people still pursue it or why they tend to segregate into two groups.

In common usage, the word "homesteading" refers to how Laura Ingalls Wilder and her family lived in *Little House in the Big Woods*. They had a parcel of land large enough to farm but not so large it would qualify as an estate or manor. They built a cabin and a barn, grew crops and raised animals, and engaged in a whole range of self-provisioning activities like cutting firewood and hunting. Based upon this famous example—and upon Nathan's and Virginia's places, which seem very similar—it appears that a homestead can be defined as a subsistence-oriented, diversified small farm.

A professional-looking owner-built home

That was easy, right?

You'll be shocked, I'm sure, to hear that defining homesteading is not that simple. There are several complications. The first is that homesteading families in the past—referred to as peasants, or yeoman, or smallholders—seldom aimed for total economic independence. Some contemporary homesteaders subscribe to this heroic-but-mythical ideal. "I'm not a homesteader!" they'll exclaim, as we sit in the house they built drinking herbal tea they grew from pottery mugs they crafted. "I have a job in town and I don't grow all my own food!" But complete self-sufficiency sounds better in theory than it feels in practice, a theme we'll return to. Peasant families throughout history traded and bartered, bought and sold goods in town, and sought wage labor when it was available.[6] In other words, subsistence production doesn't have to exist all by itself to be important—and you can count as a homesteader even if you're also a teacher or a musician or a lawyer or a plumber.

Another complication: although subsistence production is the central element of homesteading, subsistence comes in many forms. There's no single do-it-yourself task that defines a homestead as such. You might raise goats or you might raise cows or you might not raise livestock at all. In the north, you grow apple trees; in the south, oranges. In a dry place, you dig a well; in a place with rain, you build a cistern. In the past, you dipped candles from beeswax; today, you install a solar panel on your roof.

In fact, a homestead may be defined partly by a *lack* of production. Consider a family that has changed their lifestyle not so much by producing things for themselves, but by reducing their consumption. One Bear Lick couple, Ben Carvajal and Gwen Pine, live in a camper van in the woods on someone else's property. They gather firewood, haul water, and compost their excrement, but they haven't built a house and they don't grow food. Their frugality, however, is not passive. It's a conscious strategy that in the modern United States represents a difficult accomplishment—one that supports a kind of life radically different from the mainstream. Moreover, the same strategy of limited consumption was as crucial to the success of historical homesteaders as their skill in gardening or carpentry. Perhaps we should define homesteaders as much by what they reject as by what they embrace. On the other hand, Abe Hamilton, Nathan's brother, built a house that would probably sell for several hundred thousand dollars. Although it draws water from a cistern and electricity from the sun, Abe and his family live in modern comfort in this home, without a whole lot of frugality. But it appears to me they should also count as homesteaders.

Where do these complexities leave us? It still seems like a homestead is a parcel of land upon which an individual or family or group engages in some manner of subsistence production. But there is one more complication, perhaps the biggest yet: almost *everyone* in the contemporary United States relies on subsistence. The work we do in and around our homes is, in fact, subsistence production: changing diapers, vacuuming the floor, cooking supper, mowing the lawn, cleaning maple leaves from the gutters. Every household—even an apartment full of twenty-year-old bachelor gaming nerds—engages in at least some domestic labor. In most homes, this labor demands substantial time and energy—not uncommonly, on a par with the effort given to paid labor. Once economists began measuring it, they were shocked; one overview concluded that "the economic value of housework equals 20 to 44 percent of America's GDP."[7] If that sounds excessive, just imagine how much it would cost to hire people to perform *all* your household and personal chores: washing your dishes, shaving your armpits, driving you to work, scrubbing your toilet, cleaning up your daughter's puke in the middle of the night. Not only would it be bizarre to live surrounded by servants, it would be extremely expensive, which is one reason scholars conclude that subsistence accounts for such a large portion of our overall economy.

The fact that subsistence is everywhere may come as a surprise. For a long time, dominant definitions of economic activity completely overlooked domestic labor: if it didn't make dollars flow, it wasn't important. It was difficult to *not* think of "the economy" as something like "all that stuff corporations do" or "where money goes" or "the Dow Jones." Because women tend to do more domestic work, this way of seeing the economy was—and is—inherently patriarchal, as cleverly noted in the title of Katrine Marçal's book, *Who Cooked Adam Smith's Dinner?* Because household labor is such a crucial part of our well-being, this way of seeing is also, like many patriarchal perceptions, pathetically wrong. We could get by just fine without any number of the major corporations that get all the press—Disney, Goldman Sachs, Lockheed Martin—but we wouldn't last long as a species if no one prepared meals or cared for newborns.

Noticing the ubiquity of subsistence has been one of the more insightful corrections in the social sciences in the past few decades. This insight makes it harder, however, to define homesteading. If the key element of homesteading is subsistence, which most of us do, then aren't we all homesteaders? To some extent, the answer is yes. Put another way, the historical takeover of the old subsistence-based economy by the expansion of capitalism has not proceeded nearly as far as economists lead us to believe. Even if we don't build a cabin in the woods, we live in a mixed economy in which subsistence production continues to play a major role, both for specific families and in the economy as a whole.

At the same time, the answer is no—you don't really count as a homesteader just from doing normal household chores. You count as a homesteader in the contemporary United States, let's say, *when you engage in household subsistence production substantially above and beyond the norm.* This is a fuzzy definition. It does not unambiguously distinguish, in all cases, homesteaders from non-homesteaders. Because we are talking about a continuum of human behavior, and not things that are inherently discrete, like different types of atoms, this is the kind of definition we *ought* to aim for. When my dad grows a crop of greasy beans in our front yard, is my household thereby engaged in homesteading? By this definition we are—but only a tiny bit. If that was all we did, I wouldn't bother interviewing us for this book. However, because homesteading is consciously pursued, I often find that a given household doesn't practice just one or two homesteading tasks. They build their house *and* grow vegetables *and* fix their cars *and* self-medicate *and* home-school their kids. This makes the above definition less fuzzy in practice than it sounds in theory: we're not just talking about households that happen to lie at the tail end of a random bell curve of domestic labor effort.

Based on this definition, contemporary homesteading doesn't always look like *Little House in the Big Woods*. A homestead can be a twenty-acre parcel far from the beaten path—but it can also be a quarter-acre lot deep inside a city. It can feature a log cabin with deer pelts hanging from the porch beams, but it can also feature a suburban ranch house built by the family who lives there. Sometimes it looks like a conventional image of poverty: is a rural home surrounded by junk cars impoverished, or a site of skilled self-provisioning?[8] A homestead may even lack food production. Measured in dollar bills, producing your own shelter is more important in the contemporary United States than growing your own food; it takes an awful lot of tomatoes to add up to a mortgage, even if they're brandywines. Homesteading, in short, is often present in places where there are no conventional visible elements of it—no gardens, no stacks of firewood, no chicken coops, no overalls. As usual, holding a stereotype in our minds is like wearing a blindfold: we can look right at something and not see it.

*   *   *

Why are people still homesteading in Bear Lick Valley? And why do these homesteaders come in two main flavors? These are our questions. They are difficult to answer; to explain these phenomena, as I pointed out, we have to wrestle in a fundamental way with the character of the modern United States. Above all, we have to look at how the social machinery of capitalism divides people into classes and bifurcates experience, the way it shapes and limits our minds and worldviews, the way it creates not just cultural difference, but opposition and discord.

But I'm getting ahead of myself—we'll talk about that later. First, we must travel into the past. Appalachian Kentucky has a history of intensive homesteading more than two centuries long. As we'll see in the next chapter, the majority of settlers who flooded frontier Kentucky in the late 1700s were hungry for land to farm; they dreamed of being yeoman and independent smallholders. One hundred fifty years later, upon the eve of World War II, most households in Bear Lick still relied upon subsistence production, as a matter of course, for their survival.

Thus, one simple explanation for why people in this part of Appalachia homestead today is that it's a continuation of tradition, a kind of cultural relic. Is that the case? Are present-day country homesteaders like Ruth and Nathan Hamilton mostly living in ways their people have known for generations, walking a road worn by the footsteps of their forebears? Does contemporary homesteading actually have anything to say about the modern world—or is it just a window lingering open upon the past?

2 A Buzzel about Kantuck

I have been referring to Bear Lick Valley as part of Appalachia, and that is true. But there is a problem: Appalachia is not a place.

According to the current boundaries—they have been drawn differently at different times—Appalachia stretches across thirteen states, from New York to Alabama, and is home to more than twenty-three million people.[1] It includes Pittsburgh, which by 1900 was an industrial mecca, as well as Jackson County, Kentucky, which was dominated by small-scale farming up until a few decades ago. It includes Cherokee, North Carolina, home to the Eastern Band of that tribe, as well as the northern suburbs of the Sun Belt boomtown, Atlanta. It does—so I have heard—occasionally include country boys in muscle cars playing hide-and-seek with cops along the backroads. It also includes a young black woman in Knoxville who spends her days in graduate school and her evenings organizing against gentrification. A chubby, white sixteen-year-old kid from Harlan County who plays lead guitar like Jimi Hendrix. A former opera singer and intellectual from Estonia running the cash register at a West Virginia liquor store. A lesbian woman teaching math class in a high school in Asheville.

Appalachia, in short, is *many* places.

The enormity and diversity of Appalachia is worth noting, because we tend to imagine it as a specific region defined by a particular culture. The whole area has become a kind of coloring book in our minds, crudely shaded using crayons with labels like *coal mining, moonshining,* and *banjo picking.* When I moved from eastern Kentucky to Berkeley, California, at the age of twelve—so my mother could begin her linguistic studies—the city kids tried to understand my origins by referencing the *Dukes of Hazard.* They asked if we had electricity and running water. As a grown-up, I have encountered the same broad brushstrokes—but the references have shifted to more adult fare. When I tell people from outside Appalachia that my research is based there, a frequent response is, "Have you seen *Deliverance?*" That's the 1970 movie where Ned Beatty, as a whitewater rafter, gets raped by hillbillies. Or so I'm told; I haven't watched it. As political scientist Richard Couto put it, "Appalachia denotes a distinct cultural region of contradictory and incorrect popular conceptions focusing on quilts, dulcimers, and images of universal poverty and hardship."[2]

While the story of homesteading in Bear Lick Valley is set *in* Appalachia, it is not, and cannot be, a story *about* Appalachia. Even within central Appalachia, Bear Lick Valley is its own particular place: it's in eastern Kentucky like Hazard, but not in the coal fields. Mostly rural, but within commuting distance of colleges and factories. Scenically stunning, but not a center of outdoor recreation, like, say, the Blue Ridge Mountains in North Carolina or Red River Gorge just a couple counties away. What we learn here will apply in other places—but we must be just as careful to generalize from Bear Lick to Hazard as we would be to jump from Bear Lick to Baltimore.

*   *   *

Exploring the history of Appalachia is tricky, because if it's vast in space, it is even more so in time. The Appalachian Mountains, one of the oldest ranges on the planet, stretch into the unfathomable deeps of the geologic past. To tell the tale of homesteading, how far back must we go? Must we reckon with the shaping of the landscape itself, the sculpting of this maze of hills and hollers? Even in its geology, we find Appalachia is not a single place, but an intricate folded tapestry of many layers, each with its own story. In one such story, three hundred million years ago, Africa and North America, adrift on vast hidden rivers of lava, crashed together in slow motion. This collision—the most recent in a long series—rumpled a two-hundred-mile thickness of coastline like a bedsheet, helping to raise twin mountain ranges—the Appalachians on one continent, and the Anti-Atlas Mountains in present-day Morocco on the other.[3] Just to the west of the Appalachian range, a different story unfolded: in shallow ancient seas at the foot of the mountains, the glassy shells of tiny plankton rained down through clear water. For millions of years, they piled like snow in drifts that crushed themselves, eventually, into the shales and limestones of eastern Kentucky; the bones of Bear Lick Valley are built from corpses. Powerful natural processes like these are crucial to the character of the place—but to even sketch them would require volumes.

Luckily, there is a more human-scale beginning about 250 years ago, a distinct nodal point, a moment when the story took a sharp turn: a warm sunny day in June 1769, when a white man, panting and dripping sweat, climbed toward a ridgetop along one edge of Bear Lick Valley. Long rifle gripped in one hand, tree branches in the other, he pulled himself up the last few feet of slope, across a narrow, forested ridge and out onto the flat crest of the final cliff of Appalachia. There, for the first time, Daniel Boone saw what he sought: the "sweeping savannas of lush, shining grass" that made up the bluegrass region of the land of Kanta-ke. Boone had long searched for this fabled "Great Meadow," with dreams of bringing his family to a place where they could be among the first free farmers in a free land.[4] Crouched upon his perch, he finally surveyed the meadow: an Edenic wilderness of fertile, rolling hills, lush with wildlife, seemingly empty of humans, and wholly unspoiled.

*　　*　　*

Wait. Time out. For understanding homesteading in Bear Lick, that summer's day in 1769 is indeed a crucial turning point—but there's a problem. Daniel Boone did gaze over a beautiful land, nearly devoid of people, but what he saw was not a wilderness, and Boone, even though he would end up growing crops in the Great Meadow, would not be one of the first homesteaders in Kentucky. Not even close.

To understand what Boone actually saw, we have to jump back another two hundred years, to a truly monumental and world-shattering turning point. In May 1539, the Spanish conquistador Hernando de Soto landed nine boats on the Gulf Coast of Florida and disembarked 620 heavily armed men.[5] Just a few years before, de Soto had helped sack the Incan empire, and sent piles of bullion and treasure back to Spain. In return, the Spanish Crown made him governor of Cuba and sent him to do the same thing in North America—conquer Indians and take their gold.

For more than three years, de Soto's men wandered the Southeast, blazing a thousand-mile-long trail of murder and pillage across land that would become ten states, from Florida, Georgia, and South Carolina all the way west to Louisiana and Texas. Descriptions of the expedition read like nothing so much as a Dungeons & Dragons campaign run by casually savage thirteen-year-olds—with precisely the same level of regard for human life. Find yourself in a foreign land, needing directions? "Catch" some people to serve as guides. Got loot to haul? Enslave a few hundred more as porters. If they're peaceful and cooperative, you might generously "leave off collars and chains." Need to feed hundreds of hungry, mail-clad warriors? Steal the locals' food and eat it. All of it. The locals fight back? "We killed them all," wrote Luys Hernandez de Biedma of one such encounter, "either with fire or the sword."[6]

De Soto and his men didn't find much gold, but that didn't stop them from stealing any other treasure they found. In one village, they "opened a mosque, in which were interred the bodies of the chief personages of that country. We took from it a quantity of pearls, of the weight of as many as six arrobas and a half [about 150 pounds], though they were injured from lying in the earth, and in the adipose substance of the dead."[7]

In addition to gold lust, arrogant ethnocentrism, and ultraviolence, de Soto brought two things of major historical importance. First, the expedition included three men, including de Biedma, who wrote accounts of what the Spaniards did and saw. They were the first Europeans to travel through the Southeast, and their accounts are, by far, the earliest and most extensive written description of pre-Conquest American life in the region. It turns out this wasn't a land, as popular images suggest, thinly populated by hunter-gatherers. Throughout the Southeast, fertile lowland areas were covered, often to the horizon, with cultivated fields and villages; as soon as the marauders left one smoking village behind, they could often see the next in the distance. They passed through towns fortified with palisades and containing several thousand inhabitants, organized into polities with formal leaders, taxes, soldiers, and class divisions. At one point, on the edge of the Appalachian Mountains in north Georgia, a regional chief "came out to receive [Governor de Soto] in a litter covered with the white mantles of the country, and the litter was borne on the shoulders of sixty or seventy of his principal subjects, with no plebian or common Indian among them."[8]

The importance of these written chronicles is magnified by the second, and most important, thing that de Soto brought: non-human organisms. When Europeans began to voyage across the Atlantic, thousands of species shed their pelagic shackles and migrated, for the first time, across oceans. "The seams of Pangea were closing," wrote historian Alfred Crosby, "drawn together by the sailmaker's needle."[9] Some of these migrations are well known: potatoes traveled to Ireland and tomatoes to Italy; horses arrived upon the American plains. Others are surprising. In Kentucky, such common species as dandelions, honeybees, earthworms, and red clover are, like *Homo sapiens,* invasive organisms from the Old World. Even the famous Kentucky bluegrass, namesake of an entire region, came across the ocean on a boat as part of this "Colombian exchange."

In addition to piratical men, de Soto's expedition included two hundred horses and hundreds of pigs, which they herded along the way; they traveled in a "porcine cloud."[10] The most consequential organisms, however, they carried invisibly and unknowingly inside themselves: a host of microscopic species, such as measles and influenza, full of their own self-interested agendas. When humans originally populated the Americas, fifteen or twenty thousand years ago, they migrated in small groups and left behind most viral and bacterial diseases. Indians were so without contagious infections that the idea of catching sickness from another person made as much sense, according to a member of the Blackfoot tribe, as "a wounded man [giving] his wound to another."[11]

But once boatloads of colonizers began to land, epidemics scythed the Natives like fields of ripe grain. One killer after another swept through: smallpox, bubonic plague, measles, typhus, influenza, yellow fever, diphtheria, whooping cough, scarlet fever, and more. One of these epidemics alone would have spelled a calamity; together, they wrote the end of a world. In many places, these diseases went unrecorded, but where accounts survive, they are horrific. "They died by scores and hundreds," noted an observer in Peru in the 1500s. "Villages were depopulated. Corpses were scattered over the fields or piled up in the houses or huts." Closer to home, by 1650 only about twenty-five thousand Cherokees survived from a pre-Conquest population of a quarter million.[12] Scholars estimate that 90 to 95 percent of all Native Americans perished in this pathogenic onslaught—perhaps as many as a hundred million people. It was the largest dying of humans in history.[13]

When Europeans next came through the southeastern United States, a hundred years after de Soto, there were few Indians left to kidnap and pillage. They didn't see cities and villages and fields to the horizon. Too often what they saw, in the words of French explorer Robert de La Salle, after a float down the Mississippi in 1682, was "a solitude unrelieved by the faintest trace of man."[14] This is why, in the late 1700s, settlers found Kentucky to be open, a ghost land, a "dark and bloody ground." Instead of farmers living in villages, it was home to scattered, semi-nomadic bands of Shawnee—widely believed to be the dislocated survivors of the Fort Ancient people who had once populated the land. Eastern Kentucky was a "vast expanse of uninhabited mountains," and there were only, at most, two or three small Indian villages in the entire area.[15]

Thus, we return to Daniel Boone on the mountaintop. There are arguments about which cliff, precisely, he stood upon when he looked down into the prairies of the bluegrass.[16] But one of the most likely spots is an out-flung ridge that's part of a complex known as Indian Fort Mountain, just outside Berea. For reasons that remain a mystery—ritual? defense?—Native peoples apparently built stone walls around the edges of the flat top of the mountain, the largest of which ran for a thousand feet and can still be seen today. Other remnants lie scattered across the landscape near Berea, including a hundred-acre cemetery and at least two dozen ceremonial mounds, some the size of barns. The largest, the Moberly Mound, was ninety feet across and still twelve feet high after decades of being plowed and planted. Buried within were the remains of six people, including, reportedly, a man who would have stood seven feet tall.[17]

Now we know what Boone really saw. The Great Meadow was indeed mostly uninhabited, teeming with game, stunningly beautiful and wild. But it was not a wilderness—not in the sense of a place unchanged by human hands. It was, rather, an "artificial wilderness," as Charles Mann writes, "and every bit as much of a ruin as the temples of the Maya."[18] When Boone looked upon the empty country, pondering the location of his future farm, he stood upon the graves of those who farmed long before.

Without this Great Dying, there is no conquest of America by Europe, because the land would have been too full of people. There would have been no shouldering aside of Natives in a westward rush, and nothing in this book would have happened. What societies would the first farmers of Kentucky have created, if they had not fallen before megadeath and genocide?

We will never know.

*   *   *

Daniel Boone had reason to search for land. Still under British sovereignty in the late 1700s, the thirteen colonies along the East Coast were growing more crowded every year. Both game and land quickly grew scarce in newly settled frontier areas. Families were unsustainably large. Boone himself was one of eleven siblings, and fathered ten children with his wife, Rebecca. Women often bore children until it killed them, in a kind of perinatal Russian roulette. Adding to the pressure, a quarter million Scots Irish migrants crossed the Atlantic in the 1700s, fleeing poverty, and many of them headed to the western edge of settlement in search of farmland.[19]

Colonists knew there was land beyond measure across the Appalachian Mountains, but it was uncharted and hard to get to. To the north (in present-day Ohio) lived members of the Iroquois Confederacy, and to the south (in what became Tennessee, North Carolina, and Georgia) lived the Cherokee; despite the ravages of disease, both groups were still strong enough in the late 1700s to prevent their land from being overrun. In between, the Blue Ridge Mountains rose in unbroken, cliff-edged ridges hundreds of miles long; it was extremely difficult to pull a wagon over them. Would-be settlers began to eye the Cumberland Gap, a gash in the mountains made partially by a three-mile-wide crater, conveniently formed by the impact of a meteorite several hundred million years before. Long used as a pass by Indians, the Gap was part of a network of trails known as the Warrior's Path. For Boone, the Gap was a way to slip into Kentucky without passing through Cherokee lands.[20] It was, as the memorial quarter proclaims, "The First Doorway to the West."

A reluctant farmer, burdened by the drudgery and bookkeeping of settled life, Boone was a quiet man, short and strongly built, usually clad in buckskins, with long flaxen hair "pleated and clubbed" into a knot on the back of his head.[21] A huntsman and lover of solitude, he left for months at a time on "long hunts," while Rebecca Boone ran the farm in North Carolina's Yadkin Valley, on the eastern side of the mountains. Alone or with a couple of trusted companions, he would hunt and trap across hundreds of miles, building a store of beaver skins and deer hides he could sell upon his return. These hunts forged Boone into a quintessential frontiersman—an excellent tracker, marksman, and warrior, so at home with Natives that some called him a "white Indian." He has been passed down to us as a figure of romance: dashing, indomitable, roughly clad but noble of spirit, like the ranger-king Aragorn in *The Lord of the Rings*.

After his first visit, Boone took six years to return to the Great Meadow. In the early spring of 1775, he and about thirty others began chopping a rough trail through the Cumberland Gap and north into the heart of Kentucky. This first easy-to-follow track in the region, later known as Boone's Trace, helped crack open the western frontier and inaugurated a major wave of migration into Kentucky. Trampled and tamed by thousands of boots and hooves, Boone's Trace would soon become the Wilderness Road. Between 1780 and 1790, nearly one hundred thousand people poured into the region.[22] Many migrants were destitute, walking "barefoot all the way . . . carrying children and their belongings on their backs."[23] They had left behind the kings and courts of Europe, the bowing and scraping and back-breaking rent, and were drawn along the trail, like Boone, by dreams of a farm of their own.

But there was a catch. Those who cut Boone's Trace were indeed would-be settlers, seeking land for their families—but they were also paid workers. The expedition was funded and backed by the Transylvania Company, a group of elite investors from North Carolina led by Judge Richard Henderson, a patrician from a well-established family. He looked the part, if his portrait is accurate: handsome, berobed, and wielding an aquiline nose above his eloquent mouth. A businessman, a brilliant lawyer, and a vigorous defender of the existing social order, Judge Henderson had responded to an uprising of the oppressed lower classes—during what was known as the Regulator movement—by sentencing movement leaders to death.

He and his co-investors were interested in one thing: grabbing the land west of the mountains before other elites could do so. Earlier that same year, Henderson had met with Cherokee leaders and purchased twenty million acres of land from them in exchange for about two thousand British pounds' worth of goods. We can only roughly compare the value of money from so long ago with that of today, but two thousand pounds is equivalent to two or three hundred thousand contemporary dollars. For that sum, he secured a claim to thirty-one thousand square miles of land—a princely parcel the size of Ireland. It represented three-quarters of all the land in present-day Kentucky. Knowing this "purchase" was legally dubious for a number of reasons, Henderson planned to rush into Kentucky before other claimants established a strong presence there, to survey and sell plots as if he actually owned them, and thus create a reality on the ground that courts would find difficult to overrule.

After about a month of clearing trail, Boone set up camp on the banks of the Kentucky River, just north of the present-day town of Richmond and about fifteen miles from Bear Lick Valley. Judge Henderson soon joined him with a second crew of hopeful pioneers. While ordinary men worked to clear fields and build a stockade wall, Henderson spent his time inside the log block-house that had been built for him. Life in the wild "appalled him," for one thing—but mostly, his plans did not involve blistering his own hands felling trees and growing corn. He had a manservant to wear the blisters for him.[24] His hours revolved around selling land as fast as he could and penning letters to fellow plutocrats back east, trying to legitimize his claims.

Henderson knew he needed to rush. Before Daniel Boone left his first footprint in the soil of the bluegrass, other factions of wealthy, well-connected speculators were jockeying for ownership of these lands they had never seen. London investors had formed the Vandalia Company in 1705 and pestered the British government for the right to claim Kentucky. The Virginia Company followed in 1747. At the same time Boone and his companions were building Boonesborough, crews of surveyors were scattered across the bluegrass, carving the land with chain and compass into chunks of potential profit.[25] "What a Buzzel is amongst People about Kantuck," wrote a man in Virginia, feeling the swell of land fever. Less-well-connected speculators poured into the area as well, "cabiners" who would build "rude shelters and plant corn" to establish a claim, then ride or walk back east to try to peddle that claim.[26]

Another hurdle arose for Judge Henderson: not all Indians had agreed to cede Kentucky. He had placated most of the Cherokee with goods, but the Shawnee, scattered in southern Ohio, also considered Kentucky part of their territory. Like every American tribe encountering whites, the Shawnee faced nothing but bad choices. They could sit down and talk with the colonizers and lose their land, or they could fight—and lose their land. For a while, some decided to fight. During the Revolutionary War, the British, looking for allies against the rebel colonials, supplied the Shawnee with arms and encouraged them to try to retake Kentucky. One Native leader, Chief Blackfish, unsuccessfully besieged Boonesborough in 1778 with more than four hundred Indian warriors and plenty of British powder and lead. Raiding parties scalped hundreds of settlers coming up the Wilderness Road, at one point managing to run nearly every white person out of Kentucky.

During this time, a woodsman like Boone had purpose on the frontier. His skills and knowledge were crucial. He led surveyors and settlers to safety, rescued his own daughter from Shawnee kidnappers, was kidnapped himself and adopted into the tribe, escaped to warn Boonesborough of imminent siege, and in general reeled off a series of Hollywood-ready escapades and exploits. But by the mid-1780s, the last battles and skirmishes were over, and the Shawnee had largely been driven from the bluegrass. White settlement took off. At that point, the truth became clear: a frontier is only momentarily a place for frontiersmen. Mostly, it's a place for lawyers, bankers, and politicians.

In the speculative frenzy unleashed by the end of the fighting, so much land was claimed that it added up to three or four times as much land as actually existed. One result was a scrum of overlapping "shingled" properties, where more than one person claimed ownership of the same ground.[27] This litigious nightmare resulted in decades of uncertainty and court battles. In sorting the mess, men connected to the courts—or men who actually comprised the courts—found that, somehow, legal decisions seemed to fall their way. Over and over, original, non-elite settlers lost their claims because of "legal technicalities" and other juridical maneuvers.[28]

Though famous, Daniel Boone was not truly a member of the elite. He was at home around a campfire, not in parlors or courtroom disputes, which left him "puzzled and embarrassed."[29] Like most poor migrants caught in the buzzel about Kantuck, Boone ended up with no land at all, and in 1799, penniless, he and Rebecca left Kentucky for good.

Richard Henderson and his partners from North Carolina also lost most of the land they claimed, outmaneuvered by other elites. Soon after the establishment of Boonesborough, the State of Virginia—at that time in charge of the land of Kentucky—voided Henderson's land claims, "to the lasting benefit of Virginia landlords and investors."[30] But, as a well-connected member of the gentry, and a maestro of courts and congresses, Henderson lost in a different way than someone like Boone. The Virginia General Assembly gave Henderson and his fellow investors nearly four hundred thousand acres of land, as a "compensation for their trouble and expense."[31]

* * *

Within several years, almost all the best farmland in Kentucky had been hoarded by a few men. "By the end of the 1700s," according to sociologist Wilma Dunaway, "one-quarter of the entire area of Kentucky had been claimed by twenty-one land barons." In Lexington, a booming city just a few miles north of Boonesborough, "the top 10 percent of landowners" in 1810 "held an astonishing 99 percent of the taxable land." Eighty percent of Lexington residents were absolutely landless.[32] Madison County, home to both the western end of Bear Lick Valley and the town of Berea, followed the same pattern. Green Clay, born into a family of governors and politicians, cornered more than forty thousand acres—nearly 15 percent of the county. In many cases, landowners used political office to swell their estates. At the beginning of his civil service, William Irvine, Madison County clerk in the 1790s, "was the only political figure [in the county] with less than 500 acres." With the powers vested in him, however, he addressed this shortcoming, and serviced himself with an additional two thousand acres.[33]

These men quickly used their landholdings as a base upon which to form a new aristocracy. Like Judge Henderson, focused on his schemes while his manservant cooked and cleaned, the Kentucky land barons grew ever richer from the toils of the landless. They produced—or, rather, commanded others to produce—cash crops such as grain and livestock that were hauled out and sold at regional or national markets. They owned the economic infrastructure; not just the land but the ferries, warehouses, and workshops. When poor white migrants finished the long trek along the Wilderness Road and finally lifted their children down from their backs, there was no ground to set them upon that was not already owned. They woke from their yeoman daydreams to find themselves farming as tenants—renting farmland, so to speak, by giving half or more of the crops they grew to the landlords.

The exploitation endured by white tenants was not the worst in Madison County. These new elites set themselves up not just as an aristocracy, but as a slave-owning aristocracy; they owned not only the land, but a third of the human population. The cash crops they grew included not only tobacco and hemp, but human beings. Held in bondage and subject to the systematic application of terror and torture, black men and women produced much of the wealth of nineteenth-century Kentucky, only to be daily robbed of it. Green Clay's slaves watched his children grow, well-educated and well-traveled, refined and secure, while their own daughters and sons faced harrowing futures of exhaustion, heartbreak, and violence.

In many ways, Kentucky was the first frontier of the United States, settled during the birth pangs of the new nation. Although the details differ, the basic pattern of that land rush played out over and over as the United States brawled its way westward. The frontier was any zone where resources had recently been pried loose, by brutality or deceit, from those—often, but not always, Native Americans—who held them before. At that moment of prying, there is an interregnum of lawlessness and chaos. There are few cops or courts and hardly any bankers or politicians on the scene. It's still too raw and dangerous for men in suits. Anything seems possible. Dreams erupt. Rumors spill back east: The soil is light as a bank of ashes! The streams burst with salmon! Oil bubbles from the ground like spring water! The mountains throb with veins of gold! Ordinary people, desperate with poverty, risk everything—life, limb, and sanity—and rush in, hoping to snatch a share of the prize.

But, inevitably, grabbing is done best by those who have already grabbed. While the people bleed on the handles of pick and plow, established men methodically extend their laws into and around the newly available resource. In lands west of the Mississippi, wealthy railroad owners were handed hundreds of millions of acres by the federal government, as "incentive." In the California Gold Rush of 1849, the most famous frontier resource grab, the ore flowed, sooner or later, into the hands of merchants and bankers, and by 1855, most of the mines were large-scale industrial sites, owned by rich investors and controlled from the new skyscrapers of San Francisco.[34] The same song was sung in the Texas oil fields, at the Comstock Lode of silver in Nevada, across the prairie soils of Oklahoma, in the redwood forests of northern California. It echoes today, every time a new frontier is opened. As global warming melts the ice of the Arctic Ocean, speculators scramble to plant flags in the oil-rich seafloor. As soon as molecular biology extended human reach into the minute clockwork of the cell, a Kentucky-esque land grab ensued, with investors rushing in to survey and claim huge stretches of genome. Banksters litigate for unbridled ownership of internet pipelines, of airwaves, even of rainfall.[35] Time and again, elites use their power to pry open a frontier, and then they extend their power into it, re-creating class society in a new place—like a rogue artificial intelligence, downloading itself into a new substrate.

Even in Kentucky, 250 years after Daniel Boone's arrival, the frontier is not yet exhausted. In Bear Lick over the past five years, land agents from oil and gas companies quietly traveled the backroads, going door to door, using inscrutable contracts to purchase, from ill-prepared small-scale land owners, the right to frack the dark shales thousands of feet beneath the surface.

* * *

Out of all the human possibilities that could have emerged in Kentucky in the late 1700s, the one that was actually created was a brutal class society. But while men like Green Clay built a slave-based plantation system in the flatter land of Madison County, things played out differently in the hills of Bear Lick just to the east. Aside from the narrow creek and river bottoms, the land was steep and difficult to farm, with thin, easily eroded soils. In a hand-drawn map from the 1780s, recording yet another Green Clay land grab, the mountains of Bear Lick were marked, in large cursive script, "Unsuitable for cultivation."[36] There was timber, but how would you get a ten-foot-wide chestnut to market in an area with no rivers large enough to float it and (at that time) no railroads to haul it? Seeing little economic value in the land, the plantation barons broke it into parcels, and sold it off to those hungry for farms.

The hills and hollers of Bear Lick, unlike the Great Meadow of the Bluegrass, did eventually end up in the hands of people who intended to farm it themselves. At the top, some families owned a few hundred acres, and at the bottom, about a quarter of the population had no land at all.[37] But even the wealthier families had to farm and work with their own hands. Slaves, as an expensive investment on farms that were meant to turn a profit, were rare. In 1860, when Madison County contained six thousand slaves—35 percent of the population—Bear Lick Valley had fewer than ten.[38] Nonetheless, the independent smallholders that found land in the mountains east of Berea could not escape the burden of class. It shaped their lives at every turn—not least when they found themselves growing corn on slopes better suited for sledding. "At an incredibly early stage of its development," as historian Steven Channing put it, "Kentucky became a place of landlords and tenants, of rich estates for the few and second- or third-rate smaller farms for the many."[39]

The word *class* can be confusing. Sometimes people use it to refer to cultural attributes like diet or diction. Class, in that usage, is whether you drink Pabst Blue Ribbon or pinot noir. Whether you know more about Mikhail Baryshnikov or Brock Lesnar. It's okay to use the word like that. But when I say *class*, I mean a situation where one group of people force another group to work, and then take the product of that work—cotton, tobacco, coal, Nike shoes—without fair reciprocation. This stealing of labor might be easy to see, as when slave owners fattened themselves off the toil of those in chains, or it might be subtle, as when poor people have to relinquish their labor as rent because all the best land has been taken by the rich. In either case, the beating heart of a class society is one group living unfairly off another, in what historian William McNeill memorably described as "macro-parasitism."[40]

Remember that. The story of homesteading today, and of the two main groups who pursue it, is one in which macro-parasitism, brought to Kentucky long ago, still plays a central role.

3 You Can't Eat Scenery

Caleb Hayward's kitchen is small, just a narrow path wrapped around two sides of the overcrowded, full-sized dining table where we sit. The kitchen has a 1950s look, with linoleum countertops and Leave-it-to-Beaver appliances. A portable TV with a six-inch screen sits on the counter beside a well-used white plastic coffee maker. Without getting up from his chair, Caleb fills a dainty porcelain teacup and slides it to me, along with a shaker of Coffee-mate creamer and a little cardboard box of Domino sugar. Sunlight, glowing green from the forest, flows in through a pair of windows. The verdant light is surprising; the kitchen feels like it ought to be in black and white.

Caleb is in his seventies, with a strong country accent and a low, gravelly voice. I have to lean forward to catch his words. The buttons of his shirt are strained by one of those perfectly hemispherical bellies that some men grow; as we talk, his hands graze contentedly over it, like cows in a pasture. He is kind and humble. "I'm just a mountain man," he says, referring to his lack of schooling and life of manual labor. "These little kids right today that's four and five years old can tell me more about life than I can tell myself after going through it." But don't let his humility mislead you: he's a sharp and careful observer.

His wife, Ada, alternates between sitting with us and puttering around the house. But it's not her house; she has driven over today from the other side of Bear Lick Valley for a visit. They've been married for eleven years but have always lived apart and have the easy banter to prove it. "It's like dating," Ada says with a laugh.

The house is probably three hundred square feet—about the size of the living room in newer US homes. It's got two rooms and a cedar-post porch. The toilet is outside, in a classic closet-shaped outhouse. The cabin sits in the middle of a clearing in the woods, at the top of a hill, with just enough room for a vegetable garden. Caleb bought the two-acre parcel a few years ago from a "hippie woman" who built the soil and "raised a little dope," as he puts it, in a small greenhouse. He sold the greenhouse, since he didn't know how to use it, but kept the soil, which is now full of the tomatoes and squash and okra of mid-July.

Caleb is skilled at growing and building. In addition to decades of horticultural experience, he is a well-practiced carpenter; he was able to build this house in a month, framing it out of store-bought two-by-fours and keeping it simple and rectangular. He is a woodworker as well—I have to be careful every time I set my coffee down, because the tabletop is mostly taken up by an adult-sized cedar coffin that Caleb just finished crafting, sawing boards on the porch and assembling them inside his tiny house. The cedar is fragrant and eye-catching, aglow with curving lines of pink and red, like a sunset.

Caleb grew up in Bear Lick Valley before the big transition from a world of small-scale farming and handicrafts to a world of factory wages and consumer goods. He grew up, in other words, in a region full of peasants. For a smart-mouthed teenager, the word *peasant* is an insult; for historians and scholars, it's not pejorative at all. It refers to a traditional subsistence-oriented farmer, which—until the past century or so—was a category that contained a majority of the world's people. Until about 1940, it still contained almost everyone in Bear Lick Valley. In 1830 there were no manufacturing jobs in or near Bear Lick, and a century later, in 1930, there were still no manufacturing jobs. Upon the eve of US involvement in World War II, there were few paved roads, concrete bridges, electric lines, or telephones.[1] The vast social upheaval that separates the age of peasants from the age of industry had yet to churn through the region.

This is not to say that people in Bear Lick experienced life as static. Their lives were eventful and complex, as full of turns and twists as yours or mine. But the basic contours and limits of their economic lives were remarkably stable. It is much the same with us: my parents grew up in a system where their household economy was primarily based upon selling their labor in exchange for a wage; I have grown up under that same system, and—barring some epochal event, like the development of autonomous robots, or nuclear war—my son will grow up in more or less the same system.

Once the boom of World War II kicked in, everything in Bear Lick began to change rapidly, and homesteading quickly lost its economic central-ity. Caleb lived through that massive transition, and it's that transition I have come to interview him about—it's also the central story of this chapter. But before I turn on the recorder and begin pestering him with questions, we let the conversation wander. He tells me about taking his little boat down to the reservoir to go fishing, where he spends less time angling and more watching the beavers play. Ada won't join him because, like many country folks, she never learned to swim. He laments the size of the suburban houses being built along the western end of Bear Lick Valley. "Everyone has to outdo their neighbor now," he sighs. "Every house has to have twenty-two bedrooms and eight bathrooms." He asks what I think about the war in Iraq, dragging on year after year. He's not impressed with it. "I'd rather eat cornbread and drink water before sendin' them boys over there to die." He even calls out local churches for their role in supporting the invasion. Throughout, he keeps my cup brimming with coffee, and lightens the mood by joking with Ada.

"Ada," he asks, "you haven't seen my chewin' tobacco, have you?"

"Naw, I haven't."

He winks at me. "I believe that woman started chewin' my 'baccer."

"Don't tape that!" she tells me. "That's not true!"

He coughs roughly into his fist, then takes a moment to catch his breath. "Jason," he tells me, voice somber, "I'm dying." He's got cancer all through his lungs and throat—that's why his voice is gravelly and hard to hear. The coffin on the table, it turns out, is his own.

* * *

Even though they look very much alive, trees are like zombies: mostly dead. They consist predominantly of wood that is no longer living; in the trunk, only a thin layer under the bark, the cambium, is not already deceased. The rest—the hard outer bark and all of the inner trunk—is deadwood that protects the tree from infection and provides structural support. To slay a tree, even a giant, you don't have to chop it down. Just cut out a shallow ring of bark all the way around, down to the cambium—"girdling" it, as they say—and the tree will die.

That's what a rebel peasant, calling himself King John, did to a British landlord's forest in 1721. He and his followers painted their faces black and snuck out at night, like Robin Hood and the Merry Men, to strike a blow for justice. In violation of long-standing tradition, the landlord, a Mr. Wingfield, had begun charging commoners a fee for gathering firewood in his forest. The rebels ringbarked a bunch of Wingfield's trees and threatened to girdle the rest unless the fees were refunded. Fearing further loss, Wingfield gave the money back.[2]

This was but one battle in a war, fought in England over the course of about three hundred years, over the nature of land ownership. Today, we are used to the idea of land being owned in much the same way as any other personal possession, such as a shirt or a bicycle. If I own a piece of land, I can do almost whatever I please with it—kick other people off, dig it full of holes, eat the wildlife, and sell it without asking anyone's permission. This kind of land ownership, however, is a recent invention. Throughout most of history, in most parts of the world, land ownership was not so absolute; the earth, after all, is not a bicycle. In medieval England, even though the aristocracy "owned" much of the land, peasants often had a form of ownership as well—what are sometimes known as "usufruct" rights, which entailed specific privileges of access and use: they were allowed to gather firewood, hunt deer, or gather mushrooms, and even graze their livestock and grow crops in certain areas.[3]

This kind of divided ownership may seem odd, but it's similar to the legal situation along the California coastline today. Private landowners can own parcels down to the water, but—to the dismay of celebrities and plutocrats in their Malibu mansions—they are not allowed to exclude the public from the shoreline itself. Anyone who visits the beach has certain usufruct rights: you cannot build a quarry on the beach, or haul away the sand, or auction it to the highest bidder—but you may run or sun or swim or comb to your heart's delight.

Starting as early as the 1400s, and then accelerating in the 1700s as the capitalist economy developed, landlords in England pushed back against these traditional rights of usage. The British textile industry was growing as the Empire provided huge captive markets; the demand for wool skyrocketed. Landlords smelled money. Instead of being content with taking a share of each peasant's labor, aristocrats began to kick peasants off the land, wipe out rural villages, put up fences, and raise sheep—a callous process that came to be known as "enclosure."[4] As Thomas More lamented in *Utopia*, published in 1516, "your sheep that were wont to be so meek and tame, and so small eaters, now, as I hear say, be become so great devourers and so wild, that they eat up, and swallow down the very men themselves. They consume, destroy, and devour whole fields, houses, and cities."[5]

King John and his men won their round against Mr. Wingfield. But in 1723, the English Parliament passed the notorious Black Act—so named in reference to the rebels and their face paint. The act turned nearly fifty specific crimes into capital offences; peasants could now be hanged not only for being caught in a forest while disguised or girdling trees, but for poaching a deer or catching a rich man's fish. "Kill your father, or catch a rabbit in a warren—the penalty is the same!" exclaimed one critic of such draconian laws.[6] Over the following decades, the hangman's noose strangled not only quite a few Merry Men, but also an ancient, populist notion of land ownership that saw land, to some extent, as a commonly held resource.

In my first graduate seminar at UC Berkeley, I encountered this story of enclosure, of "sheep eating men." Then, in another seminar, I encountered the enclosures again. And then again. At first, I wasn't sure why we kept going back to this one set of events from one particular country long ago. But over time, I realized that enclosure in England serves as a kind of parable, a creation story for the modern world. Central to the rise of modernity is capitalism, a system where wealthy people own the means of production (such as factories and warehouses) and produce goods (such as shoes or cloth or cars) for sale on a market. And central to the rise of capitalism—according to the parable—is the process of enclosure. Imagine what it required to create the first really big textile factory. You don't just need a cavernous building full of machinery—you need hundreds of workers, rivers of raw cotton or wool, mountains of coal to run the steam engine, and endless thousands who need to buy cloth. But there's a problem: the "workers" are already busy farming and gathering. The land is already being used to grow other crops, not produce cotton, sheep, or coal. The "consumers" already weave their own cloth. For labor and raw materials and customer demand to be made available for capitalism, during these first stages, they have to be uprooted from their prior dispositions.

As Karl Marx argued in his monumental study of this new economic system, *Das Kapital,* to be available for wage labor, the worker must not command her own productive resources—in particular, land. If she owned her own farm, why would she labor for someone else? Land and people must be pried apart. "For the conversion of his money into capital," Marx wrote in a famous passage, "the owner of money must meet in the market with the free labourer, free in the double sense, that as a free man he can dispose of his labour-power as his own commodity, and that on the other hand he has no other commodity for sale, is short of everything necessary for the realisation of his labour-power."[7]

The parable of enclosure is so insightful that once you know it, you find enclosure cropping up everywhere. We already encountered it in the previous chapter: the creation of a frontier is often the first step in enclosure. A frontier isn't usually a place without people—it's a people without power, like the English peasantry. Like the Cherokee. Moreover, enclosure isn't something that only happened long ago. When the city of Lexington, Kentucky, sold its public water utility in 2002 to a for-profit company, this was a form of enclosure: a commonly owned resource was turned into private wealth. When Monsanto lawyers patent a strain of corn, they take a resource created mostly through the collective effort of generations of Mesoamerican cultivators and "enclose" it—turning it, in effect, into the domain of rich landlords.

But the original parable of enclosure is about peasants, who, to us, seem long ago and far away, irrelevant to life in the contemporary United

States. But that's not the case at all. If we got into a time machine and went back even a hundred years, we would find a planet of peasants. Now, in many parts of the world, peasants are on the endangered list. Any time a common species suddenly and precipitously declines, it is worth asking, what happened? According to the parable, peasants were kicked off the land. Given a choice, they would have passed on the factory jobs and kept their plows and their independence, thank you very much.

*   *   *

This idea—that owning land is a path to independence—is so common in America that you can't take a stroll without stubbing your toe on it. In the late 1700s, Thomas Jefferson famously asserted that the newly whelped United States could avoid strife and degeneracy by remaining agrarian; urbanization and industrialization were unhealthy and corrupting. "The mobs of great cities," he wrote, "add just so much to the support of pure government, as sores do to the strength of the human body." By contrast, "Those who labour in the earth are the chosen people of God. . . . Corruption of morals in the mass of cultivators is a phaenomenon of which no age nor nation has furnished an example."[8]

Many others since have argued along similar lines. Growing up in a household full of books, I was surrounded by their words. Henry David Thoreau's *Walden*, a classic defense of simple living, published in 1854, beckoned from the shelves. So too did the lyrical writing of Kentucky's Wendell Berry, who also sings the virtues of small-scale farming. "The question of the survival of the family farm and the farm family," he wrote, "is one version of the question of who will own the country, which is, ultimately, the question of who will own the people." In a poetic Appalachian echo of Marx, he continued: "If many people do not own the usable property, then they must submit to the few who do own it. They cannot eat or be sheltered or clothed except in submission."[9]

For those of us vexed or oppressed by modern life, these ideas are exciting—like when Thoreau argues that possessions are merely shackles. "I used to see a large box by the railroad," he wrote, "six feet long by three wide, in which the laborers locked up their tools at night; and it suggested to me that every man who was hard pushed might get such a one for a dollar, and, having bored a few auger holes in it, to admit the air at least, get into it when it rained and at night, and hook down the lid."[10] When I first read this passage, my eighteen-year-old self was like, "Yes! That's all I need! A garden—and a box!" I wouldn't be chained to a job, to paperwork, to bureaucracies. I wouldn't have to sell away all my hours. I could just *drop out*. "Money," Henry David crooned, "is not required to buy one necessary of the soul."[11]

Is this true? Is homesteading enough? Is five acres the key to independence?

If we wanted to find out what the original English peasants thought of this idea—that all you really need is a decent piece of land—we'd have to roll up our sleeves, blow the dust off the archives, and go questing for the fragments and scraps of writing that seventeenth- and eighteenth-century tillers left behind. With Bear Lick peasants, it's different. Because the transition happened within living memory, we can just sit down with the elders and ask them.

*   *   *

"What was it like," I ask Caleb, once the recorder is going, "when you were growing up?" His life, it turns out, was rich in experience, interesting, and full of close relationships; it was the opposite of lonely. But it was also "dirt poor," as Caleb put it. He was born in the early 1930s, one of nine children, and grew up on an eight-acre farm, with good-sized patches of fertile soil. The family lived in a square, four-room house that Caleb's father had framed and sided with lumbermill scraps. It had no electricity, running water, indoor toilet, or appliances of any kind.

They grew acres of crops on what we would now call a diversified small farm, the kind of farm celebrated in the writings of Thomas Jefferson and Wendell Berry. Caleb's mom was the farmer—his father wasn't around much—and she ran a tight ship. "Nobody fooled with her garden unless she said so," he said with a laugh. They raised twenty bushels of potatoes. An acre of corn. Rows and rows of cabbages. An orchard full of apple trees. They milked two Jersey cows and kept a hundred chickens, and the kids ate lots of chicken feet with cornbread and butter.

The family had enough to eat in July when the tomatoes were ripe on the vine and the corn was ripe in the husk. But what about October, when the first frosts rimed the pumpkin vines? What about January, when the land lay deep in gray sleep? And there were still months to go—the earliest crops didn't get planted until March and April. They put as much work into saving the harvest as they did into growing it; they stuffed their little plank house with food to see them through the winter. "We canned everything we raised," Caleb said. They'd pick wild strawberries and blackberries and can those, too. The space beneath every bed was filled with jars, which had to be kept from freezing. They stored potatoes in hay and apples in boxes. Cabbages could be bent over in the garden, "on the root," where they'd keep for a good while.

Caleb's mom ran the farm with skill and knowledge. She worked hard and had the help of the older children. It wasn't enough. They had to go to the store and buy soup beans in hundred-pound bags and lard in fifty-pound buckets. "We had it hard," Caleb says. "That's all I knowed. Hard work. I didn't know nothin' else."

All the other testimonies we have from the Bear Lick area—travelers' accounts, early photographs, interviews with elders like Caleb—tell a similar story. People in Bear Lick were skilled and resourceful, relying directly on farming for most of what they needed, but most of them were, nonetheless, poor. Born in the mountains in 1891, Morgan Abney remembered a time when "There was always something to fill your belly on, but sometimes it was pretty rough. Naturally, many a meal was eat with one thing on the table." In Abney's world, a wealthy family, "good livers," was a family that had more than one dish to eat for dinner. During Abney's childhood, the only way to "can" food for those cold days in January was to use a "little stone jar" and seal the lid with wax.[12]

Ruth Hamilton, Nathan's grandmother, was born in the late 1920s, a few years before Caleb, and her experience is very much the same. She grew up as one of seventeen children on a hillside farm. They plowed "plumb to the cliff line," but still had to rent some bottomland. Like Caleb, they lived in a slab house with gaps between the siding. In the winter, wind would blow through the walls, and in the morning "we had to walk down the steps in the snow." The children would take their shoes off in

March, when the weather began to warm, and not put them back on again until autumn. Some of her brothers and sisters couldn't attend high school because they couldn't afford a "decent suit" of clothes. Ruth herself didn't make it that far; she never "attended a single day of school." Travel was hard; the state didn't maintain the roads and the bridges. People had to do it themselves, using sledgehammers to bust rocks into gravel. "This road would get where you couldn't get through it," Ruth said, "'cause it would be so muddy and everything." It was, in the succinct words of another elder, "A 'poverished area."

This poverty wasn't something that people chose, like Thoreau in his lake-side cabin. It had real consequences, many of which we can glimpse in the stories above. One consequence was isolation. As Appalachian scholars have argued, mountains in themselves don't isolate people—but poverty does. Travel was hard and slow, and outsiders were uncommon. Taylor Shearer, born in 1911, talked about young boys who, at the sight of a stranger, would "take to the woods just like a gray fox." It was hard to access schooling. "Many people born in this area never set foot out of the mountain region," wrote an ethnographer who studied a neighboring county. "Schools, which met only two or three months a year, were taught by local people, many just beyond the illiterate stage and none well educated. Churches likewise were led by self-taught, local preachers whose main occupation was farming and who preached 'on the side'."[13]

Another consequence was that once they reached puberty, most women lived in a state of near-continual pregnancy or nursing. As we saw, Caleb was one of nine children; Ruth one of seventeen. Ruth herself, starting when she was fifteen years old, gave birth to eight children. This wasn't a harebrained scheme to produce farm laborers, as is sometimes claimed for peasant families; anyone who thinks that making babies is a way to get the chores done is probably a man.[14] Women in eastern Kentucky kept bearing until it killed them or they escaped into menopause. At the same time, women in more-affluent areas of the United States were already using various contraceptive techniques to have fewer and fewer offspring; average US fertility dropped from seven to three-and-a-half children per couple over the course of the 1800s.[15] Aside from the huge burden upon women's health, another effect of large families was to erode the amount of land available per mouth. From 1860 to 1930, the population of the Bear Lick area tripled, the number of farms skyrocketed, and the size of the average farm dropped dramatically.[16]

With doctors scarce, far away, and expensive, people had to provide their own health care. Folk remedies and faith healing were standard. They prayed and laid on hands. They used wild herbs. For a wide range of ailments, they applied poultices of coal oil, grease, or turpentine. "Groundhog oil"—made from actual groundhogs—would make kids gag and "throw out that hard phlegm."[17] Children especially suffered from the lack of professional medical care. A 1925 report found that out of six hundred schoolchildren, in relatively urban Madison County—home of the western end of Bear Lick—90 percent "had one or more ailments or deformities." Another survey of schoolchildren in Madison County, in 1933, found that "3,798 out of 4,980 had health-related problems."[18] Infant mortality was common during births in remote homes, and many children died from infections in the first years of life. "I had eight children," Ruth Hamilton said matter-of-factly, "and two of them deceased when they was little." Childbirth was risky for mothers as well. "Sometime the baby couldn't be born," said Eunice Allen, "and they'd lost the mother and baby."[19]

And then, during the Great Depression, things got even harder. Many families went hungry. As one interviewee put it, "Oh yeah, it was *rough* that year, buddy." "We had enough," said another, "but Lord, the people around us was hard for things. You couldn't hardly sit down and eat a good meal in comfort they's so hungry. People's so hungry."[20]

A few years ago, I visited Connemara, a remote, sparsely settled area in the far west of Ireland. It was a strikingly beautiful place. Narrow lanes wound between old stone walls, alongside dark streams full of trout. Emerald mountains rose on both sides of the road, silent and empty, tipped with bare rock; there was no sound but the moorland wind bending the foxgloves and bracken. Magpies, stark in their black and white, checkered the sky. It was a place where you wanted to linger, to bask in peace and solitude.

But then I noticed something ominous near the top of the mountains, something that wrenched my perspective and put the place into a new framework. On slopes so steep it would be hard to stand, where one stumble would ragdoll you to the valley floor, there were parallel furrows running beneath the grass. In the 1800s, before the famine, these valleys had been plowed all the way to the brim by peasants desperate for both food and rent. As locals are still likely to remark, "You can't eat scenery." In Bear Lick, it was much the same: they plowed, as Ruth said, "plumb to the cliff lines." Because the hills are now covered in young forest, you can't see the scars. But they are there all the same, like nail marks gouged into a prison wall.

*   *   *

In 1886 a twenty-three-year-old railroad station agent in Minnesota heard about an orphaned shipment of gold watches that had been sent to a local jeweler. Because the jeweler hadn't actually ordered the watches, he refused to accept them. Looking for extra income to help his rural family, the young man, Richard Warren Sears, used his connections along the railway to sell the watches to other station agents, paid off the manufacturer, and pocketed a nice profit. Within a couple of years, spurred by this initial success, Sears had written a small catalog, full of watches and jewelry and clever advertising, and distributed it through the Postal Service. He understood that the combination of rails and mail formed a new kind of network—the internet of the nineteenth century—that offered a novel way to connect customers to products. He used this network to outflank the brick-and-mortar retailers, the old-fashioned country stores that had long enjoyed near-monopoly status in small towns and country hamlets across the United States. As one early catalog proclaims, right across the front cover, "This book tells just what your storekeeper at home pays for everything he buys and will prevent him from overcharging you on anything you buy from him."[21]

By 1894 the Sears Catalog had grown to more than five hundred pages and reached millions of American homes. It listed thousands of items, ranging from kangaroo-calf ladies' boots and crushed Java coffee to "arsenic complexion wafers" and "five pounds fancy mixed candy for 35 cents." It also offered cutting-edge appliances and tools, such as a breach-loading double-barreled shotgun and a foot-powered sewing machine "so simple that it can be threaded in the dark by two motions of the hand." You could buy a wood cookstove with a ventilated oven, multiple burners, adjustable damper, and hot-water reservoir. You could even order a windmill—and a table-top corn grinder powered by that windmill.[22]

These kinds of consumer goods were the fruit of the rapidly maturing Industrial Revolution. Over time, in a trickle at first, then turning into a flood by the mid-1800s, more and more manufactured items appeared. Sewing machines, for example, had become popular in middle-class homes by the mid-1800s. By 1900 half of female survey respondents in New York City reported using condoms. On November 2, 1920, the corporation Westinghouse began broadcasting the first national radio station, KDKA; fifteen years later, 60 percent of US households owned a radio. Refrigerators became common in the 1930s, reducing the labor spent, mostly by women, in preserving food.[23] Before the development of antibiotics in the 1940s, no one could buy them, neither king nor pauper; afterward, tuberculosis and bubonic plague and gangrene could suddenly be cured—if you had money.

Caleb and Ruth and their friends and neighbors grew up poor for many reasons. When Kentucky was colonized, as we have seen, the rich took most of the better farmland. Ordinary people were in debt from buying land, or they didn't own land at all and had to sharecrop, or they had too many kids to feed. But cutting through these variables is one obdurate fact: even if they had enough land and could raise enough food to survive, the Sears Catalog made them poor. With the advent of each major new consumer product, the peasant farmers of the world fell a little more behind.[24]

Today, most of us are overwhelmed by this flood of consumer goods. Our lives are crowded with objects we don't truly need. iPods. Oversized houses. Televisions. Espresso makers. Excess clothing. Fish tanks. Our longest lasting individual legacy is not our good deeds, but the trail of plastic garbage we leave in our wake. Both my parents have had rental storage units packed to the ceiling with stuff. I've seen children—not generally a frugal demographic—so fatigued by opening Christmas presents that they lost interest and wandered outside to play with sticks. In the contemporary United States, even if we're poor and lack things we really need—quality schooling, health care, time off work—we are still burdened with excess stuff. It becomes hard to see how crucial modern consumer goods can be; the ones that really matter are all mixed in with diamond wedding rings and riding mowers, microwave ovens and embalming fluids. Under such circumstances, Thoreau's sermon on the simple life is compelling, and phrases like "sell your clothes and keep your thoughts" ring true.[25]

But many industrial products are crucial. All you need is a garden and a box to sleep in—until suddenly you need a dentist with an x-ray machine and a drill. Or bifocals. Boots in the winter. A cheap cookpot. Hernia surgery. A package of condoms. Some books wouldn't hurt, and maybe a trip overseas, to broaden the mind? Fully resisting this siren song of modern consumer goods is not hard—it's damn near impossible. Caleb's family couldn't resist. Wendell Berry didn't. Even Native Americans succumbed. Throughout eastern North America, Indian tribes helped wipe out beaver populations to feed Europe's fashion for beaver pelt hats. The beaver suddenly ceased to be just an animal and became a gateway to useful products; as one Native trapper remarked in Quebec in the seventeenth century, "The beaver does everything perfectly well, it makes kettles, hatchets, swords, knives, bread . . . in short, it makes everything."[26] Here on the Hoopa Reservation, in northern California, where I write these words, people signify and honor their heritage in many ways, but for fewer and fewer families does this involve foregoing modern goods.

There are many reasons to celebrate subsistence production; as we shall see, it continues to have a profound place in the modern world. But it no longer suffices as the sole means by which families make ends meet—industry creates too many vital objects that can't be grown in a garden or crafted by hand. This was brought home to me when my son Finn was born. Without a single, easily overlooked modern industrial product—a fetal heart monitor—he would have died in childbirth. Ultimately, this was the kind of question faced by Bear Lick farmers like Caleb and Ruth: what would you give up to save your child? How far would you travel? What would you sell?

* * *

They sold anything they could.

They sold any kind of farm produce they could find a market for, whether it was eggs, blackberries, or cream. Caleb's mom didn't give all the Jersey milk to the kids; she churned much of it into butter. "She would take this butter," Caleb said, "and walk over two miles to the store and sell it for fifty cent a pound. And she used that to buy the cornmeal and stuff that we had to have." A man named Stanley Ruppert told similar stories about his parents' search for ways to generate cash from the farm. "Corn, cattle, hogs, anything—*anything*—they could sell to, you know, make money. I can remember when mom would sell cream. She would sell three or four gallons at a time." As a kid, he'd carry eggs to the country store and sell them for "twelve, fifteen cents a dozen."

They drove flocks of geese to Richmond. They tried strawberry farming. One elder remembered gathering wild grapes and walnuts as a young girl and walking twelve miles to sell them in Berea. "As late as 1941," writes historian William Ellis, "many Madison County farm families depended on picking blackberries to supplement their income, making Madison County the leading blackberry county in the state."[27] They distilled moonshine from fermented corn, and sold that; in the early 1930s, Taylor Shearer drove around peddling gallon jars of 'shine from his car. Starting in the 1880s, people turned to tobacco—like pot today, a crop that commanded a high price and a large, dedicated group of customers. According to Morgan Abney, it "was the only cash crop that us mountain people had." They couldn't grow enough grain to sell, he said, nor enough grass to commercially raise cattle or livestock.[28]

They even sold the forest itself. Many families stripped chestnut oaks for the "tanbark," used in tanning hides. They split out staves to build liquor barrels for the bourbon makers in the bluegrass. Eventually, they clear-cut the remaining lumber and sold that. As a result of this heavy usage, by the end of the 1800s the land was eroded and abused. The woods had been "indiscriminately cut," according to a report by Berea College's Forestry Department, and the land "over-farmed, over-grazed, and burned repeatedly."[29] Even slopes at precipitous forty-degree angles had been cleared and planted. In every old photo I can find, the hills of Bear Lick Valley look hacked, naked, and raw, like a mangy dog.

In addition to selling produce and products, people sold their labor. Women sewed dresses, took in washing from better-off families, or walked into Berea to clean houses. Men worked as farmhands for those who owned more land; Morgan Abney worked eighteen years for a local landowner, earning two dollars a day for running his sawmill and a dollar-fifty for working his tobacco. Others traveled to find work on the railroads or on crews blasting roadbeds through the mountains—"driving steel," as they put it.

That's why so many farms were run by women: the menfolk were off looking for what they called "public jobs," which was any work that paid a wage. Caleb Hayward's mother was the farmer not because his father had run off and abandoned them, but because he worked in the coal fields farther to the east. Every morning, he would rise before dawn, crank a secondhand school bus, and drive two hours to the mines, picking up other miners along the way, for a small fee, until the bus was packed. Then he would work a full day on his knees at the bottom of a deep shaft, shoveling out narrow seams of coal, before climbing back into the bus and starting the long drive home.

*   *   *

Perhaps the most important question in the history of economics—and one begged by these stories of hardship—is this: "Where does material wealth come from?" Maybe it comes—as some experts in Europe thought in the 1500s—from amassing precious metals. At a glance, this seems to make sense: if I dug a forty-pound gold nugget from a riverbank, I could buy lots of stuff. If I rampaged through the Americas, stealing everyone's gold, I'd be richer yet. Today, we are likely to answer in terms of dollars: wealth boils down to how much money you have. But while I can trade money or bullion for things I need or want, these different types of currency are not really a *source* of wealth. A hunk of gold is not particularly useful, nor can it be wielded, by itself, as a tool to create other things that are useful.

In the most famous economics book ever written, *The Wealth of Nations*, Adam Smith offers a better answer to this question: material wealth comes from human labor. To get a feel for this, consider an aristocratic landowner—Green Clay, for example—sitting pretty on his forty-thousand-acre Madison County estate. But imagine he has no one to work that estate except himself and his family. Would they still live in a forty-four-room mansion? Does a steaming bath still await on a winter's morn? Who will cook the seven-course meal, with a quail stuffed into a pheasant crammed inside a goose? Who will brush the horses in the riding stables, polish the saddles, and muck the stalls? With only his own family's labor to command, such luxury is impossible. Even with all the land in the world, Green Clay would have still been just another peasant, earning his daily bread by the sweat of his own brow.

As we saw in the previous chapter, when elites in plantation Kentucky—or medieval Europe, for that matter, or imperial China, or the Incan Empire—owned land, they were only partly interested in the land itself. Owning land was largely a mechanism for controlling labor. If people need access to land so they won't starve, and you own the land, you can force them to hand over most of their daily exertions without sharing, in turn, an equivalent portion of your own exertions.

Once Adam Smith saw that the fundamental source of wealth was not veins of gold or acres of land, but the toil of human beings, it became clear that increasing the overall amount of wealth came down to one crucial thing: increasing the output of human labor. He wasted no time making this argument, opening his book by focusing on a single product: the little metal pins used in sewing, like those my mother kept by her Singer, stabbed into a fist-sized cloth strawberry. A single artisan, Smith argued, could make only a few pins per day. But contrast this with an early factory, where the process has been broken into a series of simple, repetitive motions. "One man draws out the wire," Smith wrote,

> Another straights it, a third cuts it, a fourth points it, a fifth grinds it at the top for receiving the head; to make the head requires two or three distinct operations; to put it on is a peculiar business, to whiten the pins is another; it is even a trade by itself to put them into the paper; and the important business of making a pin is, in this manner, divided into about eighteen distinct operations.

With this division of labor, the workers together produced enough pins that each one's share of the total amounted to about forty-eight hundred pins per day, clearly far more than a single craft worker could make on her own.[30]

Smith attributed this increase in labor output per hour—in labor *productivity*—to dividing the work into simple steps and having each worker focus on a single step. Although the workers' lives turn into nightmares of tedium, they also become heroically fast at their particular task. But the real reason dividing labor into simple steps unleashed a revolution is not the increased speed of the workers, it's that when work is made simple, it can be automated. It can be done by machines. And that's what the Industrial Revolution is in a nutshell: a set of techniques for reshaping production so that it can be done by machines.

Once people understood this and started systematically mechanizing production, almost everything about human life changed. The torrent of consumer goods listed in the Sears Catalog was unleashed. Ways of life that had sufficed for millennia—hunting and gathering, subsistence farming—were, for better or worse, rendered obsolete. The content of our hours was transformed. When was the last time you passed a day hoeing ragweed from an acre of corn? Or spent ten hours walking to visit nearby relatives? Or went a week without staring at a screen?

The most direct and immediate effect of mechanization is that workers can produce more stuff per hour than before. Often much, much more: a hundred times more. A thousand. Over time, as machinery is refined, the difference becomes ridiculous. In England in 1980, an actual pin factory cranked out eight hundred thousand pins per worker each day—167 times more than in Smith's prototypical factory. And the mechanization didn't stay in the factory; other endeavors, such as farming, were also mechanized. By 1860 a "threshing machine could thresh twelve times as much grain per hour as could six men"—a seventy-fold increase. A hectare of modern industrialized rice in Louisiana requires a hundred times less labor than a hectare of peasant rice in China.[31]

One consequence of this revolution in worker output is the possibility of much higher wages. This is easier to see if we step outside the fog of money and keep our eye on the labor. A handicraft worker who painstakingly built four pairs of boots in a day could be paid, at most, the equivalent of four pairs of boots. But what about a factory worker whose share of production for a day is a hundred pairs of boots? As a practical matter, the second worker could have a much higher wage. And, over the past two hundred years, wages in industrialized nations have risen dramatically. In 1914 aggressive, assembly-line automation allowed the Ford Motor Company to reduce the amount of labor in each Model T from "12½ hours to 93 minutes." This in turn allowed Henry Ford to double wages—in an effort to "stabilize the workforce"—to five dollars a day, roughly equivalent to $120 per day now.[32] "Depending on whose estimate you choose, and how you correct for inflation," notes Mark Ridley, "the average person alive in the world today earns in a year between ten and twenty times as much money, in real terms, as the average person earned in 1800."[33] While Bear Lick homesteaders were plucking grapes and walnuts one at a time and hiking twelve miles to Berea to sell them for pennies, factory workers in Detroit were thumbing through the latest catalogs and ordering washing machines and fridges, radios and electric lamps.

*   *   *

This is why, starting as early as the first real industrial boom in the United States, in the late 1800s, people migrated out of the mountains in search of jobs. They didn't just go down the road to the neighbor's sawmill or a couple of counties over to the coal fields. They also picked up and moved the whole family to factory cities like Dayton and Detroit. Over the following decades, Appalachian families followed the boom-and-bust cycles of the growing capitalist economy like an ocean tide, flowing out along the winding roads to Ohio and Indiana when plants were hiring, and flowing back when they weren't. During World War I, with factories humming, people left; during the Depression, when jobs disappeared, they came back, "perhaps believing it better to go hungry among kin," as Chad Berry writes, "than to beg in the North among strangers."[34]

In 1939 World War II erupted. Industrialization had changed war almost beyond recognition: without a flood of factory production, it is impossible to field armies of millions, satisfy the greedy appetite of machine guns, launch a thousand airplanes to salt entire cities with explosives—or, indeed, destroy a city with a single bomb. As the most industrial war yet, World War II was won on assembly lines as much as on front lines; the level of US production was astonishing. In five years, the United States cranked out "100,000 tanks and armored vehicles, 310,000 airplanes, 806,000 heavy trucks, 12.5 million rifles, and 41 billion rounds of ammunition." This output demanded millions of workers. Unemployment in the United States, more than 17 percent right before the war, dropped to essentially zero—1.2 percent—by the war's end in 1945.[35]

These home-front jobs yanked the plug, and the hollers of Appalachia drained like so many bathtubs. Unprecedented production drove unprecedented migration all over the rural South: millions of African Americans made their way north; millions more poor whites joined them. The outpouring was particularly intense from the highland South. As in the mountains of post-famine Ireland, heavily farmed side-valleys all along Bear Lick fell silent. In many hollers, only a family or two remained, to watch the forest slowly reclaim the fields. From 1940 to 1950, Jackson County, which lies partly within Bear Lick Valley, lost more than 40 percent of its population—during a time when the population of the United States as a whole increased by 20 percent.[36] The same pattern held throughout the southern mountains. "In some counties," notes historian Ronald Eller, "the movement off the land in the 1950s was so profound that it almost eliminated farming altogether. Forty counties in eastern Kentucky and West Virginia lost more than seventy percent of their farm population."[37] This is why, in the late 1960s, when hippie back-to-the-landers started coming into the mountains, looking for cheap land, they found plenty of it.

Everyone of Caleb Hayward and Ruth Hamilton's generation was affected by this outmigration. Toward the end of the war, in search of a wage, Ruth and her husband left the mountains. Following trails blazed by neighbors and kin, they found their way to Dayton, where he got hired in a Frigidaire factory, and she found work—as a sixteen-year-old—building radios and other military equipment; after the war, she got paid to dismantle that same equipment. "Half of Kentucky was right there," she said. They did their best to settle into urban life, making payments on a house and raising children. Caleb also left in his teens. He headed to Akron, where he worked mostly as a carpenter and painter, sometimes inside the factories, sometimes out. He spent most of his adult life moving around the Midwest, working in different cities.

The war also brought, for the first time, significant numbers of modern jobs to the area around Bear Lick. Many families who didn't move to Ohio moved to Richmond or Berea. In 1941 the military began construction on the local Blue Grass Army Depot, a massive base that "sucked up," as one elder put it, more than six thousand men from nearby mountain areas. After the war ended, factories began to locate in the South, in search of cheap, non-union labor; while workers were moving north in search of higher wages, business owners began moving jobs south in search of lower wages. Over the following decades, this trend has continued. In 1939 there were almost no industrial jobs in Madison County, but by 2010, such jobs had become the single largest category of employment, occupying more than four thousand workers. Ironically, given its late start, the proportion of workers employed in manufacturing in Madison County is currently twice the national average.[38] And to this day, the population of many mountain areas, including Jackson County and the eastern reaches of Bear Lick Valley, remains lower than it was during the early part of the 1900s, when the land was full of peasant farmers.

In England in 1723, when the Black Act was passed, peasants vigorously resisted losing access to land; in 1723 there was nowhere for them to go. When Karl Marx and Friedrich Engels wrote in the mid-1800s, the "satanic mills" of Manchester and Liverpool and Staffordshire—where children were literally worked to death—may not have looked any better than peasant farming.[39] In Bear Lick Valley in 1940, the story played out differently. Over the intervening decades, industry had changed far more than peasant farming; though manufacturing work remained dangerous and hellish, wages had risen. No baron or duke had to pry people like Ruth and Caleb from the land.[40] They didn't follow the parable about the rise of capitalism; they didn't blacken their faces and sneak out at night to girdle trees and poach deer. Nor did they reread their copies of *Das*

Kapital or consult the journals of Thomas Jefferson for advice. Instead, they packed what little they had, pulled on their worn shoes, gathered their children, and enclosed themselves.

* * *

That's how the story of homesteading in Bear Lick ends: people left it behind for the rapidly growing suburbs of Ohio and Indiana, or even for those of Richmond and Berea. Or, rather, that's one very common, and important, ending. But that's not the only outcome—there are others, such as those who toughed it out in the mountains, or the hippie back-to-the-landers we'll visit in the next chapter. After all, I didn't interview Caleb in Akron, and the two Berea College students who interviewed Ruth found her in a mountain cabin, not a tract home in Dayton. While the vast outmigration from the mountains made sense from a strictly economic perspective, life has many facets, and leaving felt bittersweet. People left, as my colleague Chad Berry wrote, with a "divided heart."[41] They found more money in the cities, but less freedom. More goods, but less beauty. More opportunities, but less independence. Like the current in a river, flow to the cities generated its own eddy—a counterflow of people moving back to the hills.

Ruth lived in Dayton for more than sixteen years, but the whole time she felt ill at ease. Where was God to be found, in all the bustle and consumption? "I tried to be a Christian," she said, "but couldn't hardly. It was just too numbered up." Eventually, she fell truly sick, which she took to be a tribulation from God. "The Lord, He moved back His hand," she remembered. "He let me be tried. I had leukemia. My blood just dried up. I never went to the doctor, now, but the Lord said to me, He said, 'Your blood's dryin' up.'" Then, as she lay abed, He came in a vision and told her to listen to the words that her father used to sing. And this song came back to her, showing the way:

> My eyes are on the mountaintop,
> I'm running for my life.
> I left ol' Solomon on his plain
> With all his sin and strife.

I'm to the highland bound.
I'm seeking higher ground.
He came and made it oh so plain
I'm to the highland bound.

Ruth heeded the words. In 1960, ailing and exhausted, she returned to Bear Lick, to the same cabin she lived in as a child. She slowly cleared the cobwebs and waited. Slowly swept the floor and waited. "I told the Lord, now, I said, 'This is it. If you gotta take me just do what you gotta do.'" But the mountains lifted her above the madness of the city, high into clean air, closer to heaven. And the Lord touched her again and healed her, and she has lived in that cabin ever since.

Today, Ruth's oldest son and Nathan's father, William, has pursued a subsistence-oriented lifestyle for decades. William and his wife, Ethel, live in a cabin they built from scratch, logging and milling the lumber themselves. Like Nathan's homestead, it's deep in a holler, beyond the grid. William doesn't own a truck, plows his fields with horses, and I've never seen him wear anything but a homemade button-up shirt and homemade dungarees. He has a strong, elegant rural accent. If you met him on his homestead, it would be hard not to assume he is simply living in the way he has always known—that he is just walking the road worn by the footsteps of his forebears.

But William wasn't born in the holler. He was born and raised in Dayton. He was in his teens when he first moved to rural Kentucky. Then, once he and Ethel married, they moved back to Ohio to find work, bought a house, and began to settle down. It was only then, after giving it a try, they decided they didn't want that life. William and Ethel's homesteading is not just leftover from the past. It's not inertia, or a relic.

It's a choice.

When Ruth was a child, her family homesteaded out of necessity. There was no other way for them to live, no other realistic path. Now her children, and her children's children, are engaged in many of those same activities: they grow big gardens, put food up for the winter, build houses and root cellars, make clothes. It looks like the same activities that have been going on in Bear Lick for generations—but looks can be deceiving.

My sister Orowi sometimes dresses in the traditional clothing of her father's people, the Yuroks.[42] If she had been born a couple of centuries ago, the act of putting on such clothing would have just been part of an ordinary day; unremarkable, unavoidable even. Now, that same act has different meanings. Sometimes, it's part of a ceremony, where part of the purpose is to celebrate Yurok traditions, to keep them alive. I've seen her wear traditional clothing to a school, to demonstrate for children how Yuroks used to live. This hasn't been part of Orowi's experience, but in some places, like Cherokee, North Carolina, a Native American might wear traditional clothing as part of a paid performance for outsiders. An activity that once had a certain set of meanings—donning her Native wardrobe—now has a different set of meanings, like it or not; there's no undoing this kind of shift.

Or consider the mountains of western Ireland: 175 years ago, the steep slopes were a burden upon the humans who toiled across them. Now those who walk there find them a balm. Same mountain, different meaning.

In an important sense, all homesteaders in Bear Lick—bohemians *and* country folks—are back-to-the-landers now. No one is homesteading automatically, because it's all they've ever known, or because they must subsist or starve. This is not to say it's just a hobby, something to do in the evenings, like playing golf or doing crossword puzzles. It's a potent set of economic actions with real repercussions for how people make ends meet. But since no one is driven to serious subsistence production because it's their only economic path, they must be driven there by something else. What they are up to, above all, is searching for ways to resist certain aspects of capitalist modernity. They are trying to build, in other words, shelter from the machine.

* * *

Ironically, the same Industrial Revolution that pulled Appalachians out of the mountains has made it easier to return. On the back of the increased labor productivity created through mechanization, a different kind of economy—often painfully, through political struggle—has been built. Compared with the pre–World War II United States, real wages are generally higher, even in a lower-income region like eastern Kentucky.[43]

Federal and state governments, chastened by the Great Depression, play a much larger economic role, providing at least minimal support to the poor, the ill, and the elderly through programs like WIC, the Earned Income Tax Credit, and Social Security. The labor-consuming aspect of handicrafts can now be presented as a virtue, as handmade rocking chairs or pottery mugs are marketed as art, commanding premium prices. Subsistence production itself has become easier. While they avoid modern products like televisions, blenders, and computers, the Hamiltons use four-wheelers to travel around the holler, chainsaws to fell trees, a portable bandsaw to mill lumber, and power saws to cut that lumber. At night, William wears an LED headlamp stretched over the band of his Amish hat.

But industry also *pushed* them back. Even as mechanization boosted wages enough to strike a funeral bell for the peasant way of life, wages didn't rise as much as they should have. There are many ways to detect this shortfall in wages, but one way is to note that the Industrial Revolution in the United States was actually built by ordinary people; it was, in a real sense, a people's revolution. This is not how it's portrayed. We tend to see it as a creation of "titans of industry" like Cornelius Vanderbilt, Andrew Carnegie, and John D. Rockefeller. That's what the parable of enclosure and other nostalgic treatments of peasant life suggest: the Industrial Revolution was created by elites, and rammed down everyone else's throat. Until I worked in a factory, that's how I saw it. But it wasn't elites who laid the foundations of the factories, raised the walls and ran the roof beams, set the axles and gears, and pulled the wiring. It wasn't famous men who cranked up the assembly line and kept it running. When a machine on the factory floor breaks, it's not fixed through the ingenuity and skinned knuckles of a titan of industry—it's fixed by a worker. The reason we hear about Vanderbilt and Carnegie and Rockefeller isn't because they built the Industrial Revolution.

It's because they *owned* it.

That's why workers kept only a fraction of the wealth their labor and know-how produced. As the poet Robert Frost noted, revolutions ought to be done by halves, or you turn all the way around and end up back where you started, with the "same class up on top."[44] The Industrial Revolution was no exception. As people shifted their living away from the land, the macro-parasitic class shifted the focus of their ownership accordingly; they had to go where the labor was found. To be an aristocrat in the modern world, it doesn't pay to worry about owning land. It's much better to own a factory.[45]

The exploitation built into modern industrial labor is one of the things that drove people away from the city and back to the land. After thirty years of living and working in the Midwest, Caleb Hayward finally moved back to Bear Lick. Like Ruth, he returned in part because he missed the mountains and the beauty of nature. He preferred the solitude of rural life. "I like to keep all my old junk," as he put it, "out of somebody's face." He felt that subsistence production was a valuable set of skills that ought to be preserved. "Better be takin' notice," he said, "of how to grow a garden, and how to fend for yourself. How to cook and how to can. I hope we don't have to use it again, but I'm afraid one day we might have to. And it'll be a lost art then."

But he also returned to homesteading and simple living as a way to gain a measure of economic independence. He hated working heavy for light pay. Hated to see hard-earned money drained away so easily on unneeded things. "I'm gettin' close to dying here, got my headstone, got my box built," he told me. "But just to keep me in the funeral home for twenty-hour hours—and they ain't gonna do nothin to me, 'cept put some powder on my face, put me in my box, and bring me back out here—and it's nine hunderd something dollars. That don't make good sense. Nine hunderd something dollars just to ride in an old hearse."

"That's the most expensive ride you'll ever take!" I exclaimed.

"Not plannin' on takin' it," he replied. "I don't have to take it. Get somebody to put me in my box right here. Why should I want to go from a funeral home? It don't make no sense. Everybody's out to make a quarter. Even make a quarter off a dead person."

That's exactly what he did. When Caleb passed, his family washed his body and lowered it into the coffin he had built, right there in his little house in the woods. They carried him across the porch to the bed of a pickup, drove him a couple hundred feet down the gravel drive, and buried him for free, beside his garden, in the earth he loved.

4 Never Seen So Much Hair in Your Life

Late morning in Bear Lick. Midday heat begins to gather; it has been, so far, a hot July. Virginia Webb is throwing pots on her porch. Inside the straw-bale house, which is now almost finished, she has a modern electric pottery wheel—but mostly she uses the kick wheel set up beside the porch railing, with sweeping views over the green valley below. The kick wheel is made of a wooden strutwork supporting a heavy concrete disk, about three feet across and six inches thick, laid over on its side and hanging, a few inches above the floor, from a vertical steel axle. Atop the axle, about waist high, rests the much smaller metallic wheel upon which she works the clay.

Perched on a seat taken from an old tractor, Virginia gives the flywheel quick little rhythmic kicks. The big concrete wheel turns ponderously, with a low, groaning rumble; when she stops kicking, a couple of minutes pass before it finally winds all the way down. But now, within the lacework of her fingers, a lump of red-brown clay morphs into a perfect cylinder, then blossoms into an elegant mug. With a deft motion, she pulls a wire tight and slices the mug free from the wheel, then sets it, soft and fragile as butter, on a wooden rack beside her. The rack is filled with rank upon rank of mugs; she's been working all morning.

Everything on the porch has been anointed with clay. She has an ochre streak across one temple where she swiped away a mosquito. The rough-sawn cedar floor planks are dusty with it. A passionflower vine braiding itself over the railing is polka-dotted with red droplets. Bolted to a porch beam above Virginia's head is a shelf of books and journals about ceramics, their spines highlighted with rusty fingerprints.

Her life is palpably of the earth: her straw-bale home itself is cloaked, inside and out, in layers of clay plaster dug from the land. Her garden and orchard are projects of soil, as is the little pond she uses to water them. Most of her cash income is from earth: she sells "functional ware"—mugs and bowls, saucers and plates—out of her little artisan shop and at the craft fairs for which Berea is famous. A few times a year, when she's filled it and bricked up the door, she'll stay awake late into the night feeding slab lumber into the two-thousand-degree inferno of her kiln. When a firing falls on the weekend, she'll invite friends over and turn work into play: share a few cold ones, play guitar, sing some Jean Ritchie and John Prine.

As the clay flows under her touch, she tells me of plans and projects and memories. She is learning to grow perennials and to cultivate the useful woodland species that already occur naturally on her land, a practice she calls "wildcrafting." She's set up a small water turbine, "a micro-hydro system," in the creek that cascades down the hillside near her house. At some point, she hopes to use the turbine to trickle-charge an old car she's retrofitting to run on electricity.

When I ask how she came to be so curious and open to trying new things, she pauses for a moment, glancing at the recorder, then gives an "eh, who cares?" shrug, and says, "Noah Piper put seven grams of mushrooms in me and it changed me forever. Because I had a spiritual experience, of being born again." She pauses once more, to add an apologetic footnote. "I have the internal Christian language regardless of how much I study or read. But," she continues, "the things that were happening inside of me were holy, sacred things. And I was literally born again and blessed with sacred songs." She only tripped on shrooms five or six times, but ever since—in addition to viewing life from new angles—she has become a serious student of mycology and gathers reishis and other healing fungi to make medicinal tinctures.[1]

Virginia lived in Seattle and spent time in other major cities, and when I ask how she would explain her homesteading life to a city dweller, she gives a long, lyrical treatment of the metaphysical virtues of living close to nature in a place that's not tame. "I am connected to the physical world," she says, "to the nature of the cycles and processes of things, the rhythms of the way that seasons move and when it's the right time to do this, and the right time to do that. So that I'm not living separate from physical reality, I'm not living this schizophrenic, separated, living-only-in-my-mind, ethereal kinda life. I live in my body and I live on the planet and I live with its body." She presses another lump of clay onto the wheel and quickly centers it. "I have a composting toilet that's really simple. I'm integrated with my human waste. I take that waste and I use it—like a tree drops its leaves to feed itself—I use that on my shrubs, my bushes, my berries and nut trees. I'm in connection, not just in my mind and in myth, but I'm directly connected. I walk to the spring for my own drinking water. I don't walk for my water for showers or baths or dishes, but I do for the water I drink. It's a sacred walk for me."

Virginia slices another mug free and fills the last empty space on the rack. She climbs down off the kick wheel and reaches both arms toward the porch rafters, leaning backward and audibly cracking her spine. Then she grabs an eyeglass case off the porch railing and pulls out a little zip-lock bag and a homemade ceramic pipe that was first fired one night in her kiln. Carefully packing the little bowl with her pinky, she asks, with warm southern hospitality, "Care for a toke?"

*   *   *

Alongside the back-to-the-land movement created by returning Appalachian migrants like Ruth Hamilton and Caleb Hayward, a parallel movement arose in the late 1960s.[2] This is the back-to-the-land movement we have heard of, the one that supposedly began when the hippies in their retrofitted school buses overflowed San Francisco and flooded the countryside in a Day-Glo exodus. At the same time that abandoned farm houses in Bear Lick Valley were about to collapse, the farm fields almost lost to forest, participants in this movement began to show up, looking for cheap land. Virginia Webb is a self-avowed member of this hippie back-to-the-land movement. Politically, she's left of Bernie Sanders; socially, she's left of gay marriage. "Oh yeah," she exclaims, when I ask if she would consider herself part of the counterculture. "I'm off-the-charts liberal. I'm extra-crunchy." Crunchy, as in granola.

As I mentioned in the first chapter, the hippie phenomenon has been portrayed ambivalently. On the one hand, it has been, if not celebrated, then at least mainstreamed. Things that were fringe in 1968 are now normal. Even small towns have yoga studios and Montessori schools. As late as the 1980s, no fast-food joint in Berea would hire me, because I had long hair; now the dude at the register sports a fauxhawk and a frisbee in his earlobe. In eleven states and counting, pot is legal. There's a box in the calendar for Earth Day, and probably a box in your kitchen for recycling. Counterculture spectacles that would have generated breathless headlines in 1970 now garner no headlines at all. Several times a year, for instance, music festivals with as many people, as much nudity, and more drugs than Woodstock take place—even in a state like Tennessee that fifty years ago was scandalized by a single busload of Merry Pranksters. And yes, you can buy extra-crunchy granola in any grocery store. As one editorialist concluded, surveying such mainstreamed elements, "the hippies were right!"[3]

On the other hand, the hippie counterculture is often subject to ridicule and harsh stereotypes. According to this framing, hippies were basically spoiled kids who grew up in the great postwar boom, innocent of the darkness of economic depression and global war. Carefree, lazy, and naïve, they gathered in hip urban enclaves to rebel against the uptight culture of their parents. They smoked pot, frolicked promiscuously, neglected to bathe or groom, and rhapsodized over adolescent visions and schemes. In newspaper coverage of the hippie counterculture, both then and now, there is a focus on excess and extremes. The tone runs from amusement— "their favorite dessert was hash brownies, washed down with electric Kool-Aid"—to stern judgment, where the Haight-Ashbury of "moon-faced narcissists and dropouts" was "idyllic for about five minutes" before descending into an LSD-fueled nightmare of rape and murder.[4]

This dismissive way of seeing the sixties counterculture—and sixties protest in general—has been aptly described as a "death narrative." In this storyline, sixties dissent flourished for a moment and then passed away, like a melting snowflake, leaving little trace in the world.[5] When it is noticed at all in newspapers and books, in television shows and movies, the back-to-the-land movement is more often than not seen through this death narrative lens.[6] If hippies seem ludicrous in the city—supposedly their native habitat—they must be downright laughable when they stumble off into the woods.

Clichéd portrayals of the back-to-the-land movement also happen for a practical reason: the movement is, in fact, a difficult phenomenon to study. It's scattered along backroads, tucked away in hollers, hiding out among canyons and arroyos. Even participants see only their own small part of the movement and often mistake that part for the whole. At a conference in Vermont in 1998, attended by former back-to-the-landers, the death narrative was rampant. After a "brief heyday" in the late sixties, attendees concluded, the rural commune movement "died by its own hand, impaled on its excesses." One participant, choking back tears, said, "There was a brief, shining moment when we knew it could work. . . . We knew it could work, but we blew it."[7]

As a result both of stereotypes and the challenges of research, the dominant picture of the counterculture back-to-the-land movement is based on a handful of famous, outlandish, and often out-of-control communes, places like Morningstar Ranch and Black Bear Ranch in northern California, The Farm in Tennessee, Total Loss Farm in Vermont, or Drop City in southern Colorado. When we look at the back-to-the-land movement, it's hard to take our eye away from these flamboyant exemplars, with their sex and drugs and parties, their made-for-Hollywood transgressions.

The real counterculture back-to-the-land movement remains largely unwritten. In Bear Lick Valley, we still get only one slice. But that slice is more diverse, more enduring in time, and more profound than prevailing views suggest it ought to be, which is the tale at the heart of this chapter. For instance, according to stereotypes, Virginia Webb, who appears to be a classic hippie back-to-the-lander, should have grown up in a middle-class family in a suburb of Boston or a neighborhood of Seattle. When she moved to Bear Lick, she should have come in as an outsider. But that's not what happened. Virginia didn't move into low-income rural Appalachia.

She grew up there.

*　　*　　*

When I began my research, I expected to find hippies firmly at the center of Bear Lick's counterculture back-to-the-land movement—an expectation that living in the area for years had done little to diminish. Elements of an explicitly hippie-flavored counterculture are indeed strongly present. However, alongside and intertwined with those elements are many other traditions and forms of leftist cultural dissent. One man, Joseph Rivard, who began homesteading after graduating from the University of Kentucky in the early seventies, was considered by his country neighbors to be a hippie; at the beginning of our interview, I also held that assumption. In fact, he had arrived at somewhat similar social critiques and attitudes but came to them through living on a Quaker farm during the summers, working with his hands and encountering the Quakers' long-standing progressive traditions. Another man was radicalized by his experience as a Catholic priest in Latin America during the heyday of liberation theology. A back-to-the-lander named Lori West was influenced by a hippie counterculture, but not in Berkeley or Greenwich Village—she encountered it at an international high school in Israel.

Despite their varied backgrounds, the bohemians in Bear Lick form a fairly coherent leftist social group, united by progressive political and social attitudes, as well as by the shared practical challenges of home-building and gardening and so on. But they are a multi-stranded left, among which the hippie counterculture is but one strand, albeit a highly visible one. And the visible marks can be misleading, like when I made assumptions about Joseph Rivard based on his long hair—or about a young woman with dreadlocks who lives in a yurt. It turned out that she found her formative counterculture experience in an urban Christian commune, not with a tab of acid on her tongue at a Grateful Dead concert.

The bohemian back-to-the-landers violate stereotypes in other ways as well. Some are older when they begin homesteading, like Lori West, who had a full adult life before opening a chapter as a back-to-the-lander. Others are second generation, like Cody Shulyer—the fellow we met in chapter 1 who said corporations are artificial intelligences—who was probably conceived in his parents' VW van as they drove from San Francisco to Bear Lick in 1969. Many are not from the affluent backgrounds that cliché leads you to expect, even when they are from the city. One homesteader, Cynthia Hillyer, grew up in Cincinnati with working-class parents. She hated school, had no thought of college, and went into factory work right after high school. Her first job was packing cookies for eight hours a day at Keebler; her roommates said the smell made them crave milk. Before finding her way to Berea College and Bear Lick, she spent five years working in a second factory, a vast space full of noise and grime, "making machines that made machines that made airplanes."

But most surprising of all, nearly half the bohemian homesteaders in Bear Lick Valley are, like Virginia Webb, from rural families. Raised mostly by her grandparents, Virginia grew up in a small town in Rockcastle County, just south of Bear Lick. Like so many Appalachians, they moved to Ohio to find work, but had been drawn back by the mountains and the mountain way of life. Virginia's grandma waited tables and her grandpa cooked at a restaurant by the freeway, but after work every night they drove to the country, back to the rivers and woods and wild things that felt like home. They grew all their own vegetables, Virginia told me, and kept turkeys, chickens, and a milk cow; every autumn they slaughtered a bull and a pig.

For Virginia, homesteading is the continuation of a valued family tradition, a celebration of where she is from; it gives the best parts of her childhood a living place in the modern world. In embracing subsistence production, she is choosing to walk the road made by the footsteps of her forebears—and it is, she says, a "good road, a sustainable road."

At the same time, her progressive values are at odds with the social and political attitudes of much of her family. "My dad and my uncle, my mom, all those people, even my brother," she laments, "they're very conservative people." Growing up, she was taken to fundamentalist country churches, which is why she remarked that she can't avoid the "internal Christian language" even after years of wide reading and reflection. The services were full of music she found beautiful, and, all too often, ideas she found repugnant. In this, her experience is similar to other Appalachian bohemians who feel a tension between elements of their natal culture they value and embrace, and elements—such as racism, militant nationalism, homophobia, or fundamentalism—they reject.

For some country folks, the manufacturing jobs that eventually started to show up in Madison County allowed them to stay home; they no longer had to migrate to Dayton or Indianapolis for economic reasons. For Virginia, the presence in the countryside of a progressive counterculture plays a similar role: she doesn't have to migrate to the city for cultural reasons.

*   *   *

Elijah Amaro, a tall, slender back-to-the-lander with a quick smile, first arrived in Bear Lick Valley with the Rainbow Family of Living Light. The Rainbow Family is what you would get if you distilled, like moonshine, the more flamboyant elements of sixties hippiedom into an overpowering essence. The Rainbows held their first "gathering" in 1972, a four-day event that drew twenty thousand people onto National Forest land in Colorado. The purpose of the event, according to ethnographer Richard Niman, was to "further the cause of world peace by prayer and to create a peaceful and non-hierarchical society that can serve as a model for reforming 'Babylon'"—the Rainbow nickname for modern industrial society.[8]

The gathering that brought Elijah to Appalachia took place in a remote creek valley within Daniel Boone National Forest, just past the eastern end of Bear Lick. To get there, you zig-zagged along several miles of gravel, past a dozen police cars prowling for dope, and into a hilltop field that had morphed into a dusty parking lot. The field was crammed with high-mileage vehicles of every sort, many of them worn from serving double duty as both transport and home. From this last outpost of Babylon, you plunged into the cool shade of the forest, along a trail that wound down the hillside for a mile or so to the gathering site. A steady flow of Rainbows passed by, running errands back to the parking lot: a skinny young man in Lennon glasses and jean jacket with a guitar slung across his back; a middle-aged woman wearing purple overalls, breathing hard, carrying a toddler on each hip; a Gandalf figure with a long white

beard and a walking stick woven with feathers and seashells. They called
enthusiastic greetings: "Welcome home, sister!" "We love you, brother!"
Scattered on both sides of the trail, all through the woods as far as you
could see, were tents and tarps that would serve, for a week, as housing
for more than two thousand souls.

Come dusk, people flowed down the hillsides into a central meadow,
held in the curve of a stream, where a great bonfire was ringed by an even
greater drum circle. Forty men or more, hair pleated with sweat, sinewy
arms flashing in the amber light, filled the night with a vast throbbing
beat; women, smeared and tatted with mud, writhed trancelike in the
space between the drums and the flame. Huddled together like tourists,
a few clumps of local country boys wandered the meadow, staring wide-
eyed at the bare-breasted dancers. Blowing a flute like Pan, an older man
pranced through the crowd, his skirt whirling in time with his beard. A
couple of cops, struggling to remain stern-faced, walked the camp as a
grinning escort of Rainbows forewarned everyone with affable shouts
of "six up!"

For several years, such gatherings—and the endless skein of road trips
that connected them—had been Elijah Amaro's home. But after this gathering, Elijah and a dozen other Rainbows, hoping to settle, found a cheap
piece of land in Bear Lick. They had been caught by the sixties dream of
building homes and growing food, of creating community, of finding a
permanent way to exit Babylon, instead of just squatting temporarily in
the forest between dumpster diving raids. All wooded slope, their land
had been hit by an ice storm, and many of the trees had folded under the
frozen weight into a massive tangle. "The first night I spent out there,"
Elijah recalled, "we spent all day cutting out a little thirty-by-thirty section just to set a tarp to put over a fire, and that's how we started, you
know—just a tarp and a fire pit."

The whole scene feels like a nostalgic postcard from the 1960s, but—in
another departure from the standard story—it's not. I can write a vivid
description of the Rainbow gathering because I was there, a curious ama-
teur ethnographer in my early twenties. The gathering took place not
in the sixties or seventies, at the ostensible height of the counterculture,
but in 1994, well after it was supposed to have withered and died.

The same is true of the counterculture back-to-the-land movement. Scattered as they are across the landscape and across time, bohemian homesteaders are hard to count. Without a doubt, the late sixties and early seventies saw a surge in back-to-the-land activity in Bear Lick. Some of these folks remain on their homesteads today, some have shifted to other rural places, others have moved to towns and cities, a few have passed away. There is also a penumbra of shorter-term participants who add to the head-counting challenge—people who live for a year or two on the land, then move on to another phase of life, not unlike students who spend four years on a college campus then go on to other things. But in terms of overall numbers, there are as many bohemian homesteaders in Bear Lick today as there were in, say, 1970. Over time, the steady trickle of those leaving the land has been balanced by a steady trickle of new arrivals.

This pattern seems to hold in many places across the United States, with the exception of locations afflicted with astronomical land prices, like the San Francisco Bay Area or parts of New England. Social scholar Jeffrey Jacob, for example, found a robust back-to-the-land movement when he did a large-scale national survey in 1992.[9] Although it has waxed and waned, the idea that the sixties back-to-the-land movement lasted only a few years and then collapsed is simply not true. About five years ago, I stopped keeping track of new bohemian homesteads in Bear Lick—I had done so all through graduate school as part of my research—and during that short span, dozens of homesteads have sprung up that I know little about. If I wasn't paying at least some attention, it would be easy to assume the back-to-the-land movement in Bear Lick had stalled once my own focus shifted. It's a bit like the Woodstock-style music festivals, which just kept chugging along after the media eye grew bored and wandered elsewhere.

The bohemian back-to-the-land movement not only lasted longer than supposed, but started earlier. Here in Kentucky, hints and glimpses of these earlier movements are visible. In Bear Lick itself, a well-educated woman named Eva Mullins, along with her artist husband, built a beautiful stone and wood home, known as Wood Betony, in the 1930s. Another early figure was Harlan Hubbard, born in northern Kentucky in 1900.

Hubbard was an author and intellectual who rejected the new mass consumer culture; in 1944 he and his wife, Anna, built a simple houseboat and spent eight years floating down the Ohio and Mississippi, an adventure chronicled in the book *Shantyboat*. After that, they turned to homesteading, and shared their experiences in *Payne Hollow: Life on the Fringe of Society*, a book that influenced many young people in the 1970s when it was published. Like the bohemian back-to-the-land movement today, these earlier versions were comprised of a multi-stranded left; they were, in the words of historian Dona Brown, "anarchists, socialists, and progressives; promoters of the arts and crafts, the 'simple life,' or the single tax."[10]

In the United States, with its agrarian mythos, cities have often been greeted with ambivalence, and back-to-the-land efforts have particularly deep roots. If it's hard to count homesteaders in a single valley today, it's impossible to do so for an entire nation over a span of more than two centuries. Nonetheless, we can get a rough sense of the ebb and flow of back-to-the-land activity from the written words it leaves behind. One of the most influential back-to-the-land books, *Ten Acres Enough*—forefather of a whole line of titles like *Five Acres and Independence*—was published more than 150 year ago, in 1864, when the industrializing economy lurched into pronounced boom and bust cycles. Since then, the flow of books and articles extolling the wisdom of returning to the land has risen and fallen, but never run dry. During periods of economic and political crisis, it reliably swells into a flood, peaking, for example, in the years before World War I and then again during the Great Depression.[11]

The long history of radical back-to-the-land movements shouldn't come as a surprise. Around the world and across the centuries, we find rural subsistence embraced as a means of economic, cultural, and spiritual self-defense. In 1904 in South Africa, an earnest urban lawyer named Mohandas Gandhi left the city of Durban to set up Phoenix Settlement, to be followed several years later by Tolstoy Farm, both experiments in simple, subsistence-based livelihood. Even once he became the Mahatma, Gandhi continued, until his death, to be a back-to-the-lander, interested in the possibilities of "cooperative commonwealth."[12] In 1874 in tsarist Russia, middle-class intellectuals known as Narodniks headed into the countryside—"going to the people," as they put it—to live among the peasants and persuade them to revolt against the tsar. They encountered, perhaps unsurprisingly, a difficult cultural gulf between themselves and the rural populace.[13] It goes back even farther. As early as 1649 in England, for example, in response to the enclosures, a group arose calling themselves "the Diggers" and advocating a return to rural collectivism. "It is tempting to see the Diggers as the original 'back to the land' movement," says Simon Fairlie, noting that many of them were townsfolk and "idealistic drop-outs" who "probably didn't wield anything heavier than a pen."[14]

Tempting, but incorrect. Back-to-the-land movements go back farther still—all the way back to the birth of the city. Without a city, after all, there is no such thing as the country. The countryside itself exists, of course, but the *idea* of "the country" does not. No one sees it as a particular kind of place until a city draws the contrast—and then, suddenly, the countryside becomes a distinct landscape with a distinct way of life, permanently in tension with the urban and the urbane. If the city beckons with lamplight and crowds, so does the country with starlight and solitude. No sooner had people found themselves in towns and cities, Dona Brown writes, than they "began to calculate what they had lost."[15] It wasn't long before some of them pointed their feet back toward the newly idyllic hinterlands, which had become, for the first time, not just an object of nostalgia, but a means of escape.

* * *

San Diego. May 1972. Craig Williams was twenty-four years old, a gruff, profane, handsome New Yorker with a brown ponytail and a deep, commanding voice. He was living on the beach in a sort of impromptu commune of young activists in a half-dozen rental shacks. But they weren't there to surf. On the other side of the planet, US bombers rained death upon Vietnamese peasants, and growing numbers of Americans understood that this had to stop. Amid rising clamor in the streets, President Nixon and the Republican Party were gearing up for their election-year convention, to be held in San Diego in a couple of months. Craig and his antiwar friends planned to shut it down.

I'm interviewing Craig in his second-story office in a small nonprofit environmental organization upstairs from a pizza joint and across the street from the Berea College campus. Ponytail long gone, he leans back in his desk chair and studies the ceiling, sorting memories. He spent his childhood in Queens, he tells me, where his extended family pooled their resources and bought a sprawling, four-story edifice—not an apartment, but an entire apartment building. "Every relative I had in the US," he recalls, "lived in that building, aunts and uncles and cousins. When we would have dinner, we'd go to the main dining room that sat thirty people." Despite the collectivist upbringing, in his adolescence he was an athlete, not an intellectual or activist—more frat boy than freak. In college, even as war raged and US cities burned with revolt, he remained apolitical. "I was hung up on this girl," he says, "thinking about what kind of car I could get to impress her. I had no world view. I had no sensitivity to what our government was all about, never mind what it was doing."

That changed after he dropped out of college, just in time to get vacuumed up in 1968 in the largest draft in American history. But the army didn't chuck him straight into the jungle as imperial cannon fodder; they sent him to language school, which changed his life. When he got to Vietnam, instead of shooting at people he'd been told were "evil gooks," he could "talk to them in their own language—and it just was like, *what*?" As a translator, he came to understand what the war looked like from a Vietnamese perspective, and it wasn't pretty.

When he came home after a year-long tour of duty, full of righteous anger at the murderous, self-serving US invasion, he didn't stop marching. "I did more marching," he chuckles, "after I got out of the military than I ever did when I was in." He ran the Queens chapter of Vietnam Veterans Against the War and blew through the next several years in a whirlwind of cities and couches, tear gas and chants, rock 'n' roll and women. "It didn't matter where we lived," he says. "It didn't matter what we did. Our mission was to stop the war." That's how he wound up on a beach in San Diego in '72, ready to shut down the Republican Convention. "We would have taken over the fucking thing," he says, in typically blunt phrasing. "It was over." Partly in response to this carefully laid trap, the

Republicans at the last minute moved their convention to Miami; Craig and other activists doggedly followed.

As the US invasion of Vietnam finally unraveled in 1975, Craig found himself back on the same California beach, where activists were looking for the next step. Where would they find purpose after the bombs stopped falling? "We were reading *Mother Earth News,*" he recalls, naming a well-known magazine full of articles on organic gardening and other appropriate technologies. "You know, self-sustainability, how to build a windmill, grow potatoes and intercrop 'em with strawberries. We thought, 'Well shit, we can do that.' It was the period of the Be-Here-Now-swami-guru-The-Farm-back-to-the-land, all that shit." With the end of the war in sight, "a bunch of us finally said 'Look, you know, San Diego's nice and the beach is right there but look at all these fuckin' people, we need to get outta here! You can't grow shit here, you know, let's go.' So we all packed up and moved to Kentucky." He laughs. "We had no clue what the fuck."

Within a few weeks, several carloads of urban radicals found a rambling, run-down farmhouse in the middle of a cow pasture on a hill overlooking Bear Lick Creek. They piled in and proceeded to get their commune on. Before long, the farmhouse came to be known as the Hippie Museum. "Next thing you know," Craig says, "we had like three cabins full of people and this yurt, and there were people in the warm weather would come up and pitch tipis and tents and live there the whole season. You know, there were people crawlin' all over the place. You never seen so much hair in your life. Guys coming wheelin' in from New Mexico with coolers full of psilocybin mushrooms. And everybody for like a week they'd be like *wahaaa!*"[16]

Used to the bustle of the city, many who made the rural pilgrimage took one long look at the tranquil expanse of cow pasture and said "Goodbye! We're outta here!" The rest settled in, and between outbursts of all-night intergalactic merrymaking, started trying to grow food. But there was a problem: they didn't know what they were doing. "The first garden we grew," Craig says with a smile, "we tried to grow it in the shade. I swear to God. It got like five minutes of sun a day. We had corn like that big."

He holds up forefinger and thumb, a couple inches apart. "We couldn't figure it out. Then we started reading and said, 'Oh, it needs *sunshine*.' That's how stupid we were."

This is the point at which Craig is supposed to wrap his extra pair of bell bottoms around his battered steel-string and retreat to San Diego. But the miniature corn was a result of ignorance, not lack of purpose. Fast forward a year and he lived alone in a secluded shack, beyond the end of the road, with nothing but a spring for water and a fireplace to cook on. He wrapped potatoes and onions in foil and threw them on the coals. There was no electricity, no bathroom, no radio, no TV. "I was pretty messed up, Jason," he says. "And I loved it. You could climb up these little rocky knobs and be by yourself. You couldn't do that in San Diego unless you locked yourself in a bathroom."

Soon, he met an elderly homesteader named Mitchell Abrams, who lived nearby. Abrams was one of the old-timers who decided not to leave for the factories of the North and commanded a long lifetime's worth of knowledge about living on the land. Abrams and a couple of other local men showed Craig how to really grow corn. Before long, Craig was handling crops by the acre, in fields tilled with horses. "One year we plowed up every piece of bottomland all the way back that holler," he tells me with pride. "Must have been four acres in different plots. We grew oats in one plot, we grew feed corn in one, we grew vegetables and sweet corn and crap in another one, and grew barley for the animals in another one."

Over the next decade, Craig kept learning. He found some land and refurbished an old trailer to live in with his wife, Teri, and their infant son. They planted huge gardens, raised chickens for eggs and meat, cut and split firewood, and hacked livestock pasture out of the woods. Craig became a good enough woodworker to run his own cabinet-making business. These skills are the source of an enduring sense of accomplishment. Today, he lives with his family in Berea, but subsistence continues to be vital. He built a second house on their town lot for his daughter and grandchildren, and still grows a prodigious garden every year—so big that he showers friends and family with zucchinis, tomatoes, crookneck squash, and full-sized ears of corn. Working long hours with the environmental organization, he doesn't have time to farm the old-fashioned way. But he misses it. "Cultivating fields with a team of horses, yeah. I loved it. I did. I'd like to get back to it."

Sometimes the stereotype is right: some bohemians do indeed head into the country with more dreams than preparation and make a mess. Drive their first tractor into the pond. Lay their floor joists flat, instead of on edge. Grow corn in the shade. But what do we call someone who tackles something challenging and doesn't at first succeed? A failure? A loser? A fool? The more accurate, less cynical word for someone in that position is *beginner*.

*   *   *

Many bohemian back-to-the-landers, like Craig, start as beginners. This leads to various bumbles and failures as a matter of course. But the fact that subsistence has a steep learning curve is seen less as barrier than opportunity: people *want* to learn how to grow food and build homes. They hunger for that knowledge. There is a deep satisfaction, as Craig expressed, in knowing how to do things. It makes you feel capable, confident, and independent.

Perhaps surprisingly, back-to-the-landers like Virginia Webb, who grew up in the country, also face a learning curve. They may have prior skill with subsistence tasks from helping their families weed the garden, butcher deer, or pickle eggs. But it's one thing to yank a bushel of pigweed, and another to plan and plant a whole garden. I bent plenty of nails as a ten-year-old, working on my parents' house, but that didn't mean I was capable of designing and building an entire home. To some extent, then—as is the way with adulthood generally—all homesteaders start as beginners and must journey through both the pain and pleasure of developing know-how.

Bohemian back-to-the-landers, almost as a rule, take subsistence production seriously. They are not trying to escape labor so much as create more meaningful forms of it. Consider, for instance, the garden parties. For nearly a decade, counterculture homesteaders in Bear Lick and Berea held a work party at least once a month. Each garden party was hosted by a particular homesteader or homesteading family and focused on a specific project or small set of projects. On a Saturday or Sunday morning, people arrived around ten or eleven, truck beds and hatchbacks stuffed with wheelbarrows and posthole diggers and carpentry belts and chainsaws—whatever tools were appropriate for that day's tasks. Ten people might show up, or twenty, or thirty. Working together, they'd assemble an earthen oven in an outdoor kitchen. Dig up a suburban lawn and turn it into raised beds. Shovel out a hole for a root cellar. Raise a barn. Reshingle a roof. Plaster a straw-bale house. Part of the attraction of these gatherings—and of community work parties that are a hallmark of subsistence production around the world—was the chance to learn how to do something new. In the afternoon or early evening, when folks started to get hungry and tired, they'd break for a potluck meal and a cold beer, and everyone would decide upon the host and date for the next garden party.

Although the bohemians are serious about subsistence, this doesn't always take the shape you might expect. When I tell people I study homesteading, the practical task they usually think of first is gardening. Certainly, many back-to-the-landers grow fabulous gardens. Cody Shulyer and his wife covered the earthen dam of their pond with terraced beds, where they cultivate everything from sweet potatoes and garlic to frost-hardy kiwi vines and edible weeds. Virginia Webb fills a field every year with the "three sisters"—a Native American companion-planting technique where beans trellis themselves upon corn plants, while low-growing squashes act as a living mulch, shading and cooling the ground with their large leaves. Folks gather late in the winter to order seeds in bulk and swap tips and tricks. They build greenhouses and cold frames and hotbeds to stretch the growing season. They save seeds, raise endangered heirloom crop varieties, and experiment with novel ways to control pests.

Yet in modern-day Bear Lick Valley, gardening is not the most important subsistence activity. Not by a long shot. For one thing, the soil generally sucks, especially on the cheap, hilly parcels back-to-the-landers often buy. Recall that before World War II, slopes were hacked bare, eroded, and heavily plowed—and they weren't covered in deep, dreamy loam to begin with. Raising a healthy garden in Bear Lick thus starts with serious development of the dirt, and homesteaders build their soil with cover crops and manure and layers of straw, wood chips, or leaves.

Despite these horticultural exertions, the most consequential subsistence activity—in terms of skill and labor required, in terms of overall economic impact—is the provision of housing.

Accordingly, the centerpiece of most bohemian homesteads is the owner-built home. If anything, instead of not taking subsistence seriously, as stereotype would have it, the "hippies" take it too seriously—these aren't just houses. They're art projects. Philosophical statements. Well-framed critiques of mainstream material culture. For a number of reasons—which they would happily describe for you in detail—the bohemians typically reject standard, "rectangular" building methods in favor of alternative approaches, constructing straw-bale houses, Fuller domes, earthships, yurts, tipis, and cabins of log and cob. As a result, sometimes the centerpiece of the counterculture homestead is a half-built home that ate so much labor it was abandoned; in those cases, taking a cue from Nathan Hamilton and Caleb Hayward and throwing together a simple box-shaped house would have saved a few tears. But more often than not, homesteaders manage to get far enough along to move in, and the results are often striking: passive solar houses that flood with sunlight even in the depths of winter. Ladders and lofts rising in levels, like in a child's playhouse. Minute kitchens puzzled together with the elegance of a sailboat's galley. Stairways of mortared stone whimsically inlaid with fossils, geodes, marbles, and beads. These lovingly crafted homes are part of what makes homesteads feel exotic and exciting to my visiting students. They are counterculture embodied, alternatives that encompass you, tangible dissent you can reach out and touch.

At their best, the homes are also financially striking. As Caleb Hayward lamented, house sizes in the United States are out of control. He was exaggerating for effect when he said they boast twenty-two bedrooms and eight bathrooms, but the reality is not much better. My house, slightly smaller than average when it was built around 1960, clocks in at nine hundred square feet, about the size of a racquetball court. Nonetheless, it has three bedrooms and was meant for an entire family. By 1973 the average size of a new house was sixteen hundred square feet. In 2015 that had increased to a monstrous 2,687 square feet.[17] The most direct impacts of this housing tumescence are massive debt for families, windfall profits for developers, and a vast stream of interest income for banks. The average sale price of a new home in the United States, as of May 2017, was $406,000. Even with decent interest rates, over the course of a thirty-year mortgage, a buyer would pay close to a million dollars for one of these homes. This is partly why housing now represents the single-largest budget item for most US families, accounting for 25 percent of their total expenditures; for lower-income families, the housing load is even heavier, sucking up about half of their income. Households today spend, by contrast, only 10 percent of their income on food.[18]

House prices in eastern Kentucky run lower than the national average, but they are still a burden. Ann Duncan, another bohemian homesteader from a conservative rural family, experienced this firsthand. A compact, energetic woman with curling dark hair and tanned, smile-dimpled cheeks, Ann bought a house in Berea with her husband a few years ago for $110,000. In the contemporary United States, that's a modest price; nonetheless, over the lifetime of the loan, with interest, they would have paid nearly a quarter million dollars. Instead, after their divorce, he kept the house—and the debt—while Ann saved for a down payment on five acres in Bear Lick, which she bought for $12,000. Working sometimes alone and sometimes with friends, she built a two-hundred-square-foot home for another $8,000, paying as she went. The simply designed, passive solar, off-grid cabin, with a loft and tin roof and cedar post foundation, is beautiful. It is also, after just five years, completely debt free.[19]

Elijah Amaro, a master of cheap living, followed a similar path, but took it even further. The free-form commune of Rainbows he was part of collapsed within two years—so-and-so cheated on so-and-so, et cetera—but he managed to buy a half-dozen scrubby acres of the original parcel for about a thousand dollars. For another grand, he built a cordwood cabin, laying foot-long rounds of wood—firewood, essentially—into mortar to create walls. "Yeah," he said, "I had about twenty-five hundred bucks on the whole deal and I was out on the land. I was the envy of a lot of my friends who were just like, *Jesus*—when they heard 'twenty-five hundred dollars,' that sounded attainable. I remember people wanting to know how I did that. When they came out and looked at it they're like, 'Wow, you know, it's different, it's not the Taj Mahal. But you're really out here not paying rent 'n shit, like we're having to go rent and start jobs and live on a shoestring. And, boy, if you start making money in a position like this, you get to keep it.'"

*　*　*

Above all, the sixties counterculture was—and continues to be—a project of dissent from mainstream norms of behavior and thought, a "basic questioning," as scholar Timothy Miller puts it, "of received truth."[20] Particularly in the '60s, when that counterculture blossomed, mainstream white culture was narrow and uptight. Established rules of behavior were arbitrary, oppressive, constricted, and fearful. They had to be tossed to make space for people to develop more diverse and healthy ways of being. To allow, for example, two women to live together openly and raise their children; to allow couples to end their marriage without shame and censure; to foster mature, sensible, and selective use of drugs; to embrace lives with more wandering and less shopping.

But when you discard established rules of behavior, and have yet to figure out new ones, things get pretty wild. And sometimes, they did—like at Bear Lick's Hippie Museum. The feral communes and unchained parties make such a riveting spectacle—half dance improvisation, half car wreck—that they are hard to look away from. I understand why people who live through such experiences are moved to write memoirs.[21] I understand the fascination of journalists with Drop Cities and Woodstocks and Merry Pranksters. Indeed, it has been hard to keep this chapter from filling with such stories, like the time twenty naked hippies had a mud fight in Cody Shulyer's pond so intense, the next morning all the fish floated belly up, suffocated on stirred muck. Or the time a man at a Halloween party hunched over an upright piano, pounding music from the keys with hallucinatory abandon—while perched atop a bonfire, orange flames shooting between his arms. Or, you know, the time that one guy rolled in from New Mexico with a cooler full of shrooms.

These stories are part of the hippie counterculture. But their spectacle tangles us in dismissive stereotypes about both sixties cultural dissent and the back-to-the-land movement it helped create. They provide an excuse on the part of the mainstream to shrug off the radical with ridicule: "this isn't a serious effort to figure out better ways to live—it's just people getting wasted!" This is how dominant representations of the back-to-the-land movement come to be filled with disorderly communes.

But when our eyes are drawn overmuch to the outrageous and the dramatic, when we get caught rubbernecking, we fail to see the real character of the back-to-the-land movement. As with subsistence production, when it came to communal living, the bohemian homesteaders often approached with care. While there have been a handful of zany, ad-libbed communal experiments in Bear Lick—and others, most likely, yet to come—more than 90 percent of the bohemian homesteaders have never lived that way. A free-for-all commune makes a hell of a story, but people know it's not likely to come to a graceful end. Thus, more than two-thirds of Bear Lick homesteaders choose to live on their own parcel of land in a private dwelling. The majority of the remaining third have purchased land together with others, but built separate houses, often with painstaking planning and forethought, with weekly meetings and binders and spreadsheets and bylaws. As one participant concluded, "It was not pile in one big house together, that kind of thing."

In Bear Lick, the overall shape of the back-to-the-land movement is less Woodstock and more Wendell Berry. Less Merry Prankster and more Annie Dillard. If you wanted to make a movie about it and sell lots of tickets, the images you'd film would be a sprawling farmhouse with no doors or running water, a dying pot plant in the corner decorated like a Christmas tree, people passed out half-naked in clumps and clots on the unswept floor while children paw through the kitchen for leftovers like stray dogs. But if you wanted to understand what makes the turn to homesteading such a vital social movement, such an enduring part of the American story, a more accurate image—and far more common—would be a bunch of friends and neighbors, sharing stories while they lift siding boards into place, laughing as their hammers flash together in the sunlight.

*　　*　　*

In February 1984, the US Army held a public meeting in the cafeteria of the Blue Grass Army Depot to make an announcement. The depot, you may recall, is the fourteen-hundred-acre military base built in 1941 between Berea and Richmond, that helped spur the transition to wage labor by "sucking up" six thousand local men who hadn't already left for Dayton. At the meeting, the Army said, "Hey, by the way"—I'm paraphrasing—"for decades we've had five hundred tons of chemical weapons, in seventy thousand rockets, stored inside all these cute little grass-covered concrete igloos. But now the president has signed a treaty with the Soviets saying we have to get rid of them. We just wanted to let you all know that we'll be burning them shortly. That's all. Thanks! Good night!"

One hallmark of modern, industrialized war is that competing teams of scientists get to play around, trying to out-kill each other. Along with hydrogen bombs, guided missiles, and land mines, chemical weapons are a product of such engineering contests. Between World War I and World War II, military chemists kept refining lethality and synthesizing insanity until they had built doomsday molecules like VX, short for "venomous agent X." A miniscule dot of VX on your skin will snap you into drooling convulsions for about three minutes, after which you're dead. It was wonderful news when the United States and the Soviet Union agreed to destroy such horrors. But trying to destroy them with fire was daft: in an incinerator, whatever happens in the combustion chamber goes right out the smoke stack. If the burn goes sour, and your "venomous agent X" isn't broken down perfectly? Too late—it's out the stack, jack.

Clark-Moores Middle School, with more than four hundred students, lies about a mile from the depot. Nearly fifty thousand people live in the surrounding area. Many citizens rose, at that first meeting, to voice their concerns. One of them was a gruff, balding, Vietnam vet with a deep, commanding voice. "I think you're gonna find a lot of people back in the streets," Craig Williams told an unsmiling panel of uniformed officers. "Not in Washington, but right here in Madison County, and joined by people in the surrounding counties. And the power of the people—like it did in the Vietnam War—will once again surface, and we'll put a stop to it."[22]

The US military is one of the largest bureaucracies in the world. Deeply autocratic, it is not accustomed to changing course based on comments from cabinetmakers and middle-school teachers. So how do you put a stop to something the army has already decided to do? One Berea activist put it like this: "There's two kinds of power in the world, organized people and organized money. So if you don't have money, you better organize people."[23] And that's what concerned citizens in Madison County did— they organized people. To do so, they drew upon a standard repertoire of activist techniques. They formed a nonprofit organization, the Kentucky Environmental Foundation, with a board of directors and full-time staff. They wrote grants and raised funds, organized community meetings and marches, issued press releases and wrote editorials. They built a coalition, cleverly seeking partners not in the habit of naysaying the Pentagon: not only nurses and doctors, college students, and frightened parents, but horse owners and real estate agents. Who wants to find their thoroughbreds suffocated on sarin gas? Who wants to try selling homes in the shadow of a toxic-waste incinerator?

Through such actions, the fight against incineration turned into a proper social movement. This is the kind of organized campaign most of us think of when we think about activism—one designed to change dominant institutions and domineering policies. We envision a campaign to overturn the Jim Crow laws of the American South, for example, or secure the legal right for women to vote. There is, however, another possible target of activism: not institutions or laws, but ourselves. As Elijah Amaro asked me once, "Are you going to change the world or are you going to change *your* world?" Some scholars call this a "prefigurative" approach, because it aims to directly manifest—to prefigure—ways of life and relationships that dissidents believe are more appropriate.[24] This is the path taken by back-to-the-land movements: instead of pushing for change by taking on governments and corporations directly, homesteaders aim at melioration through self-transformation.

Anyone who hopes to foster progressive social change faces this basic choice: do you try to reform dominant institutions, or do you, as the bumper sticker says, become the change you want to see? These are not mutually exclusive endeavors; key civil rights groups, for instance, such as the Student Nonviolent Coordinating Committee, tried to cultivate participatory democracy and egalitarian relationships within their membership. They tried to create, in the words of my colleague Meta Mendel-Reyes, "a democratic movement for democracy."[25]

But if these two strategies are not mutually exclusive, neither are they the same thing, and activists have often struggled to do both at the same time. Both approaches are needed, because both have characteristic strengths and weaknesses. If you choose policies and institutions as your target, you have to adopt that standard suite of tactics—forming organizations, securing funding, deploying techniques of visibility or disruption, managing coalitions, and in other ways sustaining the "mobilizing structures" that are the familiar attributes of social movements as they are usually defined.[26] To fight institutions, in short, it's expedient to become an institution. But if we're not careful, we wind up birthing a little baby autocracy, and instead of fighting for justice we find ourselves fighting over the corner office. This is partly how we end up with the bitter irony of Marxists liberating workers by subjecting them to police states. Or a civil rights movement where, too often, women did the grunt work while men reaped the credit. Or a progressive student-led movement, the New Left, that collapsed under the media spotlight and the seductive lure of celebrity.

On the other hand, one of the main drawbacks of a prefigurative activism directed at changing culture is its invisibility. Unlike a protest movement, one goal of which is to force outside attention, the back-to-the-land movement not only goes unnoticed but has little immediate need for such notice. There's no central office to call. No Martin Luther King Jr. to interview. No press releases to consult. No Edmund Pettus Bridge or Tiananmen Square or Zuccotti Park to visit. The fundamental, defining strategic choice of the back-to-the-land movement—to rework, above all, one's own culture—produces a movement that is readily overlooked and easy to belittle as a picturesque, romantic, or bizarre fringe. This is partly why journalists, hunting for an easy handle, fixate on large communes. This is partly why the death narrative has emerged as a dominant interpretation of the back-to-the-land movement, even among former participants. This is why we largely fail to recognize that—with millions of cumulative participants and going strong for at least five decades—the bohemian back-to-the-land movement is one of the largest, most enduring social movements in modern history.

And don't be fooled: this is a social movement. This is activism. Bo-hemian homesteaders are trying, with care and forethought, to change the way they live, the way they spend their time, the way they interact with others, and the way they meet their material needs. Such cultural work is challenging: culture is not just what we think, verbally, with our conscious minds—it's also what we become used to, what comes to feel normal deep down in our bodies. French sociologist Pierre Bourdieu famously referred to this embodied aspect of culture as *habitus*: a system of passed-down, semiconscious dispositions and tastes and inclinations that are difficult to notice and even harder to modify. If we're not used to eating fresh greens out of a garden, with their garnish of aphids and cabbage loopers, it takes practice to do so with comfort. If we're not used to sleeping alone in the woods, it can be scary. If we're not ac-customed to using our bodies to lift rafters, or push a wheelbarrow, or swing a splitting maul, the shift is intense. Much of the initial journey of back-to-the-landers—even those with some rural experience—in-volves a revision of one's habitus: learning to fill an evening without television. Learning to kill and eat cute animals. Learning to poop in a bucket. Learning to bathe in a pond, or a stream, or beneath the cold mountain rain. And not just learning such things but rendering them normal. It's crucial to verbally and analytically question mainstream culture; that's the first step. The second is to unlive it.

* * *

Over the twenty-five years following the army's announcement, the Kentucky Environmental Foundation—KEF, as it's known—led a grassroots effort to stop the incineration of chemical weapons. There were seven other chemical weapons stockpile sites in the United States, and the first coun-terproposal from the Pentagon was to ship Madison County's nerve gas to a different site and burn it there. But citizens from these different places reached out to each other, started talking and working together, and told the army, "No. You're not going to burn those poisons in our backyard—or in anyone else's backyard. You're not going to burn them *anywhere*." They commissioned technical studies on alternative disposal methods and found out that nerve agents can be broken down—to give the simple version—by dissolving them in hot water. If something goes wrong? It's all still there, in the tank—not outside, in a cloud, drifting toward some kindergarten. In the end, not only did citizens force the Pentagon to change technologies at four of the stockpile sites, but against all odds they forced it to open its decision making to a measure of democratic input and citizen oversight.

It should come as no surprise, given their engagement in cultural dissent, that bohemian back-to-the-landers played a major role in the fight against the nerve gas incinerator. It's easier to imagine yourself tackling a significant project as an activist if your life is already an activist project. Just ask well-known rabble-rouser and former back-to-the-lander Bernie Sanders. In the first chapter of its existence, KEF had about a half-dozen long-term staffers, and the majority of them were, or had been, serious back-to-the-landers.

Leading this effort was Craig Williams. As I mentioned in the introduction, I've changed homesteaders' names to protect their privacy—except Craig's. I can't change his name, because he's famous. For twenty years, he was director of the Kentucky Environmental Foundation. The office where I interviewed him is decorated with flyers for marches, concert posters, stacks of files and reports—and with accolades. There's a poster for a recent documentary, *Nerve,* on the anti-incineration movement, with Craig playing a starring role. Through his work with the Campaign to Ban Landmines, he has a share of a Nobel Peace Prize. In 2006 he was awarded the Goldman Prize at a sold-out gala at the San Francisco Opera House. The Goldman, the so-called "Environmental Nobel," is the world's most prestigious award for environmental activism.

But here's the thing: in 1975, when Craig left marching and organizing for plowing and building, he didn't leave activism behind. In 1984, when he put the plow down to march again, he didn't return to activism. It was activism the whole time. He never stopped trying to make the world a better place, never stopped trying to figure out better ways to be. For Craig, as for most back-to-the-landers, homesteading was not a diversion from the real work of social change. Growing his own food and fighting the Pentagon are intertwining efforts that together form a single, life-long attempt to create meaning and justice in a society all too often lacking in both.

*   *   *

When bohemian back-to-the-landers from outside the region came to Bear Lick in the early 1970s, they arrived at a fortuitous historical juncture. Many country folks had moved away over the past thirty years, hunting wages. Others stayed but gave up peasant farming to drive every morning to work at factories and stores and hospitals in Madison County. The country homesteaders who remained active were often elders, steadfastly committed to the old mountain ways, like Craig's mentor, Mitchell Abrams. Or they had done time in the cities and factories and had chosen to return to Bear Lick with a renewed commitment to subsistence, like Ruth Hamilton. Often, these country homesteaders lacked youthful companionship; the majority of their children were off chasing modernity.

This bohemian wave found open spaces not only on abandoned farmland, but in the hearts of rural elders. Emma Burress, a dark-haired woman in her late sixties with the serene air and bifocals of a head librarian, came to Bear Lick, like Craig Williams, from California. Emma was born in Berea but attended high school in southern California. In 1972 she dropped out of college at Berkeley, threw her stuff into a Volkswagen beetle, and drove east. Looking for a place to rent, she roamed the backroads in her VW until she came across an empty farmhouse—"a *beautiful* old farmhouse," she said, "on a *beautiful* farm." She walked over to the neighboring house, and an elderly farmer named Blue Parsons answered the door. "We got to talking," she said, "and you know I was just so fascinated—he had an eighty-year history of living here, that just, I mean, my mouth hung open. Well, he loved it that I thought his life was wonderful, and he had this beautiful old-time farm wife, just a very sweet, soft-spoken, beautiful, totally not-neurotic-in-any-way-whatsoever person. I fell in love with her too. So they rented it to me—they'd just met me, you know, and I was this crazy hippie thing."

Emma was fascinated by the Parsons's knowledge, but the interest ran both ways. "They were curious about me too," she recalled. "They'd heard about that city life and they'd seen stuff on TV, but here's a real live one, you know. Let's see what she has to say." After a pause, she lets out a wistful sigh. "That generation has died away now, but that was a magical time."

Joseph Rivard, a tall, willowy man with long, snow-white hair—the one I assumed was a hippie but was actually a Quaker—moved to Bear Lick with his wife, Sarah, during the same period. They found the same unexpected accord with elder neighbors. "It just sort of opened this door to this amazing museum," as he put it, "of old-timey stuff that wasn't really happening much other places. We knew people who if you got out the *Foxfire* book"—an oral history of pre-modern Appalachian folkways— "and started readin' it to them, they said, 'Yeah, that's right, yeah we used to do that, yeah, and oh, here's what comes next,' and they'd tell you what was gonna be in the next paragraph, about whatever—killing hogs or making dried beans. So it was very cool to be part of all that."[27]

Appalachia has its own traditions of rejecting mainstream customs and rules, which also helped locals accept both home-grown bohemians and bohemian immigrants from outside the area. It's easier to relax about your neighbor growing pot, for instance, if you grew up tending the fire underneath Papaw's moonshine still. According to Craig Williams, once people "got to know you and you gained their trust," they didn't care much about what you did. "Everybody knew we were doin' drugs and smokin' pot and probably growin' it and all that shit. But it was kinda like, it's alright as long as you have respect for people's property and for who they are. It was amazing." Emma Burress, who passed through several of the early communes, said much the same. "We were all piled up, you know, boys and girls, men and women, living in these big houses, and nobody ever gave us the slightest crap at all. The law didn't come, the church didn't come."

Even with this serendipitous match between parents left by their children, and children who left their parents, the cultural border between the two groups remained clear. This border changed people's lives for the better when they reached across it—but in reaching across, they did not erase it. All too often, cross-border relations were challenging. Some of Joseph and Sarah's older neighbors never warmed to them, partly because they lived together without being married, and partly because they were seen as hippies. "When we bought our place," Joseph remembered, "people said, 'Oh, these hippies have moved in.' And at that time, it was not too long after the Charles Manson thing and stuff, and hippies was like the lowest form of life."

Interacting with the younger country folks—the ones who had grown up after World War II and the transition to more modern ways—was often particularly difficult. "We were aware that there was this older local generation," said Joseph, "that had certain attitudes about how to live that really jibed with our thinking, and their children weren't that way. They were all wanting to have whatever, the fast car, the running water, the washin' machine in the house and all this stuff, and we could see that there was this generational belief system that was passing away. And we were kinda wanting to hang onto that, so we got along great with older folks. And the younger folks, they just seemed to us like they were like throw-the-beer-can-out-the-window, smart-alecky, and had more redneckyness about 'em. The older folks, they didn't know enough about political stuff to really be rednecks."

If the cultural boundary between bohemians and country folks at best is a source of pleasure and epiphany, at worst it's a source of genuine friction, mistrust, and even hatred. When Elijah Amaro and the other Rainbows began their commune experiment, they found a harsh reception in the country. "People didn't really want nothin' to do with us," Elijah said. "There was all kinds of rumors about us, you know, people think we're doin' voodoo and runnin' around naked, screwin' chickens and just all kinds of stuff." When they'd stop by the store on Bear Lick Road, they were ostracized: "There'd just be stares, dude, just like *coooold*, cold stares."

Every few months, when Elijah runs out of money, he'll find a job in one of the local factories, welding brake pads or unloading pallets for ten hours a day. This brings him into close-quarters contact with people from Bear Lick and the other rural hinterlands of Berea. He doesn't get a warm greeting from most co-workers. Partly this is because of his hippie vibe—but mainly, it's because he's black. One of the kinder responses came from a Pentecostal woman who told him that he was going to hell, and spent hours, as he put it, "twisting my arm about Jesus." But at least she interacted; most workers on the line wouldn't even look at him.

Elijah's stories are not isolated incidents. Any visible sign of differ-ence—race, religion, ethnicity, sexuality—is enough to invite, from some locals, rough treatment. The main road that runs from Bear Lick to I-75 passes through the middle of the Berea College campus. That intersec-tion of college students and locals has produced a steady stream of casual harassment: revving engines, catcalls, thrown beer bottles. Sprouting giant Confederate flags like rooster tails, heavy-duty pickups growl past campus. An African American professor at the college was approached by a white man in the Wal-Mart parking lot and asked how much she would charge to clean his house.

In response to these strains of bigotry, many bohemian homesteaders keep their distance. "There's a certain element of that local culture that I'd just as soon not interact with," said Cody Shulyer. "So I'm tryin' to find that fine line between not appearing too much like an outsider, and yet staying at a certain amount of distance so that I can have some de-gree of control over my interaction with the locals." Many back-to-the-landers said similar things. "An awful lot of the folks on this road and in this neighborhood are incredibly racist," one man told me, "and will tell a 'nigger' joke quick as anything. Not something I care to be around." Even bohemian back-to-the-landers who are themselves from country families struggle with these issues. Virginia Webb maintains, like Cody, "a certain amount of distance." As an openly gay woman with strong, progressive opinions, she doesn't always find it easy to interact with her country neighbors—even though some of them are family.

But this begs a major question, one that leads us to part two of this book: if the bohemian homesteaders are a diverse group, a multi-stranded left of different ages and backgrounds, many of whom are actually country people, how do they form a coherent social group, distinct from and to some extent opposed to, the rest of the rural population? What is it that unites them?

*   *   *

When you're crapping in an outhouse, it's easy to tell whether it be-longs to bohemian or country homesteaders. It's not the cedar sawdust you scoop from a pail to cover your tracks; both groups do that. It's not the toilet paper roll—that's universal, at least in the United States. It's not the decorative cut-out of a crescent moon in the plank door. To my nose at least, the shit smells the same, although a hound dog could surely sniff out differences in diet. Okay, you could probably tell it's a bohemian outhouse if your poop falls into a bucket to be composted. But the distinguishing feature I have in mind doesn't have to do with the act of elimination per se; it has to do with how you pass time during that act. It's the little library you'll find inside a hippy outhouse. There's a stack of well-thumbed *New Yorkers* or *Atlantic Monthlies* in the corner. Perhaps, in a clever meta-move, the owners have left a copy of *The Humanure Handbook* or *Holy Shit: Managing Manure to Save Mankind*. Sometimes there's feature-length fare: a used paperback edition of *Gödel, Escher, Bach* or *Zen and the Art of Motorcycle Maintenance*. You may even enjoy the irony of using an outhouse, deep in the woods, while reading up on net neutrality in the latest edition of *Wired*.

This distinction is even more marked inside the home. I could not predict if someone leans "hick" or "hippie" by whether or not they smoke pot, play guitar, or—for men—grow out their hair; these are not reliable markers of group affiliation. As we have seen, I couldn't even predict group affiliation based on whether or not someone was born in the city or the country. In many cases, I couldn't make the prediction based on the dwelling itself: cabin, shack, mobile home? It's not diagnostic. I could, however, make a highly reliable prediction based on a single glance *inside* their home, a glance aimed at one set of objects: do they have a big bookshelf? And on that bookshelf, do they just have the Good Book, or do they have good books?

The bohemian homestead invariably contains its own textual companion: shelves bent beneath well-used references like *The Encyclopedia of Organic Gardening, Mushrooms Demystified,* and *The Straw Bale House Book.* Alongside this "how-to" collection are wide-ranging works that address the question of "why-to": Frances Moore Lappé's *Diet for a Small Planet, The One-Straw Revolution* by Masanobu Fukuoka, Wendell Berry, Starhawk, Wes Jackson. There are classics like *Catcher in the Rye* and Dante's *Inferno,* and counterculture touchstones like *The Dharma Bums* and *One Flew Over the Cuckoo's Nest.* There's folklore like the *Foxfire* series and fakelore like Carlos Castaneda's imaginary tales of Don Juan.[28]

There are other, less visible measures of this difference. The bohemians in Bear Lick are almost universally college educated: fewer than 10 percent lack a college degree, and about half of those lack the degree only because they are still in college. Fully a third have earned graduate degrees. By contrast, among the rest of the rural population in the Bear Lick area, 80 percent have never stepped into a college classroom, and nearly a third lack a high school diploma.[29] For most, a graduate seminar would be as exotic and inscrutable as the Zócalo of Oaxaca. The bohemian back-to-the-landers in this part of eastern Kentucky are not only well-schooled relative to their neighbors, they are almost three times more likely to have a college degree than the United States population as a whole.[30]

But paper degrees are only an indirect measure of what we might call *literate intellectuality*. Many people slide through college without developing a deep, meaningful relationship with reading and writing. The bohemian back-to-the-landers are unusual not only in how many years they've spent in the classroom, but in how much they embrace the written word outside the classroom. With few exceptions, they are people who have made radical changes in their lifestyle based to a surprising extent on ideas developed through independent, nonfiction reading.

In one interview after another, they cited specific authors as a major source of the inspiration that led them to homesteading. In graduate school in Knoxville in the early '70s, one future back-to-the-lander started dreaming of rural independence after discovering the works of Helen Nearing and Ruth Stout. About the same time, Joseph Rivard remembered, "One of my friends gave me a copy of Wendell Berry's book, *Farming: A Handbook*. You know that one? It's got some poems that make it look like farming would just be so cool." Thirty years later, Ann Duncan had essentially the same experience. "In college," she recalled, "I encountered Wendell Berry, his writing, and that's what really started moving me toward the sustainability kinds of stuff." This bookishness is visible in studies of the back-to-the-land movement in other regions, as when Rebecca Gould remarks that homesteaders in Vermont "tend to produce as many texts as they do vegetables."[31]

In some ways, reading plays an even more central role for the bohemian back-to-the-landers, like Virginia Webb, who grew up in rural families. For these individuals, written works served not as a basic introduction to subsistence but were an essential ingredient in a broader education within which the homesteading they were familiar with could be understood in a new light, as a meaningful critique of contemporary civilization. Reading is thus central to the process by which they create a synthesis between the old homesteading ways they experienced as children, and newer homesteading techniques and motives. Indeed, those from conservative families often place even more emphasis on both college and reading as crucial elements of their life story. At the same time that reading leads them away from their families, in certain regards, it also leads them back home.

Hidden within that stack of magazines and paperbacks in the outhouse lies the key difference that separates the two groups, that creates two distinct social movements out of one overall strategy of dissent: the bohemian homesteaders are a literate rural intelligentsia, and the country homesteaders are not. Both groups work with ideas, trying to figure out how to respond to contemporary problems, but bohemians draw strongly on the written word, while country homesteaders rely more upon the spoken.[32]

To get a quick feel for how this works, let's do a thought experiment. Imagine you start reading some of the best popular writing on a wide range of important issues. You read, in a book like *Fast Food Nation*, about how agribusiness manipulates our palates with science, about the profits behind our expanding waistlines. In a Pulitzer Prize winner like *The Sixth Extinction*, you read about how coral reefs are being slaughtered by our tailpipes. You read about the advertising industry and body shame. About the social construction of gender. About dirt and autoimmune disorders. About the Koch brothers, ALEC, and the perversion of electoral democracy.

Now imagine that you act upon what you read, that you modify your behavior in light of all that information. Pretty soon, you're riding a bike to save money, burn less oil, and stay fit. Pretty soon, you're eating home-cooked oatmeal instead of corn flakes—to save money, burn less oil, and stay fit. Before long, you're skipping makeup and gender-normed grooming styles; you're welcoming dirt under your nails; you're wearing clothes until they're threadbare; you're refusing to turn your wedding into a shopping spree. Pretty soon, you dump your television like toxic waste at the recycling center, on your way to the march against the latest imperial incursion into the Middle East.

Pretty soon, you're a hippie.

*   *   *

This raises one of the most important questions we can ask about the contemporary United States, and back-to-the-land movements in a little corner of eastern Kentucky have led us right to it: how do some people end up highly literate while so many others don't?

This question would be easier to answer if "hippies" were all from the city and "hicks" had spent their entire lives in the country. Then stereotypes could just fill in the answers for us: hippies would read because that's supposedly something that well-off city people do, and hicks would not because reading is something rural folks supposedly don't do. But these stereotypes are wrong. Many country people read, and many urbanites don't. Many bohemians come from rural Appalachia, and many country folks have lived in cities. This isn't a difference that runs between Appalachia and other places, or between the city and the county. It runs *through* Appalachia. It runs right through other rural areas; it slices cities in two. It cuts, as far as I can tell, through the entire United States like some kind of omnipresent social disjuncture.

To answer this question—why is the distribution of literacy and book learning so uneven?—we have to embark on the next stage of our travels, leaving homesteads for a time to visit two major sets of institutions that create and reinforce this difference: schools and jobs. These institutions, we'll see, distribute literacy in much the same way that frontier Kentucky distributed land, or the industrializing United States distributed ownership of factories: by class.

PART II

Cultural Division in a Capitalist Society

5 Ain't Nothin' in Them Books

Cody Shulyer drives too fast. Sipping black coffee and steering with a forearm flopped over the wheel, he cannons his ancient Toyota pickup around the curves. We're on our way to Lexington, a city about an hour north of Bear Lick Valley, where Cody sells wild mushrooms to high-end restaurants. Two hundred dollars' worth of chicken-of-the-woods and golden oysters are carefully packed into a large cooler in the back of the truck, to protect them from the August heat. On this winding road, my little voice recorder keeps sliding off the dashboard, until I finally just hold it in my hand. I'm asking Cody what it was like to go to elementary school in Bear Lick. Because he attended schools in different parts of the United States, he has a feel for what's specific about each place.

Cody was born in Kentucky, but spent his early years moving back and forth between Bear Lick and San Francisco, where his grandmother lived. After three years in California, he attended fourth and fifth grade at Bear Lick Elementary in the late 1970s. I ask, "What was it like?" He doesn't pause to rummage through old memories—he has a summary boxed and ready to go. Clearly, he has thought about these experiences. "The school was underfunded and authoritarian and instruction consisted of memorization and worksheets, punctuated by beatings." It was "very rural," he continues, "with mostly poor students." The school building was "decrepit." Even though the school was completely rural, "there was no playground. There was no grass. We had recess on the parking lot. Yeah—actually where the dumpsters were. So we climbed on the dumpsters."

Because he was nerdy, and an outsider, schoolyard beat-downs were a regularly scheduled recess activity. Until the day a bigger kid tried to pile-drive him into the concrete and split the skin on his head. It wasn't a serious wound, but blood poured out. Horrified, the bully gathered Cody in his arms and carried him into the principal's office. Cody grins at the memory. "They didn't beat me up after that. Word got around: he's a bleeder!"

Children were supposed to do what they were told, when they were told, without explanation. They weren't even allowed to talk during lunch; it was "complete silence." The price of breaking this rule, as with many others, was corporal. "If you did talk, the punishment was to be taken to the front of the cafeteria and paddled, in front of the rest of the kids. So there wasn't a lot of talking." These stories are making me fume, but Cody just laughs. "Yeah, it was a fairly effective means of control. I mean these are fourth and fifth graders that I was hanging out with."

Cody went to sixth grade in San Francisco, one of a handful of white kids in a predominantly Asian and Latino school, then moved with his mother back to eastern Kentucky, and entered seventh grade at a combination junior high and high school near Bear Lick. Again, the lack of funding was severe. "It was the same story," he says after another sip of coffee, "a cinder block building, with a coal-fired furnace that would malfunction three or four times a semester and we'd all have to leave the building on our hands and knees because of the black smoke."

We're passing through Berea now, about to climb the ramp onto I-75, heading north toward Lexington. No more hurtling around curves on twisting mountain roads. My stomach starts to release its grip on my ribcage. Cody's saying that the same authoritarian model was in full effect at the high school. They employed, as he phrases it, "the antiquated but persistent idea that education is a downloading process: you're gonna sit still, and I'm gonna shove some stuff in your brain, and you're gonna keep it there." And what were they downloading? There were Bible readings in class, and every morning the children read the Ten Commandments off the wall and recited that cold war oath, the Pledge of Allegiance. "At that age," he says, "I was old enough to realize that was not something I felt like I wanted to participate in."

Children could be paddled not only for genuine transgressions, like assaulting another student, but also for questioning the teacher. As we pull into a parking spot beside Alfalfa's, Lexington's long-running hippie restaurant and reliable purchaser of exotic shrooms, Cody launches into a story. "I remember in the eighth grade, I had this one class, and it was the teacher who taught social studies and science. I was the only kid in the class who had ever been on an airplane. Including the teacher. But, when a kid asked how high do airplanes fly, she goes, 'Well, the highest airplanes fly at about eight thousand feet.' It was obvious she didn't know, but instead of saying she didn't know, she just picked a number."

Cody's been relaxed the whole time he's been talking, but you can tell this story still angers him. No mirth remains in his voice. "So of course I raised my hand, and said, 'No, I don't think that's right. I was just on an airplane, when I went to California, and I remember the pilot very clearly saying we're at thirty-two thousand feet.' And she proceeded to argue with me and tell me I was wrong, and I had misunderstood, and that wasn't accurate, and that I needed to stop having these outbursts in class and giving these kids the wrong information."

The teacher called the principal, who took Cody into the hallway and threatened suspension, telling him, "You need to spend some days at home." Then the principal hefted his paddle and gave Cody another beating.

*   *   *

What's going on here? This sounds like something from a Charles Dickens novel. Are these just tales of Appalachian "backwardness"? Kentucky schools were ranked forty-fifth in the nation in the 1970s, when the principal paddled Cody. And that was all of Kentucky, including wealthy suburbs in Lexington and Louisville, averaged together. Bear Lick schools, in eastern Kentucky, received about a third of the funding per pupil as those higher-funded districts.[1] So what do you expect?

In reality, while Cody's stories have extreme moments, the authoritarian schooling he experienced was fundamentally the same as that offered to most non-affluent kids in the United States, regardless of where they lived. This wasn't schooling in Appalachia, it was schooling in Appalachia, *and* on the Yurok Reservation, *and* in Birmingham, Alabama, *and* in the Latino neighborhoods of east Los Angeles. The public high school I attended in Berkeley was several steps above those in areas of concentrated poverty, but in pedagogical terms it still consisted almost entirely of grown-ups talking at you.

In the decades since, classrooms have become less authoritarian. Corporal punishment has been outlawed in more than thirty states. Kentucky schools rank much higher now than in the past, and many teachers understand that lecture isn't the best approach. But in crowded classrooms with heavy testing pressure, it's hard for overworked teachers to avoid. Schooling in the United States remains, at its core, too much like it was in Bear Lick forty years ago, where, in the words of another homesteader who experienced it, "you sit in a chair and listen to a lecture."[2]

Patrick Finn, a retired education professor and former Chicago schoolteacher, described this as "the make-believe school model," and estimated that perhaps 80 percent of students in the contemporary United States experience primarily this kind of schooling.[3] He called it make-believe because, at a glance, it looks like school is "supposed" to look. To an administrator or parent strolling the halls, these appear to be functioning classrooms: students are present and sitting quietly in their chairs. The teacher is in command at the front. Lesson plans are duly covered. This must be a good school! The majority of the kids eventually graduate, after all, and they know how to read. Just check the World Bank's annual *Development Report:* it doesn't even list a statistic for adult literacy in the United States because it's higher than 99 percent.[4]

Multiple researchers, observing different schools all across the country, have encountered this make-believe model over and over. Classrooms are marked by rote tasks and lecture, with a near-complete absence of conversation, collaboration, or debate.[5] Knowledge is "presented as fragmented facts isolated from wider bodies of meaning and from the lives and experiences of the students." Work consists of "following steps in a procedure," with "little decision making or choice."[6] Here's a typical high school assignment, observed by ethnographer Lois Weis:

TEACHER: Take out your notebooks. The title. "The Reasons for the Growth of the Cities." Put that down. It is at the bottom of page 60. "A. Industrial revolution." Skip a line. Take the next subtitle. "B. Problems Facing Cities and Urban Populations." Take the next five subtopics under that. Skip a line between each.

JOE: Just one line between each?

TEACHER: Yes.[7]

In an entire year of observation, Weis observed *a single challenge to an idea by a student*. Perhaps, like Cody, they had been vigorously disabused of any notion to dissent. When one teacher tried a more engaging approach, "he was called down to the principal's office, not to be encouraged, but to be chastised."[8] My own father, teaching in a high school in southern Georgia years ago, got in the same kind of trouble for having a boisterous classroom; he was letting the students, his principal admonished, get "out of control."

In too many classrooms, the dominant theme, from the perspective of the teacher—faced with thirty bored kids—is exactly that: control. Of his years as a "hard-bitten" teacher in a working-class school in Chicago, Patrick Finn says that "control was uppermost in my mind."[9]

From the perspective of the student, watching thousands of hours drain away in repetitive busywork, one dominant theme is resistance. The main lesson, for many students, is that life inside the institution is leavened by small insurrections. That some sense of pride and élan can be salvaged by attacking the institution that is attacking you. You can't overthrow the school, and you can't escape—but you can take turns with your friends pissing on the toilet paper in the bathroom stall. You can hide a dried chunk of cat shit in the teacher's desk. You can dip snuff and spit it on the floor in the back of the classroom and rub it in real good with your boot. Carve penises into desktops. Smuggle a joint and burn it right there in school, like a badass. These petty transgressions don't change the system, but they're funny, they're thrilling, and in the teenage brain they tower as acts of bold resistance.

The collision between these two themes, control and resistance, often produces a kind of truce. Schools don't ask for "real effort on the part of the students." In exchange, says Patrick Finn, the students "offer enough cooperation to maintain the appearance of conducting school."[10] The result is a Potemkin Village classroom, in which superficial industry masks a lack of real learning or purpose.

*   *   *

During the summer of 2010, I taught at Phillips Exeter Academy in New Hampshire. One of the most prestigious high schools in the world, Exeter sends half of its graduates to Ivy League colleges and boasts a celebrity roster of alumni, including Facebook founder Mark Zuckerberg, US president Franklin Pierce, and authors such as Gore Vidal, Dan Brown, and John Irvine. The roster also includes—in one of those small-world moments—the former mayor of Berea, Steven Connelly. As a school that primarily serves the offspring of the rich, there are times, to be sure, when the air is too rarefied. It has a billion-dollar endowment, for a thousand students; that's a million dollars per student. The entrance to the eight-story library—the largest high school library on the planet—is graced with a grand piano and curving twin staircases of travertine. There's a palatial boathouse on the river, and blackened mahi-mahi on the dining hall menu. In my dorm, full of fourteen-year-old boys, one had been in Hollywood films alongside the likes of Meryl Streep, another was in the royal line of succession in Saudi Arabia, and another was Tom Brady's next-door neighbor.

The school is so suffused with wealth I worried I might despise it. But beneath the moneyed décor, the education is a marvel. Classes are limited to a dozen students, who gather around a large, wooden table that's the centerpiece of each classroom, and learn through open-ended discussion. In other words, as a teacher, you don't talk at the students—you talk *with* them. They even have an Exeter-specific name for this approach: the Harkness Method. In this method, the classroom is turned inside out: instead of the teacher explaining the topic or the reading to the students, the students explain it to the teacher. This is just as true in an organic chemistry course as in a poetry workshop. In math classes, it's not the teacher who writes equations upon the board. The students aren't supposed to be quiescent receptacles. They're supposed to be loud, questioning, and messy. To probe and dissent. To be authors, not audience.

Another notable difference is that, unlike in public schools, no topic is off-limits. Want to talk about the insane distribution of wealth in the contemporary United States? Good! That's important. Want to cover our neocolonial invasion of Iraq? Go for it. Evolutionary biology? You don't have to pretend it's an anti-religious scam.

If this sounds ideal, it's because it is; this is what formal education can be like when cost is not the limiting factor. This is what real school looks like, and it's not a pipe dream. It exists. But this begs the question: is it fair to compare Phillips Exeter to public schools in eastern Kentucky? Yes. Yes, it is. To be sure, Exeter spends more than $60,000 per year on each student—but Exeter is a boarding school, and a chunk of this cost covers housing and feeding the students. Plus, you don't need lobster in the cafeteria to use the Harkness Method. You need small, student-centered, discussion-driven classes and teachers who are encouraged to teach such classes. We have, thanks to the Industrial Revolution, a sufficiently productive economy to afford this. That is, if wealth was not concentrated so spectacularly at the top but was distributed as widely as the labor that produced it.

At Exeter, a teacher offers three courses per semester, each with a dozen students, thus working with about thirty-six students per semester. Total. At a typical public school—not just the poorest ones—a teacher might have nearly that many students in a single class, and likely covers five or more classes per day. One veteran faculty member at Exeter told me that the success of these elite private schools was not really a matter of using some exact set of classroom practices. It was that once you limit a class to ten or twelve students, an entire array of progressive, student-centered pedagogies becomes possible that is simply unavailable to a teacher facing thirty students. At Phillips Exeter, being an excellent teacher is still not easy, but it's a reasonable expectation. In a typical public school, with typical class sizes and course loads, being even a moderately successful teacher requires heroic skill and dedication.

*   *   *

One of the main effects of make-believe schooling is that you get high school graduates who are literate but can't read.

At first glance, I suspect that looks like an oxymoron. But literacy is not an either-or proposition; it's not something you either possess or you don't, like herpes. It's a complex skill that takes years of steady practice to master. And it's a skill that make-believe schools struggle to foster. The best way to get kids reading is to let them read whatever they want and give them lots of free time to do it. They can curl up with *Hellboy* or *Twilight* or *Motor Trend* magazine or *Captain Underpants*—as long as they enjoy the reading, it doesn't matter. But where's space in the lesson plan for hours of individualized storybook wandering? Where's the standardized test that demands *The Lord of the Rings* or *The Fault in Our Stars*?

High school kids have generally spent enough time reading that they're not technically illiterate—as in, unable to sound out words on a page—but many of them are still beginners. Maryanne Wolf, director of the Center for Reading and Language Research at Tufts University, calls them *accurate readers*, as opposed to *fluent readers*. An accurate reader can, more or less, read a passage from a newspaper out loud. This, according to the World Bank, qualifies them as literate, and justifies listing the United States as a universally literate nation. However, for an accurate reader, translating the marks on the page requires continuous conscious effort. Instead of seeing pictures and ideas behind the words, they still see sequences of letters. For a fluent reader, this step of the reading process has become, through repetition and genuine engagement, effortless and automatic; the marks on the page are transparent windows into meaning.

This difference between labored "decoding" and rapid, streamlined comprehension can be seen in functional MRIs of readers' brains: the work that a non-fluent reader must do to translate writing into language shows up as extensive activity in areas of the brain devoted to visual processing. At the same time, the parts of the brain that focus on emotion and meaning are relatively quiet.[11] They're working so hard to figure out the words that they can't reach the story. You know that feeling you get when a book spirits you away into another universe? That profound experience when you emerge from a long reading session and stumble out into a world that looks different and deeper than it did before? Accurate readers have never known that feeling. Books are a realm of struggle, not epiphany.

When someone gets enough reading practice to make the transition into fluency, it usually happens when they are quite young, typically by the third or fourth grade. If it doesn't take place then, it's unlikely later in life—not because our brains lose the capacity, but because no one's forcing you to practice reading anymore, and because it's embarrassing and disconcerting as a teenager or adult to struggle like a beginner. Unfortunately, according to Wolf, "thirty to forty percent of children in the fourth grade do not become fully fluent." Instead of growing into master readers, these children slip into a "netherworld of the semi-literate."[12]

Make-believe schooling doesn't just leave students deprived of reading practice. It actively drives them away from book learning. For students who have no experience of the written word other than what they went through in school, opposition to the institution readily becomes opposition to literacy itself. They draw the logical conclusion: books are a dry well. Want to know a fragmented fact isolated from any wider body of meaning, like "what is the capital of North Dakota?" Look it up in a book. Want to somnambulate through a limp version of how a bill becomes a law, with all the corrupt drama and soul-selling edited out? That's the kind of thing—students come to assume—that you'll find in a book. As teens and young adults, they develop an identity opposed to literacy, an anti-reading sense of self. It's not that they felt the power of the written word and then rejected it—it's that no one ever really showed it to them. They don't even know it exists.[13]

They become, at best, a-intellectual, indifferent to what bookish people call the "life of the mind." They might tolerate reading when they have to, in exchange for those scraps of monopoly money we call grades. But it's not something they seek during their free time. At worst, they become anti-intellectual. They learn to see reading and writing as weak, useless, effete, and nerdy. Want to get your forehead bounced off the tarmac during recess? Then go ahead, dweeb. Read a book.

*   *   *

My first college teaching gig was at Eastern Kentucky University in 2008. Too many of EKU's students are experts at playing the make-believe school game, having practiced it for a dozen years or more before arriving at college. I know these students well; EKU is my alma mater. As I was preparing my classes, before the start of the semester, older colleagues offered avuncular, well-meaning advice. "I don't assign writing," the department chair told me. "They'll just plagiarize." A different professor said, "Don't bother giving them reading—they won't do it." This sounds belittling, but the professors weren't trying to be mean. They were just burned out. At EKU, they teach four courses per semester, packed with students who have no interest in the Russian Revolution or mitochondrial DNA. Through the sheer weight of their ingrained attitudes toward schooling, the students shape EKU, all too often, into something similar to the high school classrooms they have known.

Berea College, where I teach now, is unique. It was founded just before the Civil War as an abolitionist school, dangerously close to the slave markets and plantations of the bluegrass. It was the first college in the South to admit both black and white, both female and male. The founder, a minister named John G. Fee, endured mobs, thrashings, and the risk of death to keep the fledgling school alive. Today, Berea is just as radical, but in a way especially appropriate to our time: it serves only lower-income students and charges no tuition. Berea refuses to admit high-income students; it doesn't even allow that cash cow of elite colleges, the legacy admission. Its operating expenses are drawn from a large endowment created mainly through donations and gifts, many provided by alumni in recognition of the college's role in granting them an educational opportunity usually reserved for more affluent youth.

Because of Berea's excellent reputation, and because it's free, it receives a ton of applications. Even though the college has to turn away two-thirds of these applicants—making it one of the most selective colleges in Kentucky—the majority of those who are admitted, being poor, attended the same kind of grade schools and high schools as EKU students. In many ways, my main job as a professor is helping such students recover from the poisoned relationship with literacy they developed during their prior schooling. I teach mandatory writing seminars for incoming freshmen, and the starting point for at least half of the students—in a college writing class—is that they hate reading and writing. So I don't start writing classes with a disquisition upon thesis statements or citation styles. I start by asking the students, "Why should you give a shit about writing?"

Most of them believe they are bad writers, and it is imperative to show them that they're not. They are, instead, like Craig with his corn, beginners. One concrete way to demonstrate this is to get them to write down a number. "Think back," I tell them, "and remember all the books you have read, at Harry Potter level or higher. It can be something you read for class, or on your own." I pause to let them remember. "Now, write down a ballpark number."

The numbers vary a little from class to class, but the median number of books read among Berea College freshmen is about fifteen. Here are the numbers from one of my writing seminars: the first student estimated twenty books. After that, student by student, it was two books, six, five, seven, two, three, one, two hundred, six, sixteen, nine hundred, two, twelve, ten, twenty, and thirty. Keep in mind, these are teenagers who have been admitted to a selective college: most of their peers who are *really* turned off by book learning did not even apply to college. In each class, there are a handful of students who have active, independent reading habits, and their book number is, comparatively speaking, off the charts. And while they are no more innately intelligent than their peers, what this reading habit represents is literally thousands of hours of practice at tasks central to success in college—practice with reading, with vocabulary, with argument—that the students sitting beside them don't have. It's the unseen elephant in the room. It's one of the main things that separates students who find college academically surmountable and those who find it alien and overwhelming.

These numbers may seem shocking, but they are business as usual. One survey reported that only 31 percent of college graduates nationwide were "proficient readers." Another survey, of US adults, found that nearly half "probably do not have the skills necessary to read many types of literature." Very few read books of substantial non-fiction. Natural history, economics, labor studies, anthropology, physics, political analysis, philosophy—the entire corpus of modern science and scholarship—is read by fewer than one of every ten adults.[14]

* * *

Minus the trip to college, make-believe schooling is the formal educational experience of most country homesteaders in Bear Lick Valley.

Until the 1960s and '70s, many teenagers in rural eastern Kentucky did not even finish high school. Their goal was to drop out as soon as possible so they could begin their adult lives of working and courting. Caleb Hayward—the man who built his own coffin—quit school the moment he was old enough to get a job, in the sixth grade. "After I got to be about twelve," he said, "the only things on my mind were gettin' me a job, and buyin' me a car." He found work at a sawmill in Bear Lick, making fifty cents an hour. They didn't care if you had a diploma or not. "If you could do the job, that's all it was." After that first job, he kept working nonstop, building and painting, for the rest of his life.

In Caleb's generation, this was a normal life trajectory, and there was no shame in it. Nonetheless, he told me, he regretted his lack of book education. "I'd give anything in the world," he said wistfully, "if I could have went to school, but I didn't have too much of a choice. I've made it through the years, but some of 'em were hard. Still to this day I wish I could've done things different."

Fifty or sixty years after Caleb was in school, his experience is still common for rural Appalachian youth. I spent an afternoon with a young man named Seth Halpin, running errands in his pickup truck, right after he dropped out of Bear Lick High School in his junior year. His feelings about school were the same as Caleb's, but without the regret of late-life perspective: he sat patiently and politely in the classrooms, learning nothing of value, until he was legally allowed to leave. Despite my quizzing, he had nothing to say about school itself; it was a blank. He had no stories to tell about it.

At sixteen, he already had substantial experience with skilled manual labor like raising barns and running fences—activities he had plenty of stories about. So he quit school, got a job building wooden fences, rented an apartment with his girlfriend, and began adult life. He didn't miss the classroom; it was like a gigantic, decade-long time-out. But more importantly, he didn't miss the literate life of the mind, either. He had never encountered it.

*   *   *

Some read, some don't. So what? Some people in the United States read okay, and some read really well. Some read occasionally or only when a task necessitates it; others stay up half the night, tangled in a book. Why does it matter? It's not like the "merely" accurate readers are getting lost on the freeway or can't write a check. These days, if they need to know something about history or science, they can whip out their phone and watch a YouTube video. Sure, they're not reading Proust for fun and they've never written a ten-page paper explicating *Mrs. Dalloway*. Who cares?

Many experts conclude that we shouldn't. A recurrent theme in critiques of higher education is that it makes little sense to spend enormous collective resources training young people with skills they will never need at work, as economist Richard Vedder argued in a debate in the *Chronicle of Higher Education*. "A large subset of our population," he wrote, "should not go to college, or at least not at public expense. The number of new jobs requiring a college degree is now less than the number of young adults graduating from universities, so more and more graduates are filling jobs for which they are academically overqualified."[15] Since these people will never need to write a research paper in order to flip burgers, why waste all that educational time and effort?

There are other reasons to ask why the differential attainment of literacy and literate intellectuality matters. The bookish life of the mind is only one small part of the full range of human invention and brilliance. After all, the knowledge and accomplishments of the first two hundred thousand years of human history took place in the complete absence of literacy. In rural Appalachia today, there are still a few families, like the Hamiltons, whose members have never set foot in a schoolhouse, and yet are highly skilled, knowledgeable, and possessed of keen intellects and vibrant curiosity. As Ruth Hamilton put it, regarding her decision to keep her children out of school, "Then the Lord told me, He said, they won't have a lot of book sense. But I'll make them know how to *do*." They can pull a tractor apart and rebuild it, help a cow through a difficult birth, turn standing poplars into a cabin, and can a winter's worth of food—all without ever having read a single chapter.

I once spent an afternoon with Nathan Hamilton, replacing the clutch in my Honda. We had both repaired a clutch or two before, but neither of us had worked on a Civic. I reclined in the driver's seat and read a repair manual to see how to proceed. "Step 1," it said, "remove the transmission from the vehicle." That wasn't much help, so I started flipping to the section on removing transmissions. Meanwhile, Nathan was studying the car itself, and soon announced a quicker and easier route than the one in the book, one that didn't require fully removing the transmission. In that case, literacy went head-to-head with independent thinking, and lost.

Like many people who are not book-educated, the Hamiltons are what we might call *practical intellectuals*. They apply an expert analytical intelligence to an astonishing array of mostly practical tasks. This is a different set of tasks than the ones tackled by, say, linguist and author Noam Chomsky—but is there any basis for arguing that it is of less value? If anything, the more obviously and directly valuable skill set is that of the Hamiltons. Will the latest version of Chomsky's generative grammar see me through a cold, hungry winter? If Nathan Hamilton had been sent off to Phillips Exeter, he might have gained one broad set of skills, but only at the cost of losing the chance to develop a radically different and also valuable set of skills. And note that if he had been sent to the local make-believe school, he would have paid a similar opportunity cost, and received little in return but a crash course in fistfights, crystal meth, and gut-wrenching alienation.[16]

When I was in my late teens and early twenties I worked on a carpentry crew, building custom-designed passive solar homes all over Bear Lick Valley. The crew was a mix of country and bohemian. During lunch, I would find a shady spot and sit with a book, a practice that drew chuckles from some of my fellow workers. One day, a wiry, hard-working fellow called Bones gave voice to their laughter. "Son," he said, with the confidence of an elder guiding a wayward youth, "ain't nothing in them books you cain't learn in the real world."

Was he right?

*   *   *

Let me be blunt. The make-believe school model, and the endemic semi-literacy it creates, leaves many people in the United States—despite spending many years of their lives in "school"—with outlandishly poor formal educations. Many of the students I work with begin college, for the most part, exquisitely uninformed—unless we're talking about pop culture. They know who won last season's Super Bowl. They know the latest celebrity scandals. They can name fashionable brands of jeans all day long, even if they can't afford them. But they don't know how their own bodies work. They don't know what makes the sun shine, how the moon formed, or why the inside of the earth is hot. They don't know how carbon dioxide traps heat in the atmosphere; they've never even heard of ocean acidification. They can't name a single recent Supreme Court ruling; they don't know that John Roberts recently eviscerated the Voting Rights Act. The economic meltdown in 2008? They don't know why it happened. They don't know who fought in World War II, or why. They think we invaded Iraq because of 9/11. They are, in short, bereft of basic factual knowledge that matters.

Nathan Hamilton, having escaped make-believe school, is not bereft of factual knowledge that matters. But when it comes to book learning, he's in the same boat as my students. He doesn't know much science or history. He's curious about such things, and will ask me about them—but, without reading and writing, it's hard to go deep enough into the intricacies of a difficult topic to really learn it. His information about politics and current affairs comes from right-wing talk radio. Ronald Reagan, in his mind, is a hero, because he knew how "to talk tough and be tough." But Nathan doesn't know anything about the Reagan administration's actual policies.

None of what I am describing here is an Appalachian thing. It's a class thing, which means it's everywhere. Surveys and polls all around the country uncover the same elemental lack of learned awareness. For example, even after a doubling of scientific literacy over the past twenty or thirty years—probably owing largely to increased college enrollment—only 20 to 25 percent of Americans are "scientifically savvy and alert," according to Jon Miller, a scholar who studies public awareness of science. "American adults in general," Miller has found, "do not understand what molecules are (other than that they are really small). Fewer than a third can identify DNA as a key to heredity. Only about ten percent know what radiation is. One adult American in five thinks the Sun revolves around the Earth, an idea science had abandoned by the 17th century."[17]

Apparently, if you want to hide something, just put it in a book.

This lack of factual awareness is easy to describe, readily quantified through surveys, and has a kind of gee-whiz shock value. I introduce it here mostly as a convenient index for a more important and harder to measure outcome of failed schooling. A lack of familiarity with the basic contours of history, geography, political economy, science, and so on, while important, is only one component of a broader set of skills, capacities, and interpretive habits that often go missing when a person is weakly literate. The best overall term I can think of for this condition is *a-intellectualism*. One of the outcomes of make-believe schooling is that lower-income kids are much more likely to wind up not only with weak literacy but rendered permanently disinterested and divorced from sustained intellectual self-development—which has profound effects that not only impact individuals, but reverberate throughout society.

I remember standing at the edge of the Pacific Ocean one night on the Yurok Reservation, upon the sandbar where the Klamath River pours into the restless surf. We were hunting lamprey eels; like salmon, lampreys migrate upriver to spawn. Taking a break, I rested the eel hook over one shoulder and walked up the steep slope of the beach, to where my stepsister stood watching the stars glitter in the sky. We were both about sixteen. She had grown up attending make-believe schools near the reservation. When a shooting star drew its glowing fingertip across the night, she asked, "How are there still so many stars, when they're always falling down?" Oh, I thought, that's cute. She doesn't know that shooting stars are just grains of space dust.

A couple of years later, when she got pregnant with her first child, she didn't know what fetal alcohol syndrome was, either. Would it have made a difference if she had? Maybe she still would have partied with her unborn son—but she would have known that she confronted a choice. With subsequent children, she did know, and chose to limit her drinking while pregnant.

In this case, Bones was right: you don't have to learn about fetal alcohol syndrome from a book. You can learn about it in the real world.

*   *   *

This leaves us with a mystery. In Bear Lick and the surrounding areas, with the exception of an extremely determined and innovative teacher here and there, it was all make-believe schooling when the local hippie homesteaders were children. There were no Phillip Exeters. How did they become so literate? Why was their path different from the more common, a-intellectual one traveled by Caleb Hayward, Seth Halpin, and so many others?

For a few homesteaders who grew up in wealthier places, the answer is straightforward: they had access to higher-quality schools. At the same time Caleb Hayward was dropping out to work at the sawmill, a bohemian homesteader-to-be named Dylan Graves was attending an elementary school full of scientists' kids in Oak Ridge, Tennessee, an entire town built from scratch in 1942 as part of a sprawling nuclear weapons research complex. Dylan's mother was a college graduate and his father a chemist recruited by the Manhattan Project. He grew up in a world of affluent professionals, isolated from the surrounding Appalachian countryside. After high school, he headed to Carleton, a top-ranked liberal arts college in Minnesota—taking, almost as a matter of course, a route into young adulthood that never even crossed Caleb Hayward's mind.[18]

Most counterculture homesteaders, however, did not attend high-quality schools, and it's these people who generate the mystery. How did they become intellectual?

A few, with little adult help, find their way in a kind of real-life, pedagogical Horatio Alger story. Raised by working-class grandparents in small-town Kentucky, a future back-to-the-lander named Dean Jefferson stumbled upon a Stephen King novel when he was twelve and fell in love. Soon, he was pedaling his bike to the library to check out more—not the only story I heard involving a library and a bicycle. As a teenager, pot and rock 'n' roll led him to a biography of Jim Morrison, lead singer of The Doors, and Morrison's own voracious readings led him to an interest in philosophy and interlibrary loan, and, eventually, to Berea College.

Elijah Amaro took an even more unusual route. Raised in a non-reading household in Atlanta, he hated school and was soon channeled into "dropout prevention" classes. "All the teachers I had," he recalled, "they could care two cents about us. They pretty much knew if we stayed we're goshdarn lucky and if we left pretty much 95 percent of us were gonna end up in jail or dead." He didn't so much drop out of school as drift away into the streets. When a helpful adult suggested that he apply to college, his response was emphatic. "I was pretty much like fuck school man, institutions suck. And she was like 'If you change your mind, I'll get you an application,' and I was like, yeah, fuck you, I ain't gonna do no school."

But all along, he loved to read. "Even when I was burned out on high school," he said. "Even when I was smoking pot, I went to the libraries. I even became a book thief for a while, ganked books." Then, after a few months of sleeping under bridges, he and some other street kids thumbed a ride to a Rainbow Gathering in Ocala, Florida—and he found his university. For many alienated young dropouts like Elijah, the Rainbow Family functions as a kind of mobile, distributed, alternative school. The larger gatherings have actual libraries where you can trade in a book you've been traveling with for something fresh. The books can be pretty far out, Elijah said, with "anything from biodynamics to yoga, dumpster diving, you name it. Ram Dass, hippie-dippie books, Native American books, astrology." They might have been far-out, but they kept him reading, kept him thinking, and kept that part of his mind alight. Eventually, he did go back to school, earning his bachelor's degree from Berea College while living in his little cob cabin in the woods.

But most bohemian homesteaders, unlike Dylan Graves, didn't get to attend a high-quality school. That's not the common answer to the mystery of unusually literate homesteaders. Nor did most of them hoist themselves to book learning by their own bootstraps, like Elijah Amaro. The answer, for most, is that they encountered literacy at home.

Take Cody Shulyer. The damaging early schooling he endured pangs him. "I feel like I probably could have accomplished more in my life," he said, as we drove home from Lexington, "if I had a better elementary education. I kinda had to teach myself how to learn and teach myself how to research—I didn't have any of those skills by the time I got to college. It really hurt me. I really regret it." But this impact, while real, was limited by one crucial thing: every afternoon when he stepped off the school bus, he opened the door into a literate household. Sometimes he and his mother lived in run-down cabins where you could see daylight through gaps in the siding. They stayed for a time in that big farmhouse, the Hippie Museum, a place so "swarming with people," Cody remarked, "you never knew how many housemates you actually had." But in all these spaces, no matter how poor, the walls were lined with milkcrate bookshelves full of well-worn paperbacks.

When he was twelve, Cody sliced his knee with a drawknife and spent much of the summer straight-legged on the sofa. He started with what he could pull off the shelves: Heinlein's *Stranger in a Strange Land, The Immigrants* by Howard Fast. Soon his mom bought him a subscription to the Science Fiction Book Club—with no nearby library to bike to, getting books in the mail was a godsend—and he read his way through scores more. *The Lord of the Rings,* more Heinlein, *The Chronicles of Amber,* Isaac Asimov. What was missing in school, he found at home. Even though he laments what the make-believe schooling cost him, it ultimately didn't hold him down; he is one of the most ferociously well-educated people I know.

I heard this story over and over: I didn't get much out of school, but I was an avid reader at home. Elizabeth Brower, a homesteader in her seventies, is from a rural Appalachian family. She is one of the few individuals who seem to be genuinely and equally at home with both country and bohemian homesteaders, although she is definitely liberal in her political and social attitudes. Partly this cross-border comfort is because of her welcoming and gregarious personality, but it is also because she was able to provide for herself, through reading, a level of literate education that was unusual for rural eastern Kentucky. When the first non-local back-to-the-landers began to move into her part of eastern Bear Lick in the mid-1970s, she was immediately drawn to their educated company.

Neither of her parents had experienced college, and her father had dropped out after the eighth grade. "I didn't read until I was thirteen," Elizabeth told me, "and then my bookworm neighbor gave me *To Kill a Mockingbird,* and it just changed my life."

I asked what she meant by that phrase, "changed my life."

"Of *course* reading changes your life," she replied, like I was dense. "If you can't afford to travel in a car, you have to travel with your mind."

Libraries and bicycles. Milk crates crammed with paperbacks. Bookworm neighbors. These are the tools that allow children to overcome make-believe schooling. Among my Berea College freshmen, perhaps the strongest predictor of whether or not they have a reading habit is this: on their birthday, and for Christmas, and to mark other occasions, did an adult family member—mom, dad, Uncle Jim, Mamaw, anyone—give them books as gifts? If not, they probably don't read. So, for the final exam, I don't give them a test. I walk them to Berea's lovely used bookstore and buy each of them a book.

*   *   *

In terms of what happens at home, however, books on the shelf are just part of the story. When I was ten years old, I spent the weekend with a friend, Eddie, who lived in a two-story house beyond the end of Bear Lick Valley, farther into eastern Kentucky than I had ever been. On Saturday morning, we found a BB gun leaning in one corner of the basement. I was ecstatic. I'd never actually held a gun that shot, so I thought, real bullets. We took the gun behind the house to the edge of the woods, dug a couple of beer bottles out of the brush, stood them in line, and shot them. Chips and shards of glass flew. It was wonderful. Then, without warning, our laughter was broken by an angry bellow, and we turned just in time to see Eddie's father, red-faced and furious, striding up on long legs. He looked ten feet tall. He grabbed Eddie's wrist, lifted him off his feet by one arm, and beat him like a piñata with the other arm. I tried to shrink into the grass as Eddie squealed and pedaled helplessly in the air.

This image is a cultural Rorschach test. The child, dangling, crying out. The dad, jaw clenched, raining hard thwacks on his son's rear and thighs. What do you see? Is this an outrage? Or is it normal? Is this a violent act, perpetrated by a powerful man upon a defenseless victim? Or is this a loving parent, steering with a firm hand? Is this a failure of parenting—or its essence?

One of the most striking differences between bohemians and country folks in Bear Lick is that they practice distinct parenting styles. Country folks tend to take an authoritarian approach to disciplining their children. If they want their child to do something, they tell him to do it—and the child better comply. They don't mind raising their voice in command: "Get over here, now! I said *now*!" Kids aren't supposed to question a command or otherwise "talk back." If they do, they're liable to be threatened with a "whippin'" or a "stripin'." And if the child repeatedly doesn't do what they're told, or steps too far out of line, they can plan on getting spanked.

Bohemian homesteaders take a less authoritarian, more egalitarian approach. They rarely spank, and when they do, they often see it as a failure on their part. Even peremptory directives and raised voices are unusual. They interact with their kids largely in the way they interact with other adults: consulting and negotiating and explaining rather than commanding and hitting. "Eli, if you don't get in the car now, we'll be late, and then you won't have time to watch a movie later on." Their children often talk back; instead of following orders, they'll ask for an explanation or offer alternatives. If a kid really misbehaves, the discipline is still primarily verbal: they'll sit the child down and have an extended discussion about why she did what she did and how she can do better next time.

These disciplinary philosophies are elements in two larger approaches that sociologist Annette Lareau calls "natural growth" and "concerted cultivation." Lareau and her team of graduate students spent over a year observing working-class and middle-class families in an unnamed city in the Midwest.[19] The middle-class families—college educated, professional—engaged their children in sustained conversation, asking specific questions about their thoughts and feelings, their day at school, their visit with a friend. They engaged in debates and intellectual sparring. They worked through homework with their children—not episodically or in passing, but consistently and closely. Middle-class parents also scheduled evenings and weekends around organized activities, spending hundreds of hours ferrying sons and daughters to music lessons and football practices, and thousands of dollars on fees and equipment. You can see why Lareau called this parenting style "concerted" cultivation: it requires a lot of effort.

Working-class families—without college educations, and either unemployed or employed in lower-status jobs—were affectionate with their children and worked hard to keep them safe and healthy. But they saw little need to foster sustained conversation with their kids. Children were generally left to themselves, often in the company of siblings or neighborhood friends, to organize their own play and entertainment. If parents were occupied—watching TV or talking—children were generally expected not to interrupt. Parents would often set aside a time for children to do their homework, but seldom worked with them, or would do so for a few moments now and again in response to a specific request from a child. Working-class parents could not afford, in time or money, the same level of organized, after-school activity as middle-class parents. Lareau calls this parenting style "natural growth."

Cody Shulyer's experience in Bear Lick classrooms now makes more sense. It wasn't just some kind of malfunction. The schools were run by local people who believed that children *ought* to be treated in an authoritarian way, that they should be seen, not heard, and that paddling was an appropriate method of discipline. Cody went home to a mother who considered these practices barbaric—but most other children went home to parents who thought the school's approach was normal.

Each parenting style has drawbacks; neither is perfect. The heart of concerted cultivation is intense, sustained conversation and empowering negotiation—the direct modeling, in other words, of critical thinking and democracy not as abstract ideals, but as ways of being. This approach, however, can devolve into an arms race of betterment, a madness of over-organized activities. Kids end up sprinting from AP class to soccer practice to violin recital to calculus homework on a never-ending treadmill of desperate self-improvement. In Berkeley one July, while trying to finish my dissertation, I enrolled Finn in one of those ultra-progressive summer camps where concerted cultivation is dialed to eleven, and he came home and said, unhappily, "They made us do so many projects, I hid under the table." Under natural growth, children enjoy more free, unstructured time to shape as they will—and that's a vital thing.

The main drawback of natural growth parenting is that it provides limited guidance in the development of literacy, intellectual engagement, and the questioning of authority. It's like make-believe school, with too much talking *at* and not enough talking *with*. When directives outnumber discussions, it's hard for children to feel the power of voice, of a well-chosen word, of a finely crafted argument. There is a lack of what researchers call "literacy events"—all the moments, large and small, in the course of daily life, where the written word is normalized. Under concerted cultivation, children are given books as gifts, but parents also typically read to them past the age where they can read to themselves. Not only that, but they see their sister curled on the couch on Saturday morning, lost in *The Hunger Games*. At breakfast, they sit beside grandpa while he reads the paper and gripes about the news. They help mom check out books from the public library. I can still recall, from my own early childhood, the sound of my father's manual typewriter in the evenings: click-click-clickety-click, grrrrk, *ding*!

In a famous study in Kansas City in the early 1990s, Betty Hart and Todd Risley painstakingly documented how families from different socioeconomic classes interact with their kids. Over the course of 2½ years, they observed forty-two toddlers at home, amassing more than one thousand hours of recordings—so much data they didn't know what they had found until they crunched the numbers. The results were astonishing. The more affluent, professional parents spoke, on average, 487 words per hour to their children, while the working-class parents spoke 301, and the poorest, unemployed parents spoke only 167. That builds up. The children experiencing concerted cultivation encountered, over a four-year period, several million more words than those experiencing natural growth. There were marked differences in content as well; at one extreme, children in professional households heard "32 affirmatives"—expressions of encouragement and support—"and five prohibitions per hour." At the other extreme, the average child in the poorest families "was accumulating five affirmatives and 11 prohibitions per hour."[20] By the time they were three, these toddlers had already diverged in language use. Children in affluent families had effective vocabularies of about twelve hundred words, working-class children about eight hundred, and children in the poorest families about five hundred. A poverty of income had compounded into a poverty of diction.[21]

Before they even start reading, some children possess, as a kind of family heirloom, the dialect of written English. Others do not. Guess which kids have a shot at rising above make-believe classrooms, and which are likely to be dragged down? Which ones find within books a doorway, and which find a wall? Which ones end up in the gifted program, assuming they were just born with better brains—and which conclude they just weren't the kind of person meant to go to college, anyway?

* * *

I played a trick in the previous section. I started describing parents in Bear Lick Valley, then quietly shifted to conclusions Annette Lareau drew from some Midwestern city, then to data gathered by Betty Hart and Todd Risley in Kansas. These two places are hundreds of miles from Bear Lick; neither is in Appalachia. The shift works, however, because in all three places we find similar patterns: this bifurcation in parenting styles shows up everywhere. Study after study in the United States—and even in Europe—has found consistent differences in child-rearing practices among parents from different socioeconomic backgrounds, regardless of geographic location or race.[22]

How can these patterns be so widespread? How is it that parents on different sides of the continent, who have never met, have such similar parenting styles? This is bizarre. It's also hard to explain. Did all the working-class parents get together at some conference and decide to adopt a particular parenting style? No. Did the middle-class parents put it to a vote? No. Was it memes? Sermons? Chain letters? Of course not. But in the absence of some kind of group coordination, what creates these consistent, far-flung behavioral patterns?

One possibility is that working-class families try to adopt concerted cultivation but fall short. Concerted cultivation requires time and energy, and a hallmark of working-class life is a scarcity of both. Consider, for instance, transportation. How many professionals lose their jobs because their car won't start in the morning? Or because they can't afford a car in the first place? Such frustrations beset working-class people all the time; it's exhausting to be poor. So perhaps, amid the hassles and stresses, it's too hard to help your kid with homework in the evening. Perhaps you'd love to have a heart-to-heart with junior about his behavior, but your patience is worn, and it's easier to just smack him upside the head.

The problem with this explanation is that working-class parents aren't usually embarrassed about sparing the word and sharing the rod. My step-father, Merk, didn't see his lack of conversation with my sister, Orowi, as a failure. He just didn't see any reason to talk at length with an eight-year-old. Elva Northern, a country homesteader who grew up near Bear Lick Valley, was blunt about corporal punishment. "Sometimes," she said, "you have to get tough with a child and hurt him once to help him realize that you are the boss. I did with my son. I made a believer out of him. I whooped him all over that hillside."[23] Nathan Hamilton lamented the way that parents nowadays "let their kids run wild." He saw spanking as a last resort with his own son, but if "we really did run into a head-on collision, I'd take a switch, and I'd whip him." This is how his parents did it, and he appreciated it. "If I got out of control they'd sure set me on fire. And then it was a rough thing, but now buddy I am glad of it. I am real glad of it."

Country homesteaders, and working-class people all around the country, aren't adopting a "natural growth" model of parenting because they have failed to achieve concerted cultivation. They do it because it seems, well, natural. It seems like the proper way to raise children.

The best explanation I know for this bifurcation in parenting styles is this: as recently as the 1950s, most parents in the United States took an authoritarian approach to parenting. Bossing kids around and spanking them weren't class-specific actions—they were nearly universal. For example, in schools across the country, paddling was normal. In a typical bestselling parenting guide from the 1930s, *Psychological Care of Infant and Child,* Dr. John Watson commanded parents to be sparing in affection, lest they ruin a future worker. "Never, never kiss your child," he exhorted. "Never hold it in your lap. Never rock its carriage."[24]

What has changed over time is that expert opinion, grounded in empirical research, has shifted increasingly in favor of a more egalitarian approach. What has changed, in other words, is that people like Annette Lareau and Betty Hart and Todd Risley—and Maria Montessori and John Dewey and Benjamin Spock—have observed and examined and analyzed child development and discovered that spanking can be harmful, and that sustained verbal interaction early in life has profound effects on language development.

But how, as a parent, do you find this out? How do you learn that "many studies have shown that physical punishment . . . can lead to increased aggression, antisocial behavior, physical injury and mental health problems for children"?[25] You find out in two main ways: through reading and through interacting closely with others who have read. What's the first thing a highly literate woman—like a bohemian homesteader—does when that second pink line appears on the pregnancy test? She rushes to the library and gathers a double-armful of parenting books. And then she reads them.

Wait a second. Overall, this chapter is an attempt to explain how some end up powerfully literate and intellectually engaged, while so many others end up weakly literate and, all too often, intellectually disengaged or even anti-intellectual. Because so many kids endure schools that follow the make-believe model, what happens at home is thrust to center stage. But when we look into what happens at home, we find the same thing we were trying to explain in the first place: the different parenting styles that drive differences in literacy are themselves explained largely by differences in literacy. The cause is the effect, the effect is the cause, and round and round we go.

All too often, the drivers of such "cycles of poverty" are assumed to be some deficiency on the part of poor or working-class people. And it is true that people of lower socioeconomic status in the United States lack many things: they lack money, well-rested free time, security of employment and housing, health care, and high-quality schooling, just to mention a few. The real question is, what generates this lack of resources? In the contemporary United States—despite all the crowing from politicians about the poor being "takers not makers," and suckling upon tax dollars—most poor people are not unemployed; they work hard for their poverty. Thus, our next stop will be the different kinds of jobs available in the Bear Lick area. Because if our educational experiences as children are wildly divergent, just wait until we grow up and walk through that high school door into the workplace.

6 I Haven't Felt My Hands in Years

Delia Howell leans against the counter in the cramped kitchen of her mobile home. Fortifying herself against an upcoming shift at the factory with caffeine, nicotine, and sugar, she alternates pulls from a can of Mountain Dew with quick hits from a Camel Light. Smoke curls in the morning light. In her mid-forties, Delia is lean, almost delicate, but moves with a raw coyote toughness. When she gets lost in telling a story, her blue irises spark and shine, but as soon as she falls silent, lines of care settle back around the corners of her eyes like a flock of blackbirds.

It's a Sunday morning in early September, and the factory has called—at the last minute—an extra shift, which will push Delia to almost seventy hours for the week. It's both blessing and curse: the overtime pay is welcome; the ache in the bones is not. But it's only a half shift, so they start at ten instead of five, which leaves Delia a window of time she generously gives to my questions and my voice recorder.

Delia and her brothers, Boyd and Willie Garrett, were raised by their mamaw in the mountains just south of Bear Lick Valley in the late 1960s and early '70s. Their mother usually lived nearby, but moved constantly from one rental to another, and her men weren't always good for children to be around. Their mamaw, who never traded the green hills of Kentucky for the gray assembly lines of Ohio, proudly and doggedly cared for her three grandchildren through material poverty that sounded little different from what Ruth Hamilton and Caleb Hayward experienced in the 1930s. They crowded into a two-room tar-paper house without electricity or plumbing, with oil lamps for light and a little cast-iron "laundry stove" for heating and cooking. Delia didn't lay eyes on a television until she visited her mother in town when she was six, in 1973—a time when TV ownership was nearly universal in the United States. "I seen that TV," she laughs, "and I thought, you know, 'What's that?'"

During one particularly hard winter, about that same year, they nearly ran out of food. "It want't quite spring but winter was kind of going out and I remember we got down to where we didn't even have a bite in the house. 'N my grandma she never asked nobody for nothin'—forget it, that woman would starve." Delia sets the Mountain Dew on the counter and fidgets with a long strand of auburn hair. "And I had this little chicken, and mamaw had maybe a cup of flour. She told me, she said, 'Baby,' she said, 'Mamaw's goin' to have to kill your chicken now so we can have somethin' to eat.' And I said okay. And she said, 'I'll get you another one when spring time comes.' So she killed my chicken that night, boiled it, made a little gravy to go with it, and that was our supper. I can remember that's the poorest I've ever been. I mean it down to *nothin'* to eat."

Delia found the mountains beautiful and soothing, but married when she was fifteen and bore her first child at sixteen; since then, she has lived mostly in towns, moving frequently, like her mother, chasing steady work and cheap housing. She's raised four children—two daughters and two sons—on her own. I've never met the eldest; he lives in Lexington with his family and works at a factory there. Her second, Bonnie, just finished high school. The younger children, Ruby and Wendell, ten and eleven, go everywhere together, like a pair of shoes. Because Delia leaves for the factory before dawn, the "Irish twins," as she calls them, put themselves on the bus in the morning. Sometimes Bonnie's around to help, sometimes she's not. So, like reverse latchkey kids, they lock the door behind them. Delia's older brother, Boyd Garrett, lives in another trailer about a hundred yards away; to check that the twins make it to school, he'll step out on his porch at six in the morning when the yellow bus crunches along the gravel road.

Delia leans around the kitchen cabinets and peers into the narrow living room. "Bonnie!" she hollers. Bonnie and her boyfriend, Jared Bowen, are curled together on the couch, half sleeping, half watching television. The twins are spending the weekend at a cousin's house down the road.

"Unnhh?" Bonnie answers, with eighteen-year-old eloquence.

"I know y'all gonna sleep through church. I want you at service tonight, hear?"

"Unnhh," Bonnie answers again.

"She's not too bad about going," Delia tells me. "But sometimes I got to put my big toe in her backside."

Delia doesn't want to work in a factory. But most people in Bear Lick are stuck with hard choices. Most of them involve taking a deep breath, squaring your shoulders, and jumping headlong into decades of unrelenting work. This path, though forbiddingly steep and difficult, does not often lead to higher ground. You're not saving college tuition for your kids, burnishing your CV, or building a retirement portfolio. More likely, you're barely clearing the car payment, mailing in a late installment to the medical-bill collectors, and counting pennies to get the satellite TV turned back on.

Delia is slogging up this narrow path. She clocks ten-hour days at the factory, and brings home, in a year, half of what I do as a junior professor. But she's finally managed to catch her balance: this trailer, and the three acres of thin-soiled Bear Lick hillside where it's parked, are her own. She'll slog on just long enough to settle the loan. "I'll quit," she declares, "the day I pay that note." At that point, she tells me, she's going to shift it all around. Get some chickens. Grow a garden. Live cheap and find other ways to make money. Maybe try selling crafts. Over the years, she has sold two handmade quilts, and both times it felt like spying a crack of blue sky through the clouds.

We leave the trailer together, but Delia drives off before me, rushing to beat the Klaxon on the factory floor. I can still hear the shriek of it, feel the rumble of the machines. The sensations of the assembly line are familiar, because that's where I first met Delia. As she peels away in her rusting Taurus, bald tires spitting gravel, I think about the myriad hazards that crowd her narrow path. What if one of those tires blows and sends her into a ditch? What if a cop writes her a speeding ticket she can't pay? What if one of the twins wakes moaning in the dark, curled around a throbbing appendix? What if the factory lays off yet another round of workers? If Delia stumbles, what happens to her trailer and her patch of land? What becomes of her dreams?

*   *   *

It's the bluntest job interview I've ever had: two questions.

It's a year earlier, and I'm applying for work at a temp agency, Key Services. I'm sitting in a small, windowless room. The walls are bare and dirty. Patty, the interviewer, is politely indifferent and nearly silent; she began our interaction by wordlessly sliding a clipboard across the desk. It holds an application for Jigoku, a factory on the outskirts of Berea. The forms take nearly an hour and feel like a police interrogation. I have to sign my willingness to drive to Richmond and take a piss test. I am told to list all the jobs I have ever worked; I may "attach additional sheets if necessary." For some reason, the forms request addresses for the past ten years and permission to check my credit history. As I near the end—taking a multiple-choice exam of remedial English and math—Patty looks at the ceiling and sighs. "I'm so tired," she says. I pass the forms back to her, which she barely notices. Instead, she cuts to the real business, and asks the two questions that matter:

"Do you have steel-toed boots?"

Yes, I tell her.

"Can you start tomorrow morning?"

Yes. Yes, I can. She instructs me to show up at the factory entrance at ten-till-five the next morning and hands me a copy of the temp agency's glossy "Employee Handbook." It describes how Key Services can advance my personal and career goals, with pictures of cheerful, athletic, multiracial executives wearing immaculate corporate suits in immaculate corporate suites.

I walk out the door of Patty's office into a place that is not a corporate suite. It's a large, spartan lunchroom with concrete block walls and a gray concrete floor. Cafeteria tables are lined up in rows, like in a high school.

Shelves along one wall are packed with well-worn workmen's coolers and lunchboxes; above them, tiny windows near the ceiling let in patches of weak sunlight, but no glimpse of trees or earth. Against another wall, vending machines and dented plastic trash bins stand in a serried rank. I don't have to ask directions to the factory where I will work the next morning, because this is it. The temp agency office—the portal through which every new employee must pass—is not in the same neighborhood as the factory. It's not next door to the factory. It's inside the factory.

I had just been hired for a typical Bear Lick job. Factory work now makes up the single largest category of formal employment in the area, and—with more than eight hundred workers at its peak—Jigoku is one of the largest factories. Like many others, it's a feeder plant, churning out car and minivan struts to send to automotive assembly lines throughout the South. For people from Bear Lick who don't go to college, this is the kind of job they are likely to end up with, if they're lucky. Because of my literate upbringing, my path was different. I was writing my master's thesis at the University of Kentucky and was headed to Berkeley to start doctoral studies in the fall. But in the meantime, I was broke and needed a job for a couple of months. And I wanted to know: what's it like to work in one of these factories that people from Bear Lick drive to every day?

I'm nervous as I walk into Jigoku, in the pre-dawn darkness the next morning. I follow a flood of workers through the front entrance, past the cafeteria and the temp agency office, and through a pair of swinging double doors that lead onto the shop floor. The building is cavernous, stretching nearly out of sight in front of us and to either side, with a flat ceiling high above. Over our heads, lines of steel racks hang from a chain that winds mazelike across the plant. It's not moving yet, but soon it will. Olive-green machines the size of refrigerators stand in clusters around us like silent sentinels. Some workers are already at their stations, pulling on gloves and stuffing in ear plugs and arranging piles of parts. A short, wiry foreman puts a hand on my shoulder. He has a kind face, but he's too busy to be anything but brusque. "You're on e-coat," he tells me, and points to a half-dozen workers, mostly women, readying one of the stations. Two of the large machines frame a space between them, and into this space the overhead chain dips, bringing the metal racks down to chest level. I'm greeted with a couple of nods, and one of the women shows me a cabinet full of new cotton work gloves.

A minute later, an alarm shrieks, and the machines start all at once, like engines at a NASCAR race. On all sides, with clangs and squeals, metal is cut, bent, punched, welded, and tossed into carts to be rolled to the next station. The overhead chain jerks into motion, swinging a rack full of black, arm-sized metal parts down in front of us. Our job is to whip the painted parts off the rack as it's moving, then reload with unpainted parts before it climbs back up to the ceiling out of reach. The two machines flanking our station shoot compressed air at the unpainted parts to clean them before they're put on the rack. The chain carries the racks a hundred feet across the factory into a sealed room, where they'll dip into a coat of paint. A current passes through the paint, "electro-coating" the parts—hence the name, e-coat.

The work isn't bad, at first. It's a challenging dance, keeping pace with the chain's steady advance. The parts weigh two or three pounds each, and soon my arms begin to burn. "This is cool," I think, flexing a bicep. "After a few weeks of this, I'm gonna be ripped." But there are ominous signs. It's a little too loud and a little too fast to talk much, so I don't know who my coworkers are. I don't even know their names at first, because they don't really care about mine. I'm just a random dude whose clumsiness is breaking their flow. Across the racks from me, a young man speaks quietly to himself. Is he singing a song? Praying? Finally, I'm able to catch his words. He's repeating the same phrase over and over, in a kind of verbal twitch, like an animal gnawing helplessly on the bars of its cage. "I hate this job," he's saying. "I hate this job. I hate this job. I hate this job."

Lunch lasts thirty minutes. But the seconds start ticking as soon as the machines stop—and you've still got to walk across the vast floor to the bathroom, wash the machine oil off your fingers, piss, head to the lunchroom, grab your food. The moment that thirty minutes is done, the line starts. Like the assembly line itself, the lunchroom is full of grim determination. Gotta choke down that baloney sandwich and Little Debbie in time to step outside and hit a cigarette. If it reminded me of a high school cafeteria yesterday, today the parallel is overwhelming: I'm the new kid, and I have nowhere to sit. No one smiles or beckons. Finally, I find a spot on a bench beside two men who each have a Bible opened on the table beside their sandwich. They chew and read, ignoring everything else. An older man leans down the table toward me, as if to offer a greeting, and says, "Boy, you better run now, while you still can." I assume, for a moment, that he's teasing. But nobody laughs.

*   *   *

On the second morning, when the e-coat crew sees me returning, they offer a warmer greeting. One woman, auburn hair gathered in a ponytail, hands me a pair of gloves and asks, "Are ya sore?" Three black rectangles of missing teeth punctuate her smile. That's how I met Delia. The young man who was chanting "I hate this job" is Matt Jacobs; in his mid-twenties, he's rascally handsome with a tawny flat-top and groomed stubble. There's Melinda Jackson, dark-haired, also in her twenties. Planted to one side stands an older woman who's brisk and forbidding and feels like the owner of the e-coat station. She might weigh ninety pounds in her steel-toed boots, but she's about as easy to budge as a granite headstone. She never introduces herself, and I never quite gather courage to ask her name, so I just think of her as Mama Bird.

As the racks flow, hour after hour, I begin to see that some jobs are harder. Certain parts are difficult to grip, or weigh more, or require faster loading and unloading. Mama Bird, with seniority, claims the racks with the lightest parts. I don't mind; I want the workout. Delia and Melinda and Matt braid their motions together, shifting on the fly to keep the streams of different strut components in equilibrium. I also see that they pace themselves, letting the line carry them like a river current; they go precisely that fast, and no faster. But not Delia. She doesn't let the line push her—she pushes the line. She's a beast. For a while, I try to match her rack for rack, but it's not even close. When one of the big green machines quits blowing air, she immediately kneels, whips open a hatch at the base of the thing, plunges her arms into a snarl of pneumatic tubing, and has it back running in about a minute; the racks never cease their lurching march.

After a few days, I join the e-coat crew for lunch outside, squatting on the curb that edges the parking lot. I take a minute to rub my hands;

they're starting to hurt. One set of parts is shaped like little steel do-nuts, and every time I grab one—thumb on the rim, two fingers in the center—it gives my index finger a little tap through the glove. Now my cuticle is puffy and red. Delia sits beside me, managing to simultaneously gnaw a vending machine honeybun and light a second Camel from the stump of the first. Melinda, who seems relaxed on the line, won't even look at me, probably because her husband Kyle crouches alongside. He studies the Fords and Chevys in the parking lot with studiously flexed eyebrows; across the pavement from us, three men lean under the open hood of one pickup and talk shop.

"If Melinda gets hired on direct," he announces—if Jigoku decides to hire her permanently, so to speak, from the temp agency—"I'm gonna fix my truck." He says it'll cost three grand. I get the feeling he's not talk-ing about fixing a broken transmission; he's imagining tinted windows, crimson flames along the flanks, a lifted suspension.

Delia snorts. "Kyle, you already got forty vehicles! I'm saving my money, then I'm outta here. I'm going to sit on my ass and sell cigarettes and pop." She crumples the plastic honeybun wrapper and adds, quietly, "Or whatever I can think of to sell."

"When *I'm* done here," says Mama Bird, "I'll probably wind up a greeter at Wal-Mart. Cause I'll be *damned* if I'm gonna sit at home all day."

Down the curb on my left, men perch on their rumps in a line like frogs around a pond. Bits of talk drift across the asphalt. Gearboxes. Steak houses. Poker games. Gossip, much of it sexual, and harsh. Down the curb on my right, a woman hollers, "I need some stackers!" That's a pill cocktail of ephedrine, aspirin, and caffeine. "Somebody better sneak off and buy me some stackers or I'm gonna be a real *bitch* this afternoon!"

Delia tells us she's worried about her daughter, Bonnie. Delia got home late from grocery shopping the other evening, and when she drove up to the trailer, her headlights found bodies sprawled in the grass. "It was Bonnie and Jared!" she exclaims. "They was passed out cold." But she doesn't have time to say more; our thirty minutes are gone. As we brace ourselves to stand and walk back through the factory doors, Delia leans toward me and says, "Jason, I'm kilt."

After a couple of weeks, the foreman announces to all temporary work-ers that we will take an exam later that day. It's like he pulled the fire alarm; except for Mama Bird, my coworkers are immediately on high alert. Word on the floor was the exam determined who would be "hired on direct," which meant an immediate three-dollar-an-hour raise, plus health insurance. The e-coat line is uneasy. "There's so much in there," Delia says, "that I just don't know. I'm just not intelligent." Matt tries vague bravado: "That test don't matter!" he scoffs. "Next year, I'll be holding all the cards."

It turns out to be a longer version of the application test, a multiple-choice exam covering basic reading and math, with a dash of questions about proper American English usage. As we walk back to the line, they pester me for my score; at this point, they know I'm finishing a master's degree at the University of Kentucky. I'm reluctant to share. It's not a fair comparison. The test isn't a measure of brains; it's a measure of books. I grew up cash poor but letter rich, while they grew up with a dearth of both. When they finally pry out my score, Matt exclaims, "You coulda shared some of them points around with some of these other poor people!" Melinda, who's been chewing her lip the whole time and studying the floor, looks up and says, with bitter heat, "We got ourselves a regular smarty pants here."

One afternoon, Mama Bird steps away from the racks with a frown and slaps a fat red button mounted to a ceiling pier. The line stops with a series of ringing clanks. In her other hand, she's holding a black, freshly painted metal tube about a foot long. Delia and Melinda and Matt cluster round, examining the part. It looks fine to me, but they show me that the finish is slightly matte; it's supposed to be glossy. A floor boss trots up, glances at the strut, and snaps, "If it's black, pull it off the rack!" He slaps the button to restart the line and stalks off.

This kind of reflexive authoritarianism is standard. Most days, we don't know if we're working overtime until we arrive in the morning. Some-times we don't even know what time we'll stop; we just work until the horn blares. "Run the machine or lose the job," the workers say. Once or twice a week, the foreman directs me to a second e-coat line in a dif-ferent section of the factory; I never know why. Another worker, Sonya Broadwater, told me they stuck her in a room all by herself, sixty hours a week, month after month, going through huge boxes of tiny parts looking for blemishes. She never knew what the parts were for, why they decided to put her on that particular job, or why she was alone.

The crew watchfully runs the line for another ten minutes, enough for several sets of racks to pass through. The parts are still arriving with that matte finish. This time, Delia steps over and slaps the red button. "I ain't never buying me a Neon," says Melinda, shaking her head. This time, in the only act of bottom-up decision-making I witness, they refuse to restart the line until the problem with the paint is fixed.

My vision of getting buff from hours and hours of lifting steel turns out to be romantic. The work is indeed strenuous exercise—but it lasts far beyond anything sane. And then it lasts some more. You can literally watch a new pair of gloves fall apart on your hands; the reason they have a whole cabinet full is that we tear through several pairs in a day. After four weeks, I'm hurt. A mysterious gash of light flashes in the upper corner of my right eye. Is it exhaustion? Did I glance at one of the arc welders without thinking? My cuticle is swollen tight and green with pus; it's like I jammed an olive onto the tip of my finger. I can no longer grab the smaller parts with my fingers; I have to palm them. But the scariest part is that my wrists have started creaking, audibly, like a dry door hinge. If it's quiet, you can hear them from across a room.

Every worker I talk to has been hurt, not just at Jigoku, but at all the local factories. Ann Duncan, one of the homesteaders we met in chapter 4, worked at another Berea factory, Itami, and damaged her elbows from wielding a heavy hammer all day long for weeks on end. "When I got done for the day," she told me, "I couldn't hardly shift gears in the car. And then I'd be like aching in bed, you know, going *Good Lord.*" Elijah Amaro injured his hip in that same factory. "My mother worked at Jigoku for eight years," said one angry daughter. "It destroyed her body." Once, when I ask Melinda which particular job she likes or dislikes most, she shrugs and says, "Depends on what part of me's hurtin' the most."

Ann and Elijah and I are just passing through; very few with a college degree stay long on the factory floor. Our injuries will heal. My swollen fingertip will burst and drain, my wrists slowly cease their groaning. But what happens when you can't step away? What happens after years with no rest? This is the single most important aspect of industrial work: the character of repetitive, intense physical labor is radically different depending on how long you have to do it. Four hours on a rapidly moving line can be invigorating; it could actually count as exercise. A supposedly normal workday—eight hours—is harmful. Just getting up every morning and doing the work, over and over and over again, is a heroic accomplishment with a forty-hour week. Ten or twelve hours, day after day? Year upon year? It's living hell.

When my wrists start creaking, it scares me. During lunch, I let Delia listen to them, and ask, "Is this normal?"

"Oh, honey," she says, "I haven't felt my hands in years."

* * *

So do people take the advice the man in the lunchroom offered, and run from the factory as fast as they can? Not at all. Out of the working-class jobs that make up the majority of employment opportunities near Bear Lick, factory jobs aren't bottom of the barrel. For many workers, they're the top. Because other jobs—working in a warehouse or a call center, waiting tables or taking drive-through orders, running shingles or slaughtering chickens—are just as stressful and mind-numbing, but with lower wages and less overtime.

As in the factory, the work at these other jobs is usually repetitive. "You clean the grill, you sweep, you mop, and you run the cash register," Matt Jacobs told me; he worked at a national fast-food chain that I'll call Burger Despot for five years before getting hired at Jigoku. "The next day," he continued, "you clean the grill again, you sweep, you mop, you run the register." After about a month, there's nothing left to learn. You play games in your head, he said. Shift your posture to keep from getting hurt. Matt also worked at the Richmond store of a major grocery chain—let's call it Langeweile's—stocking shelves. He became a maestro of product handling, but nothing else. "Grab about four cans at a time in each hand," he said, "and just start throwing that shit up there." They'd walk around the store "with Sprite cans full of vodka, and just party on the job," which is the grown-up version of carving a dick into a high school desktop.

There's the same casual tyranny. At Burger Despot, they just told Matt what his weekly schedule would be. No questions. No input. He worked every Friday and Saturday for five years, like it or not. At Langeweile's, the stockers would commute to work like they were supposed to—but when the supply trucks ran late, the manager would make them clock out and come back later, even if, like Matt, they lived far away.

At many of these jobs there's little room to move above minimum wage. In this American dream, you work hard and you work long, but you're still poor. Matt walked a couple of miles to Burger Despot every day because after paying rent, he couldn't afford a car. After his first year, he got a fifteen-cent per-hour raise. There were no benefits. "None," he said. "You got free cheeseburgers." At Langeweile's, pay wasn't much better, and he hitchhiked the twelve miles to work. Many people who have one of these jobs go out and look for another, just to make ends meet, and wind up working double and triple shifts, beneath the sun and then beneath the moon. Essentially, you're a cheap replaceable part, like a pair of cotton work gloves.

At the factories, if you're hired on direct, you'll probably get ten to fifteen dollars an hour—which is higher than retail pay, but not by a lot—with some chance of raises down the road and possibly health insurance. The key difference is overtime. If you make ten bucks an hour and work sixty hours a week, you'll gross about $35,000 for a year of labor. Now we're talking! In eastern Kentucky, that's real money—and that's why so many people hang on to those assembly-line jobs as long as they possibly can.

It's not only workers who aspire to factory jobs. They are a success in the eyes of local governments as well. By usual measures, such as statistics on income and employment, Jigoku workers are the beneficiaries of mainstream economic development; they are not among the 30 percent of eastern Kentucky residents who live below the official poverty line.[1] According to this view, in which quality of life is reckoned in dollars, Jigoku looks like a success story. It looks like a solution. Every time a factory locates in an Appalachian town, it's headline news. Time to celebrate. Break out the golden shovel, gather the press, give the mayor his wings.

But the true story of these jobs is foreclosed potential and damaged lives. At best, they provide workers with a sufficiency of things, which is why people like Ruth Hamilton and Caleb Hayward uprooted themselves in pursuit of such jobs. But just because a woman owns a truck doesn't mean she isn't poor. Even when these jobs alleviate immediate material needs, they leave workers with a poverty of safety and health, of autonomy and respect, of time and purpose. They provide minimal long-term intellectual challenge, scope for creativity, or sense of meaning. They render it difficult to grow in skill and knowledge in any real way: difficult to develop a more coherent understanding of society, learn about labor organizing, figure out how to start a business, master a foreign language, travel abroad, or become an effective public speaker. They even make it difficult to find the time and energy to learn to be a better brother, parent, or partner.

Crucially, these jobs also leave workers with a poverty of literacy and literate knowledge. Thus one of their most pernicious effects is reinforcing people's childhood educational experience. Most folks who grew up in literate households and attended good colleges drive by factories without a second thought. The checkout line at Wendy's or Wal-Mart is a momentary inconvenience, not destiny. But what if you grew up with few pedagogical resources at home to overcome the make-believe classrooms? What if no one ever showed you the power of books and writing? Now, as an adult, you end up with a job that feels like more make-believe schooling, a job that actively prevents you from gaining powerful literacy and the knowledge it fosters. If, as a teenager, you didn't learn that carbon dioxide is poisoning the ocean or that Wall Street lobbyists have rewritten our banking laws, you won't have much chance to learn these things as an adult, either.

Nor will you be well-prepared to pass powerful literacy on to your children. Here, in the world of adult labor, at Jigoku and Langeweile's, we have found a major driver of that generational cycle of weak book-learning and a-intellectualism. These jobs are where the subtle class-driven shapings of childhood become carved—over twenty and thirty years of cutting—into ineluctable fate.

* * *

Many would argue that tedious, mind-numbing jobs are an unavoidable cost of modern material affluence. Want a smart phone? Want to travel in a car, train, or airplane? Internet? Contact lenses? Antibiotics? Deodorant? Refrigeration? Fresh fruit in winter? Then quit whining. These things come from factories and other factory-like workplaces. This is the attitude most Jigoku workers adopt: "Yeah, the work is rough, but at least we're providing for our families, and not sitting back drawing a welfare check." It's much easier to push through another ten-hour shift if you have concluded that factory jobs are a necessity.

Is this true? Are crappy jobs inevitable? In some ways, the answer is clearly *yes*. Without repetitive, mechanized, high-productivity labor, we would still live in a world like that of medieval Europe—or like Bear Lick Valley before 1940: a world lit only by fire, decimated by plague and infant mortality, and defined above all by the peasant's plow.[2]

But the important question is not "must we have monotonous industrial jobs?" The important question is one that may, at first glance, seem the same, but is actually quite different. "Why," we should ask, "must monotonous industrial jobs be so bad?" A boring, repetitious job—welding struts, picking strawberries, sewing shirts, flipping burgers—does not have to be a bad job. It's easy to describe the changes that would make these jobs humane. The most important step is to raise wages so people can live comfortably on, say, thirty hours a week. You can work at a factory-style job—whether on an assembly line, in a field, or in a store—six hours a day, five days a week, and still enjoy a flourishing life. The second most important step is to democratize the workplace, so workers can do things like rotate job tasks over time to prevent injury and gain new skills. It's not assembly lines or cash registers or sewing machines that are horrendous—it's the heartless way humans are yoked to them.

Now we have arrived at the real, crucial question: not, "why are there so many repetitive, mind-numbing jobs?" but "why do such jobs generally have low wages, long hours, and authoritarian governance?"[3]

It is worth taking the rest of the chapter to tackle this question, because it's central not only to the lives of people like Delia Howell and Matt

Jacobs, or to the cultural differences between "hicks" and "hippies" in Bear Lick Valley, but to the basic life prospects of billions of people around the planet. The rest of the chapter, then, will be a crash course in what's called *political economy*—the study of how power shapes economic activity—in search of answers to this question. Because if these labor conditions are the inevitable cost of material abundance, that's unfortunate—but it's not worth spending much energy bemoaning the inevitable.

But what if, as our analysis will suggest, these labor conditions are avoidable? What if they're not inevitable at all, but *created*? That is an entirely different situation. In that case, Jigoku isn't just a scene of production. It's the scene of a crime.

*   *   *

Berea College is a billionaire.

That's easy to write, but hard to feel. A billion—a *thousand* million—is meaninglessly vast. To grasp the size of a billion, sometimes I'll grab a fat book—*Order of the Phoenix*, say, the longest Harry Potter at about nine hundred pages—and slowly thumb through. Imagine *each page* is a million-dollar bill—not each piece of paper, but each individually numbered page. And that's still not a billion; you'd have to add another hundred pages to get the current size of Berea College's endowment.

Because Berea admits only low-income students and doesn't charge tuition, it relies on the endowment more than most colleges. Nonetheless, it does pretty much the same thing with its endowment as any other private college, like Harvard with its forty billion, or Stanford with its twenty. The money isn't stuffed inside the president's mattress in bundles of Ben Franklins. It is put, supposedly, to a higher use, through *investment*. The word has such a lovely ring! Investment conjures images of virtuous labor, guidance and support, uplift and improvement. Investors create new jobs and novel technologies, we're told; their exertions carry us to a better, more prosperous future. Without investors, surely, our society would reek of stagnation and desperation.

But what actually happens, when Berea College invests?

First, a little overview of how this works. Berea breaks the billion into chunks and uses the chunks to buy different things. When you buy something, you own it, and that's what Berea is really buying: not objects, but ownership. For instance, one of those chunks—roughly a hundred million—is used to buy stock in "large cap" US-based companies. This includes publicly traded corporations that are worth more than $10 billion and are expected to keep growing in value. Think Starbucks, Google, or pharmaceutical giant Pfizer. Other chunks get allocated to other types of assets, such as real estate or bonds, but about half of the billion ends up in stock. It is this stock ownership we want to focus upon, since the question at hand is "why do corporations like Jigoku create such awful jobs?"

A "stock," or "share," is simply a small piece of ownership of a company; the ownership of Jigoku, for instance, is currently broken into several billion shares. Anyone is free to buy shares of Jigoku, as long as they're willing to pay the going price. That's what the confusing term "publicly traded" means: not that a company is actually owned by the public, like a town library or a national park, but that anyone—even the public—is free to purchase stock in that company. But the company is not collectively owned by the public; it is strictly the private property of the investors.

When Berea's money managers decide what stocks to buy, they look at a whole bunch of stuff—the history of that stock, business trends, profitability, and so on—but it basically boils down to one thing: what is the potential that the stock price will continue to rise? If it looks like other investors will continue to demand stock in this company, buy it. If it doesn't, sell it. At this point, with billions of shares changing hands every day all around the globe—often faster than humans can follow—many decisions to buy or sell stock aren't actually made by people. They're made by computers. No one at Berea College actually knows, in detail, what companies the college currently owns—it's little slices of thousands of corporations, constantly shifting. But, in general, Berea owns whatever is most profitable to own. Would the college buy shares of a coal company that blows up mountains in Appalachia? If it generates a good return, the computer algorithms will say yes. Weapons merchant? Sure. Sweatshops? Why not? There's only one real criterion: does the company successfully maximize shareholder value?

Now we are ready to answer the question: what actually happens, when Berea invests? Suppose the college buys a million dollars of stock in Jigoku. Where does that money go? If you don't already know, the answer may surprise you. Berea doesn't buy the stock from Jigoku, it buys the stock from other investors—and that million bucks goes to those other investors, not to Jigoku. Generally speaking, the very first time a company sells stock, in what's called an "initial public offering," it gets the money—but after that, stocks are just traded back and forth between investors, and the company that's being bought and sold doesn't receive anything. Most of the thirty giant corporations listed in the Dow Jones Industrial Average have not offered new stock in decades.[4] So what does the college contribute, in this scenario, to Jigoku?

The answer is straightforward: *nothing*. Nothing at all. None of that money would go to the company. And, of course, the college wouldn't directly contribute anything else to the production of car parts: it wouldn't help Delia rack struts on the e-coat line. Wouldn't grease the assembly line chains or sweep the floor. Wouldn't drive a delivery truck. Wouldn't invent new metal alloys, or design better products, or devise business strategies. It would contribute nada. Zilch.[5]

And what would the college gain, in return for this negligible contribution? As a for-profit corporation, Jigoku is required by the dynamics of the stock market to focus on creating surplus wealth—and that surplus wealth goes directly to the shareholders as dividends or back into the company to enhance wealth growth for shareholders in the future. Delia and Melinda and Matt and Mama Bird and all the other people who sacrifice the hours of their lives to create that wealth have no legal claim to it. By contrast, in return for a one-time purchase, non-working shareholders own all of it. Not for a year, not for a decade, not until workers hand over some sufficient portion of their labor, but forever.

This, in a nutshell, is the basic ownership architecture of capitalism. This is the nasty truth hidden behind the euphemistic curtain of that wholesome word, *investment*. What investment consists of, in the contemporary world, is a model of ownership eerily similar to the ownership of human beings by the plantation lords of the bluegrass in the nineteenth century, or the ownership of farmland in feudal Europe by the nobility.

It is, quite simply, a legalized power to take other people's labor, without giving them a fair amount of your own labor in return. It is with good reason business writer Marjorie Kelly describes capitalism as a modern aristocratic system, one in which the divine right of kings has morphed into the "the divine right of capital."[6]

This sounds like a plot with a villain, where the antagonist is some fat-cat capitalist, cackling on the deck of his yacht while he snorts coke and tosses cash into the breeze. But I picked on Berea College for a reason: there's no villain in this story. No one is getting filthy rich. The faculty and staff work really hard to educate young people who otherwise couldn't afford it—to empower those who've been disempowered. That is *not* the mission of most colleges with billion-dollar endowments. Berea is arguably the best college in the United States at undoing the curse of class and creating social mobility.[7] There's nowhere in the world I'd rather teach.[8]

Within contemporary capitalism, to be sure, there are plenty of ruthless, greedy people. Just read Jane Mayer's *Dark Money*, an exposé of the Koch brothers, or the stories Michael Lewis tells in *Liar's Poker* about working in a Wall Street bank with men like the "Human Piranha." And most stocks are owned by rich people, not college endowments or middle-class retirement funds; the top 1 percent of households owned 40 percent of US stocks in 2013, and the top 10 percent of households owned more than 80 percent.[9] But under the current system of corporate ownership, naked exploitation doesn't require nasty people—it's produced *automatically*. When Cody Shulyer told me that we had allowed the economy to be taken over by artificial intelligences, he wasn't speaking metaphorically. He meant it as literal truth.

*   *   *

This algorithmic buying and selling of ownership forces companies to ruthlessly maximize their stock price. Capitalist corporations hunt for any edge undiscovered by their rivals, and once one of them finds such an edge, the rest must follow—or lose the game. This unceasing, inhuman competition to boost shareholder value is like a brutally powerful social engine, churning night and day at the center of modern life; indeed, perhaps more than any other single factor, it has created modern life. It profoundly shapes and reshapes our lives, driving society in particular directions, crushing some ways of being and amplifying others. Its effects are so myriad and far-reaching that it repeatedly elbows its way into discussions in my Berea College courses, even in courses on seemingly unrelated topics. Mountain-top removal mining? The southern strategy in electoral politics? CIA coups in developing countries? The character of the mass media? The war on drugs? The homogenization of the American landscape? The ubiquity of junk food? Over and over, we find that one of the keys to understanding puzzling and bizarre social problems is the ownership architecture of capitalism.[10]

To help students get a feel for how this social engine works, we play a game. Imagine, I tell them, you're CEO of a company that produces a common product, like, say, cars. It could be boots or smart phones or sewing machines; the game is the same regardless of the product. To win this game, you must do one thing, and one thing only: generate higher stock prices than the other students—and not in ten or twenty years, but *now*.[11] If you do, your company will grow and thrive; if you don't, the algorithm will dump your stock, your value will drop, and you'll eventually get bought or go out of business. Your job is to invent strategies that maximize shareholder value—and to do so with more speed, ingenuity, and intensity than anyone else in the room.

The students think up all kinds of clever strategies, usually with limited knowledge of actual automotive business methods. But in almost every case, we can find a real-world match for their daydreamed strategy. "I'm gonna hire a bunch of Einsteins," someone will holler, "and invent a completely new kind of car!" Sounds outlandish, but this is the approach at Tesla. They build machines that look like cars on the outside, but on the inside are radically different: no transmission, no muffler, no radiator, no gas tank—and thus no gas station. "I'm going to use machines to make my factories more efficient," another student will offer, "and then I'm going to slash prices so I sell more cars." This is what Ford did with assembly lines, reducing the labor required to assemble a Model T from twelve hours to ninety minutes. This drastic boost in labor output did, indeed, allow Ford to slash prices. Someone else will follow in this munificent vein and propose taking care of workers. "I'm raising wages so employees will show up on time and work hard and be loyal." Again, Ford is a good example; they not only lowered prices in 1914 but doubled wages. Today, Toyota takes a similar route, paying much more in their massive Kentucky plant than most local employers. Through such strategies, wages rise, prices fall, everyone does a little better—and all the while, shareholders reap solid returns.[12]

Some economists call these "high-road" strategies, and there are countless examples.[13] The students enjoy finding them. "I'm going to recycle all the scraps in my factory," someone will propose, "and save money." Excellent idea. A number of car companies, such as Honda, have created "nil to landfill" programs, finding "untapped revenue streams" in their garbage.[14] A penny saved is a penny earned, as my grandmother used to say. "I'll make my cars safer, so families will want to buy them!" Already done. That's airbags, anti-lock brakes, and seat belts, of course, but also the idea of "crumple zones," pioneered at Mercedes-Benz, where engine compartments are designed to collapse and absorb the energy of an impact, leaving the passenger compartment intact.[15]

These are all real strategies that companies have actually used—and it is these strategies that capitalist firms showcase when they appear on TV or testify before Congress. This is how they dress when they go out on the town: as miraculous dynamos of open-ended innovation and development, producing amazing new products that improve human life while creating a healthier planet.

But the students are just warming up. Every high-road business plan they invent is balanced with a cynical, nefarious, low-road plan. "While y'all are busy saving the planet," retorts one promisingly callous young CEO, "I'm going to use advertising to trick people into buying my vehicles." Real-world parallel? Car companies like Chevrolet research male psychology as assiduously as they do metal alloys, and gently stroke worries about manliness and virility to drive sales of oversized pickup trucks.[16] Someone will propose cutting corners on regulations, which is what Volkswagen did when it programmed diesel vehicles to run clean only when they were being emissions-tested; under normal driving conditions, they spewed thirty to forty times the permissible levels of pollutants. And this wasn't just Volkswagen, but Mitsubishi as well. And Daimler-Chrysler. And Peugeot. And General Motors. Remember, once one finds an edge, the rest must follow.[17]

Sooner or later, some student will have a breakthrough: instead of just offering cars for sale on the market, and hoping people buy them, why don't we manipulate the structure of the market itself? Instead of dropping ten million on redesigning dashboards and headlights, how about we redesign, say, tax policy? Redesign, say, Congress? Carbon dioxide, for example, has become a serious environmental pollutant. One way to rig the basic rules of the market is to ensure that the costs of dumping this pollutant into the atmosphere are not included in the price of a new car or truck, or in the price of a gallon of gas—to make sure that environmental costs remain "external" to prices. There are literally thousands of ways for elites to twist market rules in their own favor, even within a single industry. Campaign quietly against the building of effective public transportation. Make it illegal for an upstart like Tesla to sell directly to customers. Lobby against enforcement of policies that prevent mergers and monopolies. Slip "arbitration agreements" into the fine print of contracts, so that customers sign away their legal right to sue if they find out their car is defective.[18]

Some of the most important manipulations are directed at the labor market, and it's not long before my students start discovering low-road strategies that target the workforce. After all, every nickel and dime that doesn't slip out the door inside a worker's pocket is a nickel and dime of profit. And it's these strategies that directly explain Delia Howell's work situation at Jigoku, that lie behind counterproductive workplace practices that otherwise make no sense.

Consider the length of the workday. Did Jigoku do a bunch of research and discover that humans actually work more effectively during ten- or twelve-hour shifts? Of course not. So why not hire a third shift, and let everyone work more reasonable hours? There are several reasons. For example, with fewer employees, it's easier to lengthen or shorten the work week as orders rise and fall. But more than anything, it's just cheaper. Because Jigoku provides health insurance to workers who have been hired-on-direct, it's cost-effective to work a smaller pool of workers for long hours, rather than a larger pool for shorter hours. There's a tradeoff, in this instance, between human well-being and profit, and it's human well-being that takes the loss.

Or consider authoritarianism. If your concern is maximizing the production of quality goods, then a harshly anti-democratic workplace doesn't make sense, either. Aside from long hours, the main reason workers get injured is because they don't rotate job tasks. Wouldn't you want people to move around so their bodies aren't broken? Considering that workers have expertise and insight into the production process—like when Delia fixes the cleaning machines—wouldn't you want to harness their knowledge by opening avenues for their input? And how does it help production to throw a worker, with no explanation, into a room by herself?

Another common practice that makes little apparent sense, in terms of production, is the "runaway shop." Any corporate activity that's not tied to a specific location—unlike, say, a nursing home or an apple orchard—often jumps restlessly from place to place to place. This is a huge drag on efficiency. When a factory relocates, the skill of the prior workforce is lost. Everything must be moved or replaced: not just the workers, but the building, the machinery, the roads, the parking lots, the sewer lines.[19] This is how Jigoku came to Berea in the first place, as a runaway shop moving from farther north; Appalachia has often served as the first step on the road to Mexico and Malaysia.[20]

These strategies hurt people, hinder production, and reduce quality, and if maximizing the output of quality products was the way to win the game of capitalism, companies wouldn't do such things. But that's not how you win. You win by maximizing your stock price. One of the best ways to do that is to keep workers weak, divided, and scared. How much will a temp worker fuss about pay if she can be fired with a thirty-second phone call? If the authoritarianism were lifted a bit, and workers got a taste of decision making, it might not be long before they wanted input on things like benefits and work schedules. And who's going to raise a stink about carpal tunnel syndrome when the boss keeps dropping hints about how cheap the labor is in Mexico? Vulnerable workers lodge few complaints.[21]

Once my students discover the low road, they nudge and jostle each other farther and farther down the slope until they arrive at strategies like these. Even though most have never set foot inside a factory, they predict, with uncanny precision, many of the harsh labor practices typical at a place like Jigoku—or at Wal-Mart, or inside an Amazon warehouse, or at McDonald's. We're not supposed to be able to treat human affairs like a mathematical formula. Humans are more complicated than that, right? But given that single axiom—*you must maximize the company's stock price*—my students derive Jigoku like a geometric theorem.

*   *   *

This is the other face of capitalism, a brutal, psychopathic face not featured in stump speeches and corporate branding campaigns. Both are real: capitalist firms do invent useful products, make labor more efficient, cure disease, solve problems. But these nation-sized organizations, with their unprecedented productive and technical capacities, don't exist to help humanity; that is not their goal. The one rule that binds them all is to generate wealth for shareholders who, in most cases, contribute little or nothing to the creation of that wealth.

Once we spell this out in plain language, it is quite obviously insane. And many other modern insanities suddenly make sense: why are we watching ourselves destroy the planet's climate, apparently helpless to intervene? Why, even as the economy grows and grows, does it seem harder to afford health care and education? Why is the subway station a thousand feet from the White House lined with people who live in sleeping bags and cardboard boxes? How can it be that the top eight people on the planet own the same amount of wealth as the bottom four billion?[22]

Capitalism is, at the same time, one of the best things we ever did to ourselves, and one of the worst. By revolutionizing production, capitalism makes it possible to dream of ordinary people living affluent lives without endless toil. But then capitalism, through exploitation and despoliation, crushes that same dream. This is not hyperbole. Based on growth in the productivity of labor over the past fifty years, an average worker in the United States today could work *half* as many hours as her parents did in

1970 for the same income they made. Or she could work the same hours she does now, for *twice* the income of her parents. Or pick any combination between those two, such as working thirty hours a week for sixty hours' pay. But instead of benefiting from this increase in wealth, people in the United States work, at mostly stagnant wages, for longer and longer hours. From 1973 to 2000, according to sociologist Juliet Schor, the "average American worker added an additional 199 hours to his or her annual schedule." And it's only gotten worse since then.[23] The additional wealth that workers created was taken from them—through a thousand legal scams and policy tricks and market manipulations—by those who own.[24]

Here we find the answer to one of the central questions about life in Bear Lick, the question I posed earlier in this chapter: why do so many jobs have low wages, long hours, and authoritarian governance? These job features exist, simply put, because of the parasitic ownership structure of capitalism. Absent this parasitism, in other words, workers could produce affordable cars and bathtubs and strawberries and haircuts without being overworked, oppressed, and injured.

Indeed, the pressure to exploit is so unrelenting that it leads to a follow-up question—one that's crucial to understanding the modern world, but also counterintuitive and thus seldom asked. It's also a key question in explaining the difference between country and bohemian homesteaders. The question is this: in a place like Bear Lick, are there any good jobs at all? Are there jobs that lift people up rather than beat them down? The jobs at Jigoku, though deeply immoral, are shaped by a hard logic; within the context of capitalist ownership, they make sense. It is a decent job, ironically, that is difficult to explain. Any time a worker has a living wage, a solid pension, reasonable work hours, or a humane workload, that's unrealized profit. From the perspective of CEOs and shareholders, every decent job is a stand of virgin timber that somehow escaped harvest. If there are good jobs, something must shield them from that harvest. Perhaps they contain, hidden within, the seeds of a better society.

*   *   *

Eight feet above the ground, perched astride a stout wooden beam, Ann Duncan seems to float midair in the early October forest. Her chestnut hair is pulled under a Kentucky Wildcats baseball cap, chubby carpenter's pencil jutting above one ear. I straddle a second beam, parallel to hers, about ten feet away and a couple of feet higher. We're running rafters that will support the tin roof of her new woodshed, which she's building an easy stone's throw from her tiny house.

Ann's five acres of Kentucky hardwood wrap the south-facing base of a tall hill. She hasn't cut the forest, and her cottage nestles between soaring pillars of white oak. There is no lawn, just a tawny jumble of last year's leaves, and waist-high thickets of huckleberry and sassafras climbing the steep slope toward the hilltop. Below, across a crooked little creek bed—nothing but dry stone this time of year—a neighbor's pasture stretches beneath the hot sun, dappled with purple ironweed and goldenrod. The warm breeze stirs oak leaves above our heads; if I close my eyes, it sounds exactly like ocean waves breaking upon the shore.

Before I arrived, Ann precut a dozen rafters and stood them against her beam, like you might lean a broom in the corner. She grabs one and raises it, slowly, hand over hand, straight up; once it's high enough, she swivels the top down toward me. I lean out to grab it, beam grinding into my thighs, and reel it in. The rafter is heavy—fourteen feet of rough-sawn tulip poplar Ann bought from a neighbor who runs a sawmill. Poplar is a warm, butter-colored wood, and rough-sawn lumber is thicker, tougher, and shaggier than store-bought; it retains a bit of the wild tree.[25] Ann has already drawn pencil lines across the tops of the two beams, and all we have to do now is snug the rafter to those lines and toenail it into place.

We talk while we work. Ann grew up poor in West Virginia in the late 1970s and early '80s, in a decaying, hundred-year-old farmhouse on the edge of town. They stuffed newspaper into cracks in the walls and walked down the road to use the bathroom at a gas station because the plumbing was ruptured. Her mother earned money working at a church-based kindergarten, but her father was gnawed by paranoia, anxiety, and depression, and seldom left the house. "He was just like a storm," Ann says, fishing in her tool belt for a nail. "A whirlwind. Lots of shouting and manipulation." But he did putter around the house, slowly chipping away the dilapidation.

All around us, shafts of sunlight lance through gaps in the forest canopy. Ann pivots a second buttery rafter into my outstretched hand. Both her parents were evangelical Christians. "It was all about Jesus," she says. "'Jesus is your best friend,' that kind of thing." They went to church three times a week. Cloistered and isolated, Ann didn't know anyone who wasn't a socially conservative Republican. But her parents were also college-educated and bookish, and Ann found escape in their bookshelves. "There were certain books I wasn't allowed to read," she says, driving a nail with quick, efficient strikes. But she found Laura Ingalls Wilder and *Anne of Green Gables,* and then fantasy novels like *The Magician's Nephew,* and then myth and history. And then, in 1995, books carried her even further afield, serving as her ticket to college. She was offered a full scholarship at Harvard—but her parents, afraid she might "backslide spiritually," steered her toward Berea, thinking it was a Bible school. While it has deep Christian roots and Christian elements, Berea is in many ways a typically secular liberal arts college, and it didn't take long—living in a dorm with women from around the world—for Ann's fundamentalist worldview to shatter. "I had to chuck the whole thing," she says with a laugh, "right out the window."

Ann married the same day she graduated—reducing two difficult parental visits to one—and settled in Berea. Her husband, Dave, made almost enough money as an activist lawyer, and Ann covered the shortfall with a series of part-time, white-collar odd jobs. She managed the office at a nonprofit, transcribed medical records, and edited dissertations via email. She had difficulty imagining kids; the global human prospect felt fragile and ominous. The future cast a shadow across her womb. When her marriage ended, after seven years, she rented an apartment in town and needed to boost her income. "I was having a hard time," she says, "even with a college degree, trying to find full-time work." That's how she ended up on the assembly line at Itami, swinging a sledge until it almost broke her joints.

We drop another rafter into place, wiggle it flush to the line. I hold my end while Ann sinks a 16-penny nail diagonally through the rafter into the beam, locking them together. With precut boards, it's quick work, and we're over halfway done. Behind us, what had been, less than an hour ago, a volume of empty air above the forest floor is now sectioned into a lattice of rafters; our labor has transformed it into a measured, engineered, humanized space.

Even though Itami has no connection to Jigoku, and doesn't even make car parts, the two factories, by pursuing similar low-road strategies of wealth extraction, have converged upon a common form. They are mirrored entities, like McDonald's and Wendy's. Ann has never stepped inside Jigoku, but she would know the place. As at Jigoku, people entered Itami initially through a temp agency, and thus they went to work every morning desperate to be hired for a job they were already doing. The hours were long and exhausting and everyone was injured—but the overtime meant bigger paychecks than at other local jobs. Ann pauses to lift her baseball cap and wipe sweat from her brow. "You see people that have been working in the factory for twenty-five years," she says, "and have locked into it with car loans and house loans and boat loans."

For the first few months, Ann thought she could make a go of it. She envisioned writing poems in her head while her body did the work. But after half a year, she realized she had to stop. "It was just too boring," she says. "A lot of creativity dies in that kind of environment. Life is too precious, and I didn't want to stay in a factory my whole life." She plucks another nail from her apron, taps gently to set it in the rafter. "The money wouldn't have mattered. I remember one morning when I walked in and that bell went off and I was like, 'This is purgatory.' It was like I had just left there, and then there's that clock. And there's the same people. And those clothes and that smell"—she belts out a big rueful laugh—"and it's *not going away!*"

So she quit. But not before laying a groundwork. She took the GRE and applied to a graduate program in social work at the University of Kentucky. She kept working through the spring, saving up, and made the down payment on this patch of Bear Lick hillside. At that point, she walked away from Itami, pitched a tent on the land, and spent the summer building her home. She knew lots of women interested in carpentry and tiny houses, and many of the bigger jobs—framing, insulating—were tackled at all-women work parties. Then, over the next two years, she earned her master's degree. "Some nights, I was too tired to drive all the way back from Lexington," she says, reaching for the final rafter, "and I would just sleep in my car in the hospital parking garage." Once she finished the degree, she found a job working as a counselor at a state-funded agency serving poor people in the Bear Lick area. "I've been working there for five years," she says with a grin, as we balance the last rafter on the ends of the beams. "And I love it."

It turns out there are jobs in Bear Lick that lift you up more than they beat you down; Ann's job as a therapist is just one of them. Virginia Webb's career as an artisan—throwing pots on her porch—is another. Others, like Craig Williams, make a living as activists. Nathan Hamilton does well building custom log cabins. Like Ann, I left Jigoku for graduate school, and found my way to a college teaching job; between Eastern Kentucky University and Berea College, there are more than seven hundred faculty positions in the area, making it one of the more common higher-quality occupations. Matt Jacobs also left Jigoku, bouncing through a series of crappy jobs until he eventually found work as a rodman on a surveying crew.

While these jobs typically pay better than poverty wages, most of them are not notably high-paying; these aren't good jobs, generally, because of fat paychecks. They're good because—in contrast to so many jobs in which profit extraction has been maximized—they provide less-tangible benefits like variety over time, a measure of independence, flexibility of schedule, scope for learning and creativity, and a sense of meaning. Matt spends his days tromping through the woods, sorting out the crazy, overlapping land claims leftover from Kentucky's initial round of colonization. He enjoys being outdoors, but also relishes the endless "puzzle solving" of surveying. "You're constantly improving and learning how to do the job better," he said. Virginia Webb spoke about pottery in similar terms. "There's room for growth," she told me. "What are you gonna do with your form, and the function of your pots? How are they gonna look, what kind of glazes are you gonna do? You can experiment here and there. You can grow as an artist, or you can grow as a businessperson. You can work with kids part-time. There's all kinds of things you can do with pottery."

These are real jobs, not utopian visions. Ann's work as a therapist is crowded with paperwork, deadlines, and emergencies. Sometimes she's on call all night long. It's so stressful she gets sick to her stomach. And she only makes about thirty grand a year—no more than she made at the factory. So why does her face light up when she talks about this job?

When I ask, her reply is blunt: "It's meaningful." She helps Bear Lick residents who suffer chronic mental illness, often as a result of poverty's multifaceted deprivations. "It's a tough clientele," she says. "I can't believe what these people went through when they were kids. Both men and women. Some of them locked in a shed with no food, and raped, beaten. Parents just out drunk for days. They'd break their arm, and nobody'd take them to the doctor. That kinda shit. The whole area is riddled with pills. And everybody looks a lot older than they really are."

To do this challenging work, Ann must constantly develop and deepen a wide range of skills. Hour after hour, day after day, she gets paid to practice listening better, thinking better, speaking better. She has to keep study-ing therapeutic science, improving her writing, mastering new healing techniques. And these aren't just specialized job skills you leave in the office at the end of the day—these are tools for living. In this job, unlike at the factory, Ann continually grows more powerful; through reaching out to others with a steady hand, she lifts herself.

Therapy is both a calling, she says, and an art. "There's so much to learn and so many approaches you can take," she tells me, as we climb down from her newly framed roof, the forest above making an ocean of the autumn wind. "If you really do it with your heart and with creativity, you can make a difference. Even with the most broken people."

*   *   *

Somehow, hundreds of jobs in the Bear Lick area have been shielded from the degradation of labor that is a defining feature of capitalism. Perhaps surprisingly, some shielded jobs exist *within* capitalist corpora-tions—even within Jigoku. Mainstream explanations for why certain workers are treated well claim it's a reflection of contribution: labor mar-kets ensure each worker is paid what they are worth. Those with uncom-mon or highly valued skills will, supposedly, command a higher wage or salary.

But how a given worker is treated is less a function of how much they produce, and more a matter of power. Because they actually make the goods, all workers—even those in the most deskilled, easily filled positions—actually possess awesome power. But they can only access that power when they organize and negotiate together. This is a challenging task, and one that executives have done their best to disrupt. In the 1940s and '50s, many people in the United States resisted exploitation by forming unions; about a third of all workers were organized. For several decades, however, this has been a losing battle, and today only about 10 percent of workers are unionized, and fully half of those are government workers.[26]

There are, however, other sources of power for employees. Whenever people work together to produce a complex good or service, the labor is necessarily broken into different tasks. Some workers engineer or design, some administer, some track the accounting, some assemble, others repair, deliver, or clean. All the steps are crucial, but certain positions within this "division of labor" provide more power than others. Those who administer, especially those at the very top—the CEO and other elite executives—wield tremendous power, a power based less on how well they perform their jobs than upon their position in a hierarchy. This power is reflected in compensation grossly out of proportion to their actual contribution. Indeed, because they are present day-to-day, while shareholders are distant and dispersed, executives within modern corporations have sucked up a lot of the wealth that ostensibly should have gone to shareholders. Executives increasingly represent a dominant force within the macro-parasitic class.[27]

Some less-exalted workers are also hard to exploit based on their position in the division of labor. Those engaged in creative tasks like product design or computer programming are hard to supervise; their work entails a degree of expert autonomy. Consider Gilbert Bailey, a Berea College graduate who ran the computer infrastructure at Jigoku. He worked long hours but was paid nearly four times more than workers on the line, treated with respect, and granted a great deal of independence. According to market mythology, this is because his skills are both valuable and uncommon—but it has just as much to do with the fact that no foreman can glance at him and see how well he's performing, because they don't understand his job.

To get a sense of the key role of power in protecting a worker, consider that Jigoku floor bosses also get paid handsomely and enjoy autonomy, even though they don't have a highly specialized skill set; they get paid a lot because it's difficult to guard the guards. Or consider this: if Jigoku executives could purchase a computer program that would effectively monitor Gilbert's every key stroke, reducing his independence and his quality of life, would they be tempted to do so? Sure. If they could outsource his work to India, and decimate his wage, would they do so? Yes. What if they could replace him altogether, with an artificial intelligence? If it's cheaper, sure. Why wouldn't they? They would be happy, in other words, to use policy and technology to manipulate the supply and demand of skilled labor, and to seek ways to cut wages regardless of the intrinsic value of the labor. Under capitalism, no worker is permanently immune from exploitation—except perhaps those at the very top of autocratically governed corporations.

Every well-paid position, remember, is a harvest waiting to be reaped.

* * *

But there is another reason why certain Bear Lick and Berea workers are shielded from unrelenting exploitation: they have non-capitalist jobs. The dominant narrative is that capitalism and so-called "free markets" are just the way the economic world is ordered, period. If you lived through the end of the cold war and the collapse of the Soviet Union, you probably recall how this was framed: capitalism and communism went head-to-head, and capitalism won. Debate over. A college student recently asked Speaker of the House Nancy Pelosi—who counts, in the contemporary United States, as a leftist politician—about his generation's loss of faith in capitalism. Her chuckling reply? "I have to say, we're capitalists—and that's just the way it is."[28]

But, as it turns out, not every enterprise is designed for the sole purpose of channeling human labor into the hands of absentee owners and CEOs. To discover alternative economic models, we don't have to resort to fantasy, and we don't have to look back to the Soviet Union: there are thousands of examples all around us, right now, in our cities and towns, our neighborhoods and backyards. Because even though capitalism is *politically* dominant in the contemporary United States, in many ways it's not *economically* dominant. If we tallied all the productive activities that make up the economy, capitalist firms would account for only a fraction—probably less than a third.

Wait, what? For a system that has no alternatives, that's a lot of alternatives.

They come in many flavors, but they share one thing: they are *real* alternatives. They exist. They're not pie-in-the-sky utopias where—as I heard a revolutionary announce once at a Marxist gathering in London— "everyone gets a swimming pool." They are not perfect. They are full of real people, including some who are hard to get along with or suck at their jobs. But the problem with capitalism, recall, is not primarily that individuals who participate in it are dysfunctional or incompetent or mean. The core problem is that it's a system—like feudalism, or slavery, or sharecropping—premised upon exploitation. These non-capitalist economic activities, with their varied ownership architectures, have their shortcomings—but they generally do not have macro-parasitism built in as a fundamental design goal.

We have already encountered some of these alternatives. When homesteaders like Caleb Hayward and Ann Duncan build a house or a woodshed, they are working to produce things they need. They're doing a job. This kind of labor is easily overlooked, but it's important, it's widespread—and it's largely non-capitalist.[29] We'll talk more about homesteading as an economic alternative in chapter 8. Or consider nonprofits. Like Jigoku, these are corporations, but they're built around a different ownership architecture—one in which no individuals have ownership rights; a nonprofit owns itself, and no one has legal power to take any surplus wealth. And they're everywhere: Craig Williams, for example, works as an activist at a nonprofit, Ann Duncan works for one as a therapist, and I work for one as a teacher. In the United States as a whole, there are more than 1.5 million nonprofits, accounting for nearly 10 percent of total wages.[30]

These may be interesting examples of non-capitalist production. They may be economically important. But are they really alternatives to capitalism? Don't they run into that problem where industrial products, like those in the Sears Catalog, drew people off the land? We can't have an economy based on pottery mugs and pet chickens and therapy sessions and environmental activism, can we? We're not going to grow electric cars and pacemakers and condoms in a garden bed, no matter how heavily we apply the mulch. Don't we need large-scale, industrial, high-tech corporations?

Sure.

But they don't have to be capitalist.

*   *   *

Because a fundamental problem with capitalism is unfairly concentrated ownership, alternatives necessarily involve more-equitable and democratic forms of ownership. The main historical name for this is *socialism*, which is where, in the words of the *Oxford American Dictionary,* the "means of production, distribution, and exchange" are "owned or regulated by the community as a whole."[31]

Community ownership takes many forms, but the most widely recognized is government ownership, also known as state socialism. One reason we've heard of this kind of socialism is that it's been thoroughly vilified in the United States. We've been told, often by those who are paid to say so, that government involvement in the economy is a bad idea. Government is inefficient, incompetent, corrupt, and incapable of innovation; production, obviously, should be left to the private sector.

Sometimes, to be sure, government is inept—but so too are capitalist corporations. Been on the phone with Comcast lately? In many cases, government production of goods and services works just fine. Is government incapable of innovation? What about the Apollo program, which put footprints on the moon? The astonishing field of molecular biology arose on the back of basic research at government-owned public universities. The roots of modern computing can be traced to a government project at a mansion named Bletchley Park, outside London, where cryptographers built analytical machines to crack German codes during World War II. Indeed, most of the components in your smart phone have socialist roots. The touch screen, for instance, was developed by a physicist, Sam Hurst, who was a Berea College graduate from deep in the mountains; his research took place in government labs at Oak Ridge, Tennessee and the University of Kentucky.[32]

Is government production inefficient? Many top-ranked global airlines are government-owned, including Air France, Singapore Airlines, and Qatar Airways.[33] Or compare capitalist-centric health care in the United States with government-provided health care in other developed countries. In 2015 the United States spent more than $9,000 dollars per person on medical care. Most other developed countries, such as France, the United Kingdom, and Japan, spent only about $4,000—and yet their citizens are healthier and live longer. We paid more, quite simply, because of higher prices for the same medicines and procedures. Massive profits aren't cheap.[34]

State socialism gets such a bad rap in the US media it's easy to overlook all sorts of interesting stories. A hundred years ago, tired of getting ripped off by eastern capitalists, the farmers of North Dakota organized, took over the state legislature, and created a number of government-run entities, including a bank, which is still going strong today.[35] Unlike a commercial bank, which is chartered to maximize share price, the official purpose of the Bank of North Dakota is to serve the people. As a result, it doesn't swindle customers at the bottom, and it doesn't shovel money to shareholders and politicians at the top. Among other things, it gives loans to college students at lower rates than commercial banks, supports local credit unions, and avoids the aggressive and risky speculation pursued by Wall Street banks. In 2009, as politicians were injecting those capitalist banks with billions of dollars in taxpayer life support, the Bank of North Dakota made a record profit. And where did that profit go? Not into the silken pocket of a banker. Instead, over the last two decades, the Bank of North Dakota has transferred almost $400 million, more than $3,000 per household, into the state's general fund, providing "support for education and other public services."[36]

Another example. The city of Chattanooga, on the edge of the Appalachian Mountains in southern Tennessee, has a municipal electric grid—owned by the city itself. An electric grid represents what is known as a "natural monopoly," because it makes no sense to build more than one; just imagine a town with multiple competing networks of utility poles and electric lines. Whoever owns the grid thus commands a default monopoly, and many communities have insisted on government-owned electric utilities, to prevent price gouging. In 2007 Chattanooga started threading fiber-optic cable along its grid to create a "smart" system, in which power could be rerouted around trouble spots to prevent blackouts. But as the cable was installed, they realized it could carry internet traffic. Now, residents of Chattanooga pay their city government a fraction of what they used to pay Comcast, their internet speeds are many times faster, and the city has become a booming southern mecca for tech companies.[37]

One historic critique of state socialism is that it represents, to use economist Friedrich Hayek's famous phrase, "the road to serfdom." Government ownership of the means of production, in this view, leads to the kind of tyranny suffered by the Soviet Union. And it can, indeed, be a challenge to make governments democratic. But it's also a challenge to make *corporations* democratic. The greatest threat to democracy and freedom in the contemporary United States is not state socialism. It's not the Post Office or firefighters. It's not our public librarians or schoolteachers, our forest rangers or the virologists at the Centers for Disease Control. It's the power of ultrarich people like the Koch brothers, based largely in their ownership and control of capitalist firms. Our road to serfdom doesn't begin with letting government control corporations, but from letting corporations control government.[38]

*   *   *

State socialism, however, is not the only way to set up community ownership. Instead of ownership by government—or by distant, restlessly speculating investors—how about companies owned by people who have meaningful relationships with them? A corporation could be owned, for example, by its customers, with each customer holding a single share and a single vote. This model is surprisingly widespread; one survey, by the University of Wisconsin's Center for Cooperatives, found twenty-nine thousand "consumer co-ops" in the United States in 2009, accounting for $75 billion in wages and benefits.[39] They're all over the place. Many cities have a customer-owned grocery store, like the Good Foods Co-op in Lexington, Kentucky. The outdoor retailer REI is owned not by investors, but by customers. One of the most well-known consumer co-ops is the Green Bay Packers. Most NFL teams are a rich man's piggybank and plaything, but since 1923 the Green Bay Packers have been community owned. No one makes a profit, the concessions are staffed by volunteers, and a big chunk of the proceeds goes to local charities. As sportswriter Dave Zirin gleefully notes, "Even the beer is cheaper."[40]

Consumer cooperatives have a long history. For example, in the early twentieth century, when city folks began enjoying electricity in their homes, capitalist firms figured there wasn't much profit in electrifying rural America, because you had to run so much cable for each customer. So they didn't. That's why Caleb Hayward's family didn't get electricity until the 1940s. But even then, they didn't get it from a capitalist company: rural America electrified itself, with help from New Deal financing, by forming consumer co-ops. These still deliver most of the electricity in non-urban areas, covering 75 percent of the land in the United States and serving forty-two million customers—including those in Bear Lick Valley.[41]

One of the most common types of consumer co-op is the credit union, which is a bank owned by its customers. There are currently about seven thousand credit unions in the United States, together serving more than a hundred million members.[42] One of them is Park Credit Union, which runs a branch office in Berea. Like the Bank of North Dakota, Park offers better banking services than for-profit banks because they have little motive to bilk customers—who, after all, are the owners. They have no need to slap you with ludicrous fees, cram an opaque mortgage down your throat, or proliferate accounts in your name without telling you. Compared with capitalist banks, Park pays its members better interest on savings and charges them lower interest on loans. The company also, according to employees I have spoken with, treats its workers better than capitalist banks.

In perhaps the most intriguing ownership model, a corporation is owned by those who have both the closest relationship to it and the strongest moral claim to its wealth: the workers. When I first encountered this idea, it seemed unthinkably radical—and yet, such businesses exist all around the world. There are more than two thousand companies here in the United States owned entirely by their workers, including the book publisher W. W. Norton; the New Belgium Brewing Company in Colorado, maker of Fat Tire Ale; the major southeastern grocery chain

Publix, with more than a thousand stores; and W. L. Gore, the company that makes water-resistant Gore-Tex fabric.[43] One of the larger factories in the Bear Lick Area is a cable manufacturer called Okonite; you can spot their products heading along I-75, wrapped around gigantic wooden spools and strapped onto flat-bed trucks. In sharp contrast to Jigoku, Okonite is owned, 100 percent, by the people who work there.

Worker-ownership can be set up in many ways. In the most well-developed examples—such as the grandmother of all cooperatives, Mondragón, owned by seventy-five thousand workers in the Basque region of Spain—each worker has a single ownership share and participates, through deliberation and vote, in the governance of the company. In watered-down versions, like Okonite, different workers own different amounts of stock and the company is governed, as in a typical capitalist firm, by unelected executives.

Nonetheless, even watered-down worker-owned enterprises behave differently than capitalist corporations. Unlike Jigoku, Okonite doesn't hire through a temp agency, and pay starts at about twice that of most local factories. During the Great Recession in 2008, when orders plummeted, Jigoku quickly laid off about a third of its workforce. As a result, my next-door neighbor lost his job—at a time when no other jobs were available—and, within a few months, his family lost their home as well. Okonite, instead of firing people, shifted to a thirty-hour work week. Everyone took a pay cut, but no one ended up unemployed and destitute.[44]

These worker-owned businesses are also notable because, like capitalist firms, they compete within markets; some scholars refer to these businesses—as well as consumer co-ops—as "market socialism."[45] When they go head-to-head with capitalist firms, worker-owners do quite well. Is this really a surprise? We know autocratic governments are dysfunctional—but somehow when it comes to business, we suddenly think dictatorship is best? The evidence does not bear that out. When democratic ownership is joined with democratic governance—one worker, one vote—you get firms that are more formidable than capitalist ones. They pay better, last longer, and produce goods and services more efficiently.[46] This makes sense. Worker-run businesses seldom embrace the kind of crazy workforce-abusing strategies that so many Americans endure. Profit that

isn't reinvested in the firm is not skimmed off by parasitic absentee owners and renegade executives but distributed to the laborers who created
it. Overall, workers simply care more about a company when they own
it. Where would you work harder and with more satisfaction—at your
own company, or at one for which you're just a disposable tool?[47]

We can engineer bacteria to secrete spider silk, launch a robot through
the rings of Saturn, and build machines that record thoughts as they erupt
inside our living brains. Yet we're supposed to believe we can't design an
alternative to capitalism? To an economic system that's basically gussied-
up feudalism? In reality, as we have seen, there are many ways to build
fairness and democracy into the economy. So many, in fact, that I can't
even mention all of them here. Just in the past several decades, we've
seen the invention of myriad new ownership forms, such as collectively
generated open-source products like Wikipedia and the Linux operating
system. Or time banks, like the one in Louisville, where people use the
internet to build a network of modern barter—and where, with a kind
of beautiful elegance, an hour of human effort is considered equivalent
to an hour of human effort, regardless of whether it's babysitting, building cabinets, or lawyering. I recently traveled to Puerto Rico, and instead
of paying a hotel corporation for lodging, I paid a kind and affable man
named José. Airbnb, a privately owned company, took a small cut—about
3 percent—but most of my money went directly to the person providing
the service. There's more: B-corps. Community Land Trusts. Co-housing.
Nonprofit manufacturing. Guaranteed minimum income. Participatory
municipal budgeting. Peer-to-peer solar electric trading. Cooperative wind
farms. The innovations are legion, and stunning.[48]

And thus, we have an answer to that major question posed earlier in
this chapter: the jobs at Jigoku are defined by long hours, low pay, and
autocracy largely because of the architecture of capitalist ownership. But
they don't have to be. Such conditions are not integral to industrial production. We can enjoy the kinds of flourishing lives made possible by
modern goods like antibiotics, tractors, books, washing machines, and fetal
heart monitors, without consigning two-thirds of the planet to slavery in
a Satanic Mill or the abject poverty of unemployment. We can't build a
perfect society, of course. But a much better one? Clever people all over

the world have already created the economic building blocks. They're lying all around, just waiting for the rest of us to wake up and make use of them.

*   *   *

In the meantime, the economy we have is one in which the labor of the many is too often siphoned away by the few—and this top-heavy economy shapes us. All of us. It worms itself deep into you, intimately molding and carving; it has done no less to me. As second-wave feminists of the 1960s pointed out, even that which is most private and personal is political.[49] It's no fun to find politics inside your body and your mind, influencing what you know and believe, defining the degree and nature of your success, choosing which life pathways are readily available and which are difficult to even perceive—but that's the reality.

Under this economic system, working-class people in Bear Lick and Berea are struggling; I've described their lives as being like a hike up a steep, rocky, narrow trail. Some of them, through sheer effort and discipline and luck, manage to avoid taking a fall. But there are so many ways to fall, and so few things to catch you. A recent headline captures this perfectly: "Escaping Poverty," it said, "Requires Almost 20 Years With Nearly Nothing Going Wrong."[50] As a therapist, Ann Duncan works directly with those who bear the brunt of this unfair system. Many of them end up, she says, trapped in a cycle of "hard living." Emma Burress, a bohemian homesteader who worked as a therapist in eastern Kentucky for thirty years, doesn't mince words. "Jason," she told me, in a calm, matter-of-fact voice, "this is a devastated society."

It's comforting to think of poverty as being mostly about a lack of money. If that were the case, poor people wouldn't have enough stuff—but underneath, they would basically be healthy and safe, like an adorably disheveled orphan in a Norman Rockwell painting. All they need is a little more stuff! If that were the case, poverty wouldn't be worth so much worry. But being poor isn't just about money, and it doesn't just leave you short of possessions. It injures you. It shortens your life. It turns hard work into failure, heroic effort into debt. Most insidious of all, it gets into your mind and the minds of those closest to you, shaping and limiting your knowledge and your worldview. It doesn't just damage your back and your knees and your hands—it damages, in a word, your culture. And then that damage, in turn, makes it harder to fight back against the system that damaged you.[51]

When Ann left the assembly line to attend graduate school, Delia remained, as so many must, hanging on desperately to that factory paycheck. But their fates began to diverge long before. Ann grew up cash poor, but—unusually—book rich. This allowed her, eventually, to find work that shielded her, to some degree, from exploitation. Delia grew up in a far more common situation, bereft of both income and letters; compared to Ann, she was hardly shielded at all.[52] At this point, they seem like different kinds of people. They know different things, they use different words, they see the world from different angles. Ann looks and talks like someone who belongs in a professional office, and Delia looks and talks like someone who belongs on a factory floor.

But they didn't start that way. And they didn't diverge because one worked hard and one didn't. Because one was smart and the other dumb. They're both remarkably tough, sharp, and industrious. Both are from poor country families; both are Appalachian. They're close enough in age to belong to the same generation. They live only a couple of miles from each other, driving along the same country road in the morning, and watching the sun set over the same mountain in the evening.

But they might as well live on different planets. If Ann gets sick, she'll still have a career; if Delia gets sick, she won't even have a job. As Ann learns about healing, Delia gets hurt. As Ann hones her craft, Delia is on that line, hanging struts on the racks as fast as she can. She must fulfill all the most important needs of human life—loving, learning, remembering, creating, communing—in the few shattered hours that remain each day after her labor is done.

7 Hard Living

It's early November, and unseasonably warm. Indian summer lingers. Gathered around the dying embers of last night's campfire, Boyd Garrett and three companions sprawl in lawn chairs under a shady oak beside his trailer. A Sunday morning breeze stirs the ash, twirling little gray vortices into the air. Boyd keeps a half-acre of open grass around his trailer, but it's just a clearing surrounded by forest. The leaves swish like rushing surf, but not for long—the trees are aflame with a thousand scarlets and ochres of autumn. Their limbs will soon stand naked and stark in a frozen sky.

The men trade insults and tall tales, reckonings and insights, puns and punch lines. Their masculine banter is like that on the local factory floors and construction sites, with a similar style and range—witty, quick-moving, and seldom straying far from women and sex. Among other things, they discuss homosexuality and religion and race, three points of divergence between country and bohemian homesteaders. They passed the morn pitching horseshoes—spinning the iron crescents toward the posts with expert ease—but the day has grown hot and the beer has grown cold. Boyd, Delia Howell's older brother, holds court like a jolly pirate captain, with an unruly golden beard spilling across his thick neck and long hair drawn beneath a red bandana. A T-shirt stretched across his chest announces, in neon-yellow letters, "DICKIE-DO AWARD: my tummy sticks out farther than my DICKIE-DO."

Boyd lives on a two-acre parcel just down the gravel road from Delia; you could almost throw one of the horseshoes from his front porch to hers. Some homesteads look like Virginia Webb's, with a hand-sculpted cottage, ducks wandering among the marigolds, corn and beans and squash intertwining in verdant profusion. Some look like Nathan Hamilton's, with a barn full of stables and horse tack, a soft-eyed Jersey cow grazing beside the root cellar, rows of potatoes measuring the valley floor. Boyd's place looks like neither. The centerpiece is a rusty Elcona mobile home, baby-blue paint faded in the sun, parked in an island of patchy, slate-crusted crabgrass. A grid of concrete blocks pokes up like gray tombstones on the roof, holding down a sheet of black plastic to keep the rain from leaking through.

Nonetheless, Boyd's land is, by any fair accounting, a homestead—a place created substantially through the labor of those who live there. Boyd didn't build the Elcona, but he bought it used, towed it to the land, sat it upon a block foundation, and added two cedar-post porches, one on the front and one on the back. He and his brother, Willie Garrett, connected the electric lines and installed the septic system. After about a year, Boyd and a friend, Steve Lewis, built a tiny house on a corner of the property. It's ten feet by eight, framed with two-by-fours and sided with free slab pine from the same Bear Lick sawmill where Ann Duncan bought her rafters. It's just big enough for a sliding glass door in one wall and a full-sized Confederate flag on the other, but it fits a kitchen sink, a dorm fridge, and a twin mattress where Steve sleeps. The unpainted siding will rot within fifteen years, but that's okay—the whole thing cost less than five hundred bucks. Aside from a pair of rose bushes, Boyd never bothered with gardening. Cultivating shale is no joke, but mostly he just followed the contours of economic logic: what he needed, above all, was affordable housing, and that's what he created.

Growing up, he faced the same hard choices and limited options as Delia. To save their mamaw the cost of feeding him, he left home when he was sixteen and found work in the coal mines to the east. He followed the shaft into the darkness one morning, but the groaning ceilings and lung-spearing dust were terrible and terrifying; at the end of the day, he followed the shaft back into the light and never entered a mine again.

Like Delia, he chased crappy jobs and crappy housing all over eastern Kentucky, until one day a pallet of grape juice toppled from a forklift in a warehouse, nearly crushing his knee and tearing ligaments around his spine.

Ever since, he's lived "on disability," shorthand for various Social Security programs that support those too injured or sick to work. The amount you receive is based on how much you paid in Social Security taxes before you stopped working; if you held a higher-paying job, you get higher benefits. With a patchy work history at low-wage jobs, Boyd survives on less than $1,000 a month. Ten years after the accident, he walks with a cane half the time. Some evenings, Delia finds him curled on the floor of his trailer, yanked fetal by back spasms.

* * *

At the moment, the men are recollecting childhood. "I loved school," Boyd recalls. "I was good at spellin'. I liked the writin'." Even on days when snow fell deep, and his mamaw said they could stay in bed, Boyd would pile on the clothes and fight through drifts to meet the bus.

Gary Lane, a short, tightly built man, leans back in the lawn chair beside Boyd. He recently returned from a motorcycle trip to Myrtle Beach, where he picked up the Dickie-Do shirt as a souvenir for Boyd. "I wasn't never good at school," he announces, a forgotten horseshoe balanced on one knee. "I couldn't listen to the teacher. All I could think about was eatin' pussy."

On Boyd's other side sits Willie, Boyd and Delia's younger brother. He's less jolly pirate and more zombie ravager, with a gaunt, stern face and hard eyes. Sitting across the firepit is Steve Lewis, who still lives in the tiny slab cabin across the yard but has started spending time over at Delia's. With unconscious familiarity, each man holds a sweating silver can of Natural Light.

The conversation pauses at the growl of an approaching engine. After a moment, a Toyota pickup drives by, gravel popping beneath the tires. It's Joseph Rivard, the bohemian who lived on Quaker farms during his college summers; his homestead is only a quarter-mile down the road. Just past Boyd's property line, he slows and pulls his truck off to the side. Then he climbs out, tall and lean, white hair pulled into a braid, and bends down to pluck a half-dozen beer cans from the edge of the road. He tosses them noisily into the back of his truck and drives off without even a glance in Boyd's direction.

Boyd studies the dust from Joseph's truck as it swirls in the sunlight. "I ain't never figured Joe out," he says after a bit. "Is he straight?"

"He's got a pretty wife," answers Willie, flipping his cigarette butt into the firepit.

"My woman's got a gay friend from work," says Gary, after a swig of beer. "She brought him home the other night and they just laughed like they were best girlfriends." Another swig. "Don't bother me none, long as they don't talk gay stuff."

"They say Lee Majors was gay," Steve remarks, "and *he* had a pretty wife."

"We know about gay," Boyd puts in. "We got a gay cousin."

"Yeah—cost me double pussy," says Willie. "I picked up this pair of girls at the Maverick, went by Monty's and got a case of Bud and some cigarettes. Them girls was okay doubling up on me. All I needed was a place. So I went by our cousin's—he was supposed to be out of town. We walked in there and him and his partner was buck-naked on the floor buttfuckin' each other. 'Bout made me puke. Them girls was outta there fore I could turn around. They was yellin' from the truck, 'Take us home! What kind you think we are?'"

Boyd crumples his empty beer and tosses it toward a loose pile of cans near the closest horseshoe post. He works his way out of the lawn chair and limps up onto the back porch and into the trailer, leaving the door open. Emerges after a minute with a plastic jug of American Pride Vodka in one hand and a six-pack of Natty Light dangling from the other. He passes cans all around, eases down with a groan, and twists the lid off the vodka.

Willie lights another cigarette, takes a draw, asks, "What do y'all think about the nigger in the White House?"

"I think he's got a smart wife," says Gary. "And tall. That Michelle Obama's over six foot, I'd say."

"She's smart *and* pretty," Boyd adds, passing the vodka jug to Gary. "Got them long legs that go all the way to her butt."

"Everybody's legs go all the way to their butt," Steve says.

"Everybody's Christmas tree," Willie mutters, "needs a Barack Obama hangin' from it."

"Country's in a mess, that's all I know," says Boyd. "Man can't do nothing about it. Even a good man. Maybe God can."

"Goddammit!" Gary says. "There ain't no God out there. There ain't *nothing* out there. I hate preachers and I hate God."

Boyd chuckles, unoffended. "That's Gary. But I don't feel that way. I believe in God."

Steve clears his throat, spits, changes the subject. "You know the name of that spot between a woman's asshole and pussy?" This draws a snorting laugh from Gary. "*Taint*. Taint ass 'n taint pussy."

"But it's a damn good place to rest your chin while you're getting your face wrankled!" Gary shouts, raising his beer in salute.

"That," says Boyd, "is the most redneck thing I ever heard."

"I ain't saying this out of no disrespect for my mama," Steve continues. "She was a good woman, God bless her. Had seven of us boys to raise. That wasn't easy. But a man spends nine months getting out, and the rest of his life trying to get back in."

"Unless you're gay," amends Boyd, gesturing down the road with his beer, in the general direction of Joseph's truck.

"World's going to hell," says Willie. He draws on his cigarette, shadows pooling in his cheeks. "Men marrying men. Women marrying women. It ain't right."

Gary's gazing up at the yellowed oak leaves waving in the breeze above his head, scratching the stubble on his chin. "I like an eighteen-year-old girl now and then," he muses. "They ain't skanky like older women."

Boyd snorts. "Oh, now the bullshit's gettin' deep! Gary, you ain't had no pussy in so long, you don't remember how."

"I remember good and I'm good at it."

Boyd smiles and reaches over to chuck Gary gently in the shoulder with his beer. "It's been so long that probably the last time you had any you *was* an eighteen-year-old girl." Still smiling, he looks around the yard, one way, then the next. Doesn't see what he's looking for. "Monster!" he hollers. "Hey Monster!" After a moment, an old brown Chihuahua with a missing front leg and a rhinestone collar climbs sleepily out from under the porch, stretches, and limps slowly over to jump in Boyd's lap. He sets his beer on the ground beside his chair and affectionately tugs her ears. She circles a few times, then lays in the cradle of his arm and falls back into sleep.

*   *   *

There are four bohemian homesteads on the same road as Boyd and Delia, one of them right next door. But, with few exceptions, they don't hang out together. Thirty years ago, in his late teens, Gary Lane used to show up at some of the parties at the Hippie Museum commune, on the other side of Bear Lick. And my father, who has a lovely way with all kinds of people, has stopped by occasionally to visit Boyd over the years; now, whenever he drives by, Boyd hollers, "I love you George!" But mostly, the two groups segregate. Obviously, this has something to do with education and income. Something to do, in a word, with class.

As we have seen, the United States is very much a class society, which profoundly influences people's lives and well-being. Indeed, class is arguably the single greatest social problem we face—not just as a nation, but as a species. The political clout of certain corporate elites, just to give one major example, has been the main barrier to dealing effectively with global warming.[1] But it's hard to figure out what class is and how it really works. Consider the term "working class." Delia and Boyd would generally be considered working class. But, like them, I also must work for a living; without work, I have no income. Why aren't professors, then, seen as working class? Or compare a master plumber and an adjunct professor: the plumber likely gets paid three or four times as much as the adjunct. Who's working class and who's middle class, in that scenario?

One result of such contradictions is that this crucial aspect of social life remains unclear. It shapes and impacts us, but also eludes us. Even scholars and scientists scratch their heads in puzzlement. Medical researchers, for example, often shy from examining class-based differences in health and health care because they lack a coherent definition of class. Is it income? Is it type of work, like white collar versus blue collar? Is it culture? If they can't define it, they can't measure it, and if they can't measure it, they can't research it.[2]

This is one reason why the division between "hicks" and "hippies" is so important: not only does it slice through most of the rural United States, but it's an expression of one of the most important processes—class—in the modern world. The divide between someone like Boyd Garrett and someone like Joseph Rivard represents a basic intellectual challenge: if we can figure out what it is and how it works, we have grasped something fundamental about our society. And if we can't? It does not bode well for our chances at building a better, more just world. It's hard to fix a problem you can't diagnose.

We've already explored some aspects of how class works. The distribution of money and ownership in the contemporary United States is largely a function of power. At the very top, those who exploit many others become incredibly wealthy. For the rest of us—those who crank the gears of production, rather than own them—income is shaped largely by the degree to which we are either shielded from or exposed to exploitation. In my current job, for example, at a nonprofit college, I am relatively well-shielded; when I worked at Jigoku, I was not.

This uneven exposure to macro-parasitism, I would argue, is really the central driving force of class difference in the contemporary United States. But if that were the whole story, class wouldn't be all that difficult to understand. There are contradictions and complications, like the problems noted above with the terms "working class" and "middle class." One of the biggest complications is that—setting aside millionaires and billionaires, segregated in their enclaves and retreats—differences in income don't really divide people. Boyd Garrett barely scrapes by, while his friend Gary owns a roofing business and can drop twenty-five grand on a Honda Goldwing, but they get along just fine. Joseph Rivard, who works occasionally as a stonemason, lives on an income as modest as Boyd's, yet they hardly know how to talk to each other. What makes it hard for these two men to relate is not different incomes, but strikingly different levels of literate education.

Class, then, involves the distribution of both money and literacy. The distribution of these two forms of wealth overlaps considerably: if you grow up affluent, you generally have access to resources that make it easier to achieve powerful literacy; and if you grow up in a powerfully literate family, it is easier to access jobs that will keep you affluent—jobs that are relatively shielded from exploitation. On the flipside, if you grow up poor, it's harder to get a good education; and if you grow up without a good education, it's harder to get a good job.

And yet, while the distributions of money and education overlap and reinforce one another, the two are not identical. Individuals can and do buck these trends. Berea College enrolls plenty of poor kids who, despite long odds, are determined to learn. More-typical colleges enroll plenty of affluent kids who, despite a host of advantages, are determined *not* to learn. Joseph Rivard's two granddaughters, growing up in a household with more books than dollars, have a better shot at powerful literacy than Gary Lane's grandkids, who will grow up in homes with door-sized televisions and brand-name clothing, but few bookshelves.

This leaves us with a key question: how can it be that the class divisions people actually *feel* turn more on differences in education than income? How can reading and writing—which have been widely distributed activities for only a couple hundred years, at most—stand at the heart of deep cultural divergence and segregation? How can that one thing make it so difficult for Boyd and Joseph to hang out together? They live on homesteads carved from the same patch of Kentucky forest. They are both, in their way, refugees from the mainstream. They both have ponytails, enjoy a cold beer, pluck a guitar now and then. Why don't they share a campfire and swap stories? Why don't they trade labor and know-how and help each other out?

That's the question at the heart of this chapter. To answer it, we'll look at a series of cultural differences—in diet, trash disposal, and attitudes toward sexuality—each more divisive and difficult to resolve than the one before. Within each one, we'll find that literacy plays a defining role.

First, a note on terminology. Despite the above complications, the most useful simple label for people like Delia Howell and Boyd Garrett and Caleb Hayward and Ruth Hamilton—those who bear the brunt of exploitation—is still "working class." The most useful simple label for those who must work for a living but are somewhat shielded from the most aggressive forms of exploitation—folks like Ann Duncan or Virginia Webb or Craig Williams or myself—is still "middle class." Although imperfect, these are the phrases I will use.[3] But if you have to work for someone else in order to receive an income, you are, in a very real way, a member of the working class. The majority of us, in other words, are working class. If we focus, however, not on the cultural differences that split the working class into factions, but on *real* differences in wealth and power, the truly momentous class division in the United States is between—to use the common phrase—the 99 percent and the 1 percent. Or, to be more accurate but less catchy, between the 99.99 percent and the .01 percent. That's the real rupture, the master fracture. That's the fault line that portends cataclysm.

*   *   *

The shopping carts at Berea's Wal-Mart are full of soda pop and corn dogs. Wal-Mart is where I buy groceries, so I have spent many an hour waiting in the checkout line, observing what people eat. Most carts contain a smattering of whole foods—a head of broccoli, a bunch of bananas. But these are usually lost in a crowd of junk food: Red Baron Deep Dish Mini Pepperoni Pizzas, Stouffer's Macaroni & Cheese, State Fair Corn Dogs, Wild Grape Pop Tarts, Little Debbie Marshmallow Pies, cases of Mountain Dew, half-gallon tubs of Cool Whip. If I spot a cart that shows systematic avoidance of processed foods, I usually know the shopper; chances are they're a member of Berea's highly literate minority—a professional staff or faculty member at the college, an activist, a bohemian homesteader, or, sometimes, all three wrapped into one.

Like the reading material in outhouses, shopping carts serve as a diagnostic tool of cultural divergence.

Among progressive scholars, the dominant theory about why poor people eat junk food is that it's cheaper. Thanks in part to government subsidies, the bargain calories are supposedly found in foods confected from mass commodities like corn syrup, soybean oil, and white flour.[4] Working-class families are trapped, according to this theory; they have no choice but to rely on these cheap calories.

This is a popular argument. I've heard it voiced not only by scholars, but by graduate students, bohemian homesteaders, and well-read undergrads; it's an argument, ironically, spread through articles and books. It's an attractive position because it avoids the risk of blaming low-income families for their predicament and places responsibility explicitly on the villains: poor people in the United States are forced to survive on low-quality food because of ruthless, profit-seeking mega-corporations.

Problem is, it's not true. Or, rather, it's only partly true. Let me illustrate with a story. Every fall at Berea College, I teach a writing course for incoming freshmen. Berea's student body is entirely non-affluent, and many would feel at home around Boyd's campfire or in Delia's trailer—or with the African American or Latin American versions of Boyd and Delia. They struggle with writing not because they're dumb, but because they seldom read or write; many of them have developed, through make-believe schooling, an anti-reading sense of self. To help them feel engaged in their writing, I let them select, as a group, a topic they find interesting. Sometimes, they choose food—and when they do, we jump in a couple of vans and head down to Wal-Mart.

"Okay," I tell them, once we're in the store, "everyone grab a cart and pretend you're at home, shopping with your family. Go get the stuff you normally eat." While they're off "shopping," let's note that if you ask them what they think about junk food, they'll say, without hesitation, "It's bad for you! You shouldn't eat a lot of it." It appears they possess all the knowledge they need.

Turns out, things are a little more complicated.

When they return, we circle the carts—with me wondering how long it will take a manager to kick us out—and take a look. The carts are like those in the checkout line: full of processed food. "Now, can you tell me," I ask, "which items in your cart are junk food?" This is where it gets interesting. They know a gallon of ice cream is junk food. They know the two-liter Pepsi and box of Maple Iced Donuts are junk food. But they don't know that most of the rest of the processed food is also junk. They don't realize that a breakfast cereal like Cinnamon Toast Crunch is manufactured from the same three ingredients—flour, sugar, oil—as the donuts. Or that a jug of Juicy Juice, nutritionally, is just soda pop without the fizz. They'll flag frozen pizza as junk food but not mac and cheese; Cool Ranch Doritos, but not Beefaroni.

Then we go deeper. We read nutrition labels together. The first time, I got a shock: the student I was reading with didn't know ingredients were listed in order of predominance. "No worries," I told her. "Now you know." But it prompted me to check with the rest of the class—and discover that none of them knew. Fifteen students, and not a single one was clued-in to this basic fact about food labels. I was dumbfounded. For a moment, I didn't know what to say, and so we had a moment of silence, there in Wal-Mart, in our circle of shopping carts.[5]

Part of my job is to have a sense of what students know and what they don't—but this surprised me. It shouldn't have. A nutrition label is an excellent example of a text that distinguishes between powerful, fluent literacy, and merely accurate literacy. All my students can sound out the words and numbers on a label—but that doesn't guarantee they feel the meaning. What is a trans-fat? Is thirty-nine grams of sugar a lot, or a little? What's dextrose? Or maltodextrin? Like poetry, food labels are word puzzles, full of unstated rules and hidden meanings and semantic games, and my students have too few people in their lives who can help them navigate the genre. They don't know the numbers are often distorted by unrealistically small serving sizes—a serving of ice cream, for example, has long been listed as "half a cup," rather than the real-world portion of "half a quart per *Game of Thrones* episode."[6] They don't know there's a big difference between sunflower oil and palm kernel oil. They don't know what sodium nitrate is, or why you should care. They don't know that "all natural" has almost no meaning whatsoever when it's printed on a label, or that "cholesterol free," "gluten free," and "no sugar added" are legalized doublespeak, not synonyms for "healthy."

My students have a sense that junk food is bad for you. But they don't possess the tools to identify it.

The idea that junk food is cheaper than healthy food is also only partially true. If we compare Chef Boyardee and instant mashed potatoes from Wal-Mart with swordfish and arugula from Whole Foods, then sure, it is. But that's not the right comparison. Let's stay right inside Wal-Mart. Even here, if you want to eat avocados and pecans and organic soymilk and fresh blueberries out of season, you'll spend more. To be sure, it's easier to eat healthy if you have enough money to toss anything you want in your cart. But, if you're stretching dollars, how about eggs, dried or canned beans, chicken thighs, carrots, and sweet potatoes? Those are all just as cheap, if not cheaper, than highly processed food products. Oats are roughly half the price, per ounce, of America's bestselling breakfast cereal, Honey Nut Cheerios. Water is cheaper than soda pop. "The alternative to junk food," as author Mark Bittman puts it, "is not grass-fed beef and greens from a trendy farmers' market, but *anything other than junk food:* rice, grains, pasta, beans, fresh vegetables, canned vegetables, frozen vegetables, meat, fish, poultry, dairy products, bread, peanut butter, a thousand other things cooked at home."[7]

But wait! This prompts a final objection from the left: "Okay, maybe poor people can buy healthy food for cheap. But they don't have time to cook."[8] Sorry, but that doesn't fly, either. For seven years now, since Finn was three, I have been a single parent with a more-than-full-time job. I understand not having time to cook. I'm not humming around the kitchen in the evening, searing plums and mincing shallots and hand-churning butter. I don't marinate or fricassee or engastrate. But I can fry eggs and peel bananas almost as fast as opening a box of Pop Tarts. Drain a can of black beans and dump in some olive oil and salsa faster than I can heat a frozen pizza. Toast cheese on whole wheat bread, peel some oranges, chop a cucumber. Boom. Meal done.

The dominant theory is not totally wrong: the real reason poor people buy junk food is, indeed, because profit-hungry mega-corporations make them do it. But corporations don't accomplish this, for the most part, using prices. After all, they don't want people purchasing cheap food—they want them purchasing food that's cheap to manufacture but expensive to buy, like that box of Honey Nut Cheerios. And most working-class people aren't carefully reckoning pennies per calorie, anyway. The way corporations get us to fill our carts with junk food is through low-road strategies of manipulation. They hook us with sugar and salt and carefully engineered mouth-feel; they aim cartoons and jingles at children; they assault shoppers with a bewilderment of mislabeling. They get away with this trickery, quite simply, because so many of us lack the education we need to recognize we're being tricked.

*   *   *

Teresa Schroeder is a master farmer. On a stunningly beautiful hilltop farm, overlooking Bear Lick Valley, she grows vegetables and fruits and herbs for sale at the Berea Farmers' Market. Aside from her pickup truck, she doesn't use industrial inputs: no pesticides, no fertilizers, no designer seeds—not even a tractor or tiller. It's all done by hand. She doesn't make much money, but she lives frugally in a tiny home, and brings in a little extra by teaching permaculture workshops around the United States and Europe. And she doesn't have to do all the work by herself; there are usually several young apprentices living on her land.

A couple of years ago, two country boys, both in their early twenties, came to stay on Teresa's homestead for the summer. They worked on family farms in a neighboring county and wanted to learn about alternative agricultural methods. Teresa met them at the top of the steep gravel drive and directed them to the tent where they would sleep. As they unloaded gear from the bed of their pickup, it turned out they hadn't just packed clothing and sleeping bags—they had also brought several dozen cases of canned Vienna sausages and Mountain Dew. Why? Teresa was planning to feed them. Eventually, they blushingly confessed: they had never lived with hippies before, and they were worried about eating hippie food.

Trepidation about exotic food is normal. Our palate is sculpted when we are young, and food we did not encounter regularly as children often feels weird. In the United States, we're not accustomed to eating insects, but drinking cow milk seems normal; in some parts of the world, it's reversed, and a glass of milk is as appetizing as cold mucus. I confronted my own gustatory shaping on the Yurok Reservation as a teenager: the first few times I ate lamprey eel—a slimy, boneless, bloodsucking fish with a rasping suction-cup mouth—I was able to swallow it, but it freaked me out. It was only after eating it over and over that it lost the revolting novelty and became just another thing on the plate.

If you grow up eating lab-designed industrial products, by the time you're old enough to make your own dietary choices, switching to healthy food will be physically challenging. It's hard to shift taste preferences in general, but it's especially hard with junk food, which has been scientifically engineered to crank our innate flavor cravings. After twenty years of bathing your tongue in soda pop, water—the very stuff of life—seems lifeless. Compared with Cool Ranch Doritos, eating a carrot is like chewing damp sawdust. A leaf of spinach? Please. Leave the mulch in the garden.

This dynamic is laid bare in the Berea College cafeteria, where price and availability are both irrelevant; students may fill their plates with anything they like. Meal after meal, many of them walk past the whole foods—the kale and garbanzo beans and boiled eggs and peanut butter and oatmeal—homing in on the pizza, pop, and never-ending flow of soft-serve on tap. As one student said, with a shrug, "It's just what I grew up eating."

People are not only tricked by agribusiness into eating junk food—more importantly, they're tricked into feeding junk food to their kids. Without powerful literacy, it's hard to perceive this profit-maximizing game for what it is; hard to recognize the extent to which your taste buds have been kidnapped by Nestlé and General Mills and Unilever; hard to access well-developed analyses and critiques of the food industry that are crucial to your self-defense. Books like *Fast Food Nation* might as well not exist. As another student remarked, "I didn't know what was in the food until I came to college and started reading."

But this game isn't just played out in our heads. Our taste preferences aren't purely cognitive; they're embodied. They are *felt* as much as *thought*. What's happening, in other words, is that our parents' lack of education gets built into our bodies as deep-seated dietary norms. What begins as a set of capitalist tricks grows into a seemingly permanent, natural part of who we are. These low-road business strategies don't just boost shareholder value—they morph into culture.

In Bear Lick Valley, as in eastern Kentucky generally, this corporate-generated culture is killing people. Diet-driven illnesses such as heart disease, stroke, and diabetes together comprise the region's largest source of sickness, physical suffering, and early mortality: people are eating junk food literally unto disability and death. I know a thirty-year-old mother who is going blind from diabetic retinopathy, and yet will sit down to-night—like a nicotine addict smoking through her tracheotomy hole—to another supper of Fanta and Hamburger Helper. The national obesity rate, at one in four, is way too high—but in Appalachia, it's higher still. In the Bear Lick area, more than half of adults are seriously overweight.[9] The combined burden of preventable diseases is so severe that, for the first time in modern history, life expectancy is falling in certain parts of the United States—particularly Appalachia. Indeed, as Olga Khazan writes in *The Atlantic*, "The eight counties with the largest declines in life expectancy since 1980 are all in the state of Kentucky."[10]

A lack of money makes it harder to eat healthy, but you can still do it. A lack of literacy? That makes it truly difficult to protect yourself, even if you have money. This shows clearly in national statistics. The single best predictor of an individual's life span in the contemporary United States is not income, which is usually treated as the main determinant of class and poverty. It's not how frequently a person exercises, or whether they have health insurance. It's not even whether or not they smoke, even though cigarettes chop, on average, an entire decade from a smoker's life. The single best predictor of how long a person will live is the number of years they have gone to school.[11]

* * *

On a cold December eve, as skeletal trees stand silent in the frost, Boyd Garrett hobbles across his back porch with a white plastic trash bag slung over one shoulder. I offer to help, but he waves me off. He carries the bag slowly past the horseshoe pit and piles it into an old fifty-five-gallon steel drum, which is already close to overflowing; Delia and Steve dump their trash here as well, and it fills quickly. The barrel's surface is a lacework of rust and corrosion; at the base, where heat and rain have gnawed gaps in the metal, varicolored ash spills out in alluvial fans.

Boyd braces a hand on his knee, squats with a grunt, threads his other hand through one of the holes at the bottom of the drum, and holds a lighter to the garbage. Within three or four minutes, ropes of thick yellow smoke writhe in the night sky. It's beautiful and hypnotic. Another couple of minutes and a cone of fire crowns the barrel. It begins sucking air in a gulping roar. It looks like a rocket trying to bury itself nose-first in the earth. Rivulets of melted plastic begin trickling from the fissured base, bubbling and spitting rainbow flame. Boyd pulls up a lawn chair and fishes two beers from his coat pocket, the curls of his beard glowing like tiny bronze rings in the firelight. As I grab a second chair, he passes me a brew, and we study the dance of oddly hued flame, follow sparks as they chase each other through billows of smog. The sudden wash of heat is welcome in the winter night. By the time the flames begin to subside, the barrel itself glows a dull orange, like a jack-o-lantern, and ragged punctures in the steel form themselves into shifting constellations of luminous faces.

Boyd burns trash in part because that's the way it's always been done. His mamaw burned their trash when he was a child, as did her father before. It's just another Sunday afternoon chore. No big deal. On a dry evening, Bear Lick Valley sometimes looks like a battlefield, with a half-dozen columns of black smoke propping up the sky. Sure, Boyd says, the smoke probably isn't good for you—"so don't stick your face in it, dingbat."

Boyd also burns trash because it saves money. Not long ago, there was no waste service in Bear Lick; if you didn't want to burn your trash, you had to haul it to the dump a half-hour-drive away and pay a fee. Now, in half the valley, you can spend about twenty bucks a month for a truck to collect your garbage. But instead of paying a company to deal with his waste, Boyd deals with it himself. Like growing tomatoes or installing solar panels, burning trash is a form of subsistence production. Nor is it the only method of subsistence disposal in Bear Lick: junk appliances, which don't burn well, are pushed over steep roadsides into creeks. Tires are rolled into sinkholes. Candy wrappers and plastic pop bottles get tossed from truck windows. But fire is the easiest method, even for large-scale items: if you've got a mobile home that's too rotten to sell, for instance, wait until the middle of the night, and light it up.

Above all, however, Boyd burns his trash because he doesn't really know what's in the smoke. He doesn't know that poorly combusted plastic produces dioxins and furans and a host of other mutagens, teratogens, and carcinogens. That dioxins are some of the deadliest chemicals in existence. That one smoldering trash barrel can pump out more dioxin than a factory-sized municipal incinerator that serves ten thousand homes. That the nauseating fogs of diapers and milk jugs that regularly creep across Bear Lick Valley help turn Kentucky into the nation's leading cancer state.[12]

If Boyd really knew these things, he wouldn't even consider taking a lighter to his plastic trash. Think about it like this: if I offered Boyd twenty bucks a month to go down the road once a week and force Joseph Rivard and his family to swallow a little bit of rat poison, would he do it? Of course not. This is a man who can hardly watch the news because the parade of suffering makes him weep. But feeding poison to his neighbors is what happens, in effect, every time Boyd fires up that barrel.

Burning trash is a lot like eating junk food: they both look like economically sound decisions, but they're actually driven, fundamentally, by educational dispossession. They make sense only as long as everything happening at the molecular level remains hidden in books, esoteric and invisible. A similar dynamic underlies many other behaviors common in Bear Lick. Consider, for example, smoking. If poor people were choosing what to put into their bodies based on price, then they'd just breathe air for free, and cigarette smoking would be a sign of affluence, as it was back in Victorian England. But the distribution of smoking tracks best with education, not money: while 46 percent of people in the United States with only a GED smoke, among those with a graduate degree the rate is just 6 percent.[13]

Or consider breastfeeding. Nursing an infant can be difficult, if not downright impossible, especially for working mothers—and if a mother chooses to feed her baby with formula, no shame. But, in an absence of sound knowledge, genuinely unhelpful rumors about breastfeeding proliferate. Some of the notions I have heard in Bear Lick about breastfeeding are that it's gross, it's a sin, "it makes your tits floppy," and breastfeeding "a girl baby will make her gay." At the same time, some parents who are wary of putting a breast in an infant's mouth are comfortable letting them suckle sugary drinks, including soda pop out of a baby bottle. This has contributed to an epidemic of tooth decay so extreme and unprecedented that, in an attempt to spread awareness, rural dentists—sick of yanking rotten teeth from the mouths of toddlers and fitting dentures for teenagers—popularized the phrase "Mountain Dew mouth."[14]

Dietary habits and cigarette smoking and breastfeeding practices represent real cultural differences, but, for the most part, they don't drive people apart. It can be tricky to be socially intimate with people who eat differently than you, but it's not an unbridgeable difference. Trash burning, by contrast, is a point of genuine contention. If you have a good sense of what's in the smoke and how genetic damage builds over time into cancer, a neighbor burning trash feels like criminal assault.[15] If you grew up in a bookish family that socialized with other bookish families, you've probably known not to burn plastic for so long it doesn't feel like something you had to learn; it just feels like common sense, even though it's not. On the other hand, if you don't have a clear idea of what's in the smoke, and if burning trash is just what you've always done, you wonder why your snobby neighbors are so uptight. Why don't they mind their own business and quit telling other people how to live?

At the same time that trash burning separates people, it also knits them together. "Injustice anywhere is a threat to justice everywhere," Martin Luther King Jr. famously wrote, scribbling on scraps of smuggled paper in an Alabama jail cell. "We are caught in an inescapable network of mutuality," he continued, "tied in a single garment of destiny. Whatever affects one directly, affects all indirectly."[16] In the case of trash burning, the garment of destiny binds us most intimately. Four months after he drove by and grumpily gathered beer cans, Joseph Rivard passed away from an aggressively malignant cancer. As is generally the case with environmental toxins and illness, it is impossible to determine the exact line of causation. But there is a chance that Boyd's educational dispossession—which filled the sky, week after week, with formidable poisons—wove itself, in time, into a tumor inside Joseph's brain.

*   *   *

A man strides to a podium on the floor of the Berea City Council chamber. He's in his fifties, handsome and strongly built, wearing a long-sleeve red button-up and tie. The chamber is packed. Behind him, others wait in line for their turn to speak. On the pew-like seats, running in diagonal rows across the room, citizens sit shoulder to shoulder. The council members listen, silent and somber, from behind a long, raised

bench bracketing two sides of the room; against the opposite walls, p
stand three and four deep. Others who couldn't squeeze in stand outs
in the hallway. For a government meeting on a weekday evening, this
turnout is unprecedented.

"I didn't come prepared to speak," the man begins, "but I will speak a
few words. My name is Don Wheeler. I'm a local pastor here in Berea. I'm
the least qualified probably to speak of all that I've heard speak tonight."
He talks quickly and smoothly in a strong baritone with a slight Kentucky
accent. As he feels out what he wants to say, his hands explore the edges
of the lectern. The audience is quiet. "But I want to just ask us a question tonight: where is God in all of this? I know there's many Christians
represented here tonight, and as we make decisions—and especially you
that are on the panel tonight and you call yourselves a Christian—you
must vote the Bible." He is finding his rhythm now and turns to address
the audience. "Any time that you vote for a politician, or make a vote for
anything, you must ask yourselves, 'What does God have to say?'" One
hand lifts from the podium, drumming in time with his words. "Many
people that have spoken tonight have talked about business. Well I came
on business for the King."

The audience stirs. "Yep," says one man. "Amen," adds another.

"I don't care about big business. I came on business for the King. And
that's the thing we must concern ourselves with. Sweet and bitter water
does not flow from the same fountain." Wheeler is preaching now; he has
made the podium into his pulpit. Every word rings with passion. "And
I just came to say to you tonight that God calls homosexual activity, in
his word, an *abomination*."

The chamber erupts in the loudest applause of the evening.

"God will not . . ." He pauses to let the ovation subside. "God will not
take to heaven what he has called in his word, abomination."

A shout: "That's right!"

"Get that in your spirit tonight, if you don't get anything else that I
say. He has called it in his word unholy, unclean, unnatural—and he will
not take to heaven what he has called those things." Wheeler finishes
with a reproving finger in the air, then opens his hand and waves it over
the crowd in benediction. "God Bless you. I love you every one."

s, Kentucky has passed progressive laws protecting vari-
liscrimination in employment, housing, and access to
ful, for instance, to fire someone because of their race,
n, sex, age, or disability. This same statute also out-
yee because of their religion; it even prohibits firing
..ey smoke. No Kentucky law, however, offers these
.. protections if you're gay. It is legal to fire someone, kick them out
of an apartment, refuse to serve them at a restaurant, or bar their entry
to a public pool because you disapprove of their private intimacies.[17]

As a result of this gap in state law, there has been a push by activists
in Kentucky over the past few years to enact "fairness ordinances" at the
municipal level. These proposed laws add sexual orientation to the list of
already protected identities and conditions. In 2011 one such ordinance
was proposed in Berea.[18] This turned out to be divisive. Over the next
three years, the city held a series of hearings at which citizens could speak
their minds; the one described here, held in May 2011, was the first.

It was also the smallest. At a hearing in 2014, held in a bigger venue,
450 people showed up; two hundred of them stood outside listening via
loudspeaker. All kinds of people spoke. High school students and elders.
Some who fought through stage fright, others who orated with practiced
ease. Some with country accents, some without. By 2014 liberal activists had distributed blue T-shirts that declared "Another Kentuckian for
Fairness," while conservatives distributed red ones that said "Just say
NO to favoritism." Thus the people of Berea arranged themselves into
two groups, like opposing fans at a basketball game, with red shirts on
the right side of the room and blue shirts on the left. It made a striking
image—a community physically divided—but the words people spoke
were even more striking. They revealed the cultural breach that runs
through this chapter as vividly as an x-ray of a broken femur.

Some concerns people expressed about the proposed ordinance had to
do with the specific wording, modes of enforcement, or cost to the city,
which are always relevant questions to ask about a proposed law. But let's
set them aside; a few individual testimonies notwithstanding, the debate
wasn't really about the law itself. It was about queer sex.

The majority of those in the red-shirted camp agreed with Pastor Wheeler: non-straight sexuality is an abomination and a sin. Simple as that. Sometimes this came out in a roundabout way, like when one man attempted to argue that "homosexuality" didn't make evolutionary sense because of the "law of survival of the fittest"—because "homosexuals can't reproduce," he said, they are clearly unnatural.[19] Another pointed to a town-and-gown divide: "There's more to Berea than that ivory tower right down here." But often the anti-gay position was bluntly stated. As another local pastor said, "I don't hate no one. God tells me not to hate them." But, he continued, "God tells me to hate the sin." Another man claimed that "homosexuality is a choice, plain and simple." Where, he asked the audience, do we draw the line? A number used ominous, meme-like phrases: this is all part of "the homosexual agenda" and "gay recruitment." An elderly country woman who had run a wedding chapel for forty years said firmly that "if a law like this was passed, it would force me to close that weddin' chapel."

These ideas, common in the town of Berea, are ubiquitous in the rural countryside. In 2004, by a margin of three to one, Kentucky voters passed an amendment to the state constitution outlawing gay marriage. In one of the rural counties that constitutes Bear Lick Valley, fully 90 percent of voters favored the amendment.[20]

The speaker before Don Wheeler was also a native of eastern Kentucky. An author and historian, Jason Howard is a slender man in his middle years with short brown hair who radiates both thoughtful poise and boyish vivacity. "I stand before you today," he said, "not just as a Berean, but as a gay man, one who risks being discriminated against based on my sexual orientation." As a writer, Howard drafted his words, and read from a printed page.

> I did not choose my sexual orientation no more than I chose to be born an eastern Kentuckian. When I lived outside this region for nearly six years, I was occasionally profiled by my accent. Some found it charming while others scoffed, thinking it a mark of illiteracy and ignorance. I defended our region in those moments, testifying of our rich literary heritage, and the hard-working, good-hearted people in our towns and communities.

But here, back home in these mountains, I find myself being judged by
my sexual orientation and I have too often been made to feel like an exile
in my home region.

If Berea passes this ordinance, he concluded, it would be "fighting back
against the reactive culture that often prevails in our region, one that is
fearful of progress and change."

Those who spoke from the blue side of the aisle grounded their comments in a wide range of arguments and evidence. Some cited the egalitarian history of Berea College; others spoke of the necessity of anti-
discrimination laws during the women's suffrage and the civil rights
movements. A biologist debunked the "evolutionary" argument. A number of speakers described being harassed. One young man recalled how
high school classmates had shown up on his front porch in the night,
wanting to fistfight. A local pastor who is openly lesbian said, "I walk
around with an extra layer of fear all the time." "I would like to think,"
another woman said simply, "that I am not a partisan issue." But on this
side, too, the argument often came back to scripture. One man who spoke,
a bohemian homesteader who grew up in a conservative family, said his
views changed during college. "I used to believe homosexuality was an
abomination," he told the audience, but then "I got educated at Berea
College. The bottom line is, to be a Christian, it's very simple. There's
one rule: love your neighbor. And it's funny how people can't do it."

Underlying the arguments of those wearing blue shirts is one basic
idea: homosexuality is a healthy and normal part of the diversity of human sexual expression. For them, abominable sex is not queer sex—it's
sex without consent.

In Bear Lick, differences in diet are a minor cultural division, albeit with
important ramifications for people's health. Contrasting methods of trash
disposal or parenting styles are trickier to navigate. The stark difference
in attitudes brought into the open at the fairness ordinance hearings is
the kind of thing that *really* divides people. These are deeply held and
antagonistic beliefs about basic facets of existence: "homosexuality is
healthy and normal," versus "demons will burn you in hell forever." For
many, the position on the other side is not just difficult to sympathize
with—it's repulsive.

In the end, the fairness ordinance lost. But the fate of one local statute is less important than the clashing cosmologies it revealed. This is not just a single, isolated difference of opinion; I could have written this section based on similar opposing views about any number of issues—race, immigration, foreign policy, drug policy, prisons, guns, gender, abortion, sex education, coal mining, global warming, and so on and on. This is essentially the same cultural schism that divides "hicks" from "hippies" in Bear Lick Valley. But here it is, cutting through the town as well as the countryside. Nor does it stop, as I've noted before, at the borders of Berea or Appalachia. It cleaves the nation. Right versus left. Red versus blue.

It's not unusual, of course, for different groups of people to hold different world views. If you cross the ocean to some faraway land, you expect to meet folks with odd and curious beliefs. That's not what's happening here. These aren't just *different* world views—they're *opposed*. Mutually incompatible. Hostile. In a faraway land, we find people who are strange. But just down the street, in our neighbor's home—if we ever actually visited—we find people who are estranged.

In the case of attitudes toward queer sexuality, this schism appears to be a collision between the old-fashioned and the newfangled. Between tradition and change. Between ancient scripture and postmodern text. Is it? The answer, in a word, is no. But understanding why will take more than a word; it will take the next four sections. To begin, we must travel far away from eastern Kentucky, to examine the industry of persuasion that has been built around a peculiar and dangerous modern technology.

* * *

On December 7, 2011, President Obama threw a holiday party at the White House. Welcoming each guest, he came in turn to a jowly Alfred Hitchcock look-alike, and offered an unusual greeting. "I see," the president said, "the most powerful man in the world is here." Rather than dispel the claim, the man's response hinted at the source of his power. "Don't believe what you read, Mr. President," Roger Ailes replied. "I started those rumors myself."[21]

Like Alfred Hitchcock, Ailes was, in his way, an auteur of thrillers and horror films. He grew up in a blue-collar family in an Ohio factory town in the 1940s and '50s, with one of those tough-guy fathers who beat his children not until they started crying, but until they stopped. Ailes was afflicted with hemophilia—the disease where your blood won't clot—and spent even more time in front of the television than most children. He didn't just watch, however; he analyzed how shows were put together, dismantling production techniques in his mind like some kids dismantle radios or lawnmower engines. In 1967, as the twenty-seven-year-old executive producer of a talk show in Philadelphia, Ailes met presidential candidate Richard Nixon. Restless for wealth and acclaim, he was quick to notice that Nixon had a pressing need for his skills. US politicians face a quandary: to get elected, they need both the financial support of rich patrons and the votes of commoners. But how do you persuade ordinary people to vote for you, when your actual policies are designed to help your wealthy benefactors at the expense of everyone else? How, in other words, do you defend oligarchy in the midst of electoral democracy?

Ailes had concrete ideas about how to resolve this dilemma. For one thing, he was familiar with the mental landscape of the white American working class—their ideological vulnerabilities, their ethnocentrism, their lack of countervailing literacy. He also understood, in a way that older men like Nixon did not, the intimate power of television. He knew, for instance, that television is a drug. We all have a sense of this: if there's a TV on in the room, it requires an effort of will to tear your attention away. It's easy to treat this as a trivial thing, much like cigarette smoking was treated when I was a kid and people casually puffed in elevators and restaurants and hospital waiting rooms. But, generally speaking, it's not a good sign when a behavior is physically difficult to cease. Indeed, television viewing fits several of the formal criteria psychologists use to define addiction. For example, it's an activity we tend to do more frequently than we want. And we do it frequently indeed: in 2016, Americans watched television an average of five hours per day.[22] That's almost a full-time job. After sleep and work, it was the thing we did most. We spent more time hanging out with our screens, by far, than we did hanging out with our children, partners, and friends, or than we spent exercising, gardening, reading, traveling, or dancing.[23]

Ailes also knew that a defining feature of television viewing was utter passivity. Unlike most activities, watching television requires neither effort nor skill; even toddlers master it instantly. As a result, although it has the appearance of presenting information, television is a poor tool for learning. It's like the worst elements of a make-believe classroom—the never-ending lecture, the impossibility of interaction—stuffed into a box. In a make-believe classroom, specific content hardly matters; content is overwhelmed by format. Math class and history class and biology class all run together, like in a *Peanuts* cartoon, into a single lifeless drone. Television is similar: what's most important is not the specific subject matter, but the fact that it's presented as a stream of rapidly shifting images that never stops.[24] If one image sparks an insight in your mind, the next washes it away, like ocean waves endlessly erasing your footprints from the sand.

Researchers have measured such effects. In one incisive study, Anne Cunningham and Keith Stanovich found that frequent television viewers not only had less knowledge about the world than those who abstained, but the knowledge they had was more likely to be incorrect—a correlation that held for a wide range of subjects, from World War II to the economy to religion. Frequent readers, by contrast, were more knowledgeable not just about high-brow, bookish subjects, but were more likely to know "how a carburetor worked, who their United States senators were, how many teaspoons are equivalent to one tablespoon, what a stroke was, and what a closed shop in a factory was."[25]

The more you watch, the less you know.

Now, obviously, television viewing does put information into our minds, in some fashion. If I watch a show or a movie, I can recall at least part of what I saw a few months later. But in terms of fostering education? Education is not just retention of facts or images, but the building of comprehension. It is less like memorizing, say, how to spell a set of words, and more like learning how to speak a language. And for that kind of growth, television is simply too passive. We can test this with a quick reality check: with few exceptions, my freshmen students have watched thousands upon thousands of hours of video—and yet most of them are, as I have noted, exquisitely uninformed about the world. If watching videos—whether on a TV or a phone, whether on NBC or YouTube—was a reliable educational method, our youth would enter college as prodigies and polymaths.

After persuading Nixon of the power of television, Ailes went on to help him win the presidency.[26] He did this by carefully manipulating the images beamed directly into millions of living rooms. He realized it didn't matter who politicians actually were, or what policies they supported—it just mattered how they *appeared* on screen. So he micro-managed Nixon's television coverage. Place cameras below eye level, he directed, to make the candidate look more powerful. Exclude reporters and journalists whenever possible, to maintain control of the narrative. Ailes even directed the candidate's conjugal body language. "If Nixon put his arm around his wife in public or held hands with her when walking once in a while," Ailes wrote, "it would do much to endear him to women all over the country."[27] Above all, he knew politicians didn't have to give details about policy or answer difficult questions—or even tell the truth—if they were equipped with the carefully crafted one-liners we would eventually come to know as *soundbites*. On the TV screen, little self-contained moments of drama and wit trump serious discussion every time. "The general public," he said of this strategy, "is just not sophisticated enough to wade through answers."[28]

After Nixon, Ailes worked as an image-fixer for a slew of Republican politicians, including Ronald Reagan, George H. W. Bush, Rudy Giuliani, and Donald Trump. He helped craft the factually inaccurate but effective attack ads widely credited with foisting Mitch McConnell upon the voters of Kentucky.[29] Eventually, this political work culminated in the founding of Fox News in 1996—but he, and others like him, had begun weaponizing television long before then. In the Nixon White House, as early as 1970—only twenty years after the beginnings of widespread television ownership in the United States—staff passed around a memo titled, "A Plan for Putting the GOP on TV News." In the margins, Ailes scrawled notes and recommendations, noting that this was "basically an excellent idea." The memo began by noting that "Today television news is watched more often than people read newspapers, than people listen to the radio, than people read or gather any other form of communication. The reason: People are lazy. With television you just sit—watch—listen. The thinking is done for you."[30]

At this point, using mass media to manipulate people is like building an internal combustion engine or printing a circuit board: it's a mature industry with a reliable and highly profitable array of products.[31] There's a standard business model: ultra-wealthy investors like Joseph Coors and Richard Mellon Scaife and Charles Koch and Rupert Murdoch provide behind-the-scenes funding to entrepreneurial idea-men like Roger Ailes and Paul Weyrich and Ralph Reed and Grover Norquist. That funding is used to build factories of influence and misinformation like Fox News and Sinclair Broadcast Group and the American Legislative Exchange Council. The resulting products take many forms: confused and anxious viewers, expertly honed talking points, well-coached politicians, and cunning statutory language that's cut-and-pasted from one state legislature to another. These products, despite their apparent variety, serve a single goal: manufacturing social support, within an electoral democracy, for the aristocratic power of those ultra-wealthy investors.[32]

There was a time when I thought the internet might render someone like Roger Ailes obsolete. But in the past several years, social media has been captured by this same industry of manipulation, and the production facilities now include armies of hackers, swarms of Twitter bots, and Russian troll farms with thousands of workers. The "Pizzagate" story, where people were convinced that Hillary Clinton was running a child sex-ring in the basement of a DC pizza joint, is a typical product.[33] These well-funded "psychological operations" have altered the outcomes of elections around the world, including in the United States. In addition, knowing the addicting power of moving images, corporate websites scramble to place videos before our eyeballs at every turn, and to make sure each video is followed, immediately and automatically, by another; video already accounts for nearly 80 percent of internet traffic, and its share is growing rapidly.[34]

The internet is an astonishing invention; through smartphones, we could have possessed, in our pockets, an easily accessed library such as the world has never known. Instead we ended up, mostly, with a tiny, omnipresent television. This is a missed opportunity, but it's also—in terms of building a fairer, healthier society—a tragedy. Because if you don't know how to use the library, you have little defense against the television.

* * *

The fairness ordinance debate appeared to be a collision between old and new. One side, indeed, is notably modern. Less than seventy years ago, we lacked basic empirical knowledge about human sexuality. Sex was so fraught with judgment and taboo that scientists knew they would be called perverts and worse if they tried to research it. Funding was scarce, judgment abundant. As recently as the late 1950s—well after science had probed the inner workings of the atom—William Masters and Virginia Johnson wrote that, when it came to sex, both "science and scientist continue to be governed by fear . . . above all fear of bigotry and prejudice."[35] Researchers who didn't hesitate to jab electrodes into a living brain chickened out when it came to mapping the clitoris or taking notes on orgasms. As a result, sex was something people mostly learned about by stumbling through—groping, so to speak, in the dark.[36]

This lack of knowledge was a burden to all, but weighed especially heavily on those with any sort of non-straight sexual orientation. In small towns and rural areas, queer people were likely to live in fear and silence and self-repression, full of shame and wrestling with basic questions about why they felt different. For researchers, gathering honest data on "homosexuality" was career suicide. Homosexuality was not seen as a variety of sexual expression—it was an actively prosecuted crime. Gay men in particular were subject to imprisonment, torture, lobotomies, electroconvulsive "treatment," and chemical castration.[37] And, like any popularly reviled group, gay people were politically useful. Long before Fox News, one answer to the problem of getting ordinary people to vote against their own economic interests was the cold war and the red scare that peaked in the 1940s and '50s. It wasn't just supposed communist agents, however, that Americans had to guard against. As Guy Gabrielson, Republican national chairman, wrote in 1950, "perhaps as dangerous as the actual Communists are the sexual perverts who have infiltrated our government in recent years." Thousands of federal employees were fired as part of this "Lavender Scare."[38]

But over the past several decades, researchers have finally begun to weave human sexuality into the tapestry of established scientific knowledge. They have measured and probed, interviewed and filmed, tabulated and sampled. One of the first to bring objective methods to the study of queer sexuality was Evelyn Hooker, a professor of psychology at UCLA. Like most people in the 1950s, she accepted the dominant idea that homosexuality was a mental illness. After developing a friendship with a former student, who turned out to be gay, she began to question this idea, and—risking her career—designed a project to put it to the test. In 1954 she administered psychological assessments to sixty men, thirty gay and thirty straight—the first time anyone had done research on gay men who weren't locked in an asylum or a prison. When she shuffled these sixty assessments and had them reviewed by top experts, they couldn't tell which subjects were gay and which straight. "At that time," Hooker later wrote, "every clinical psychologist worth his soul would tell you that if he gave projective tests he could tell whether a person was gay or not. I showed that they couldn't do it."[39]

Hooker's pioneering study was the first of many. At this point, thanks to emancipatory science undertaken by thousands of researchers, we know much more about the diversity of human sexuality.[40] We know that queer orientations and behaviors are not associated with psychological disorder. We know they occur in human cultures around the world, past and present. We know that sexual orientation has a strong biological component; it is, to a large extent, not a choice. We know that LGBTQ individuals are no more likely to be pedophiles or rapists than heterosexuals. We know that children raised by queer parents are just as healthy as those raised by straight parents, if not more so; in one study, those raised in lesbian households reported absolutely no sexual abuse whatsoever. We also know—now that biologists have relaxed about publishing what they have long privately recorded in their field notes—that sexuality in animals is incredibly diverse. At this point, homosexual and queer behavior has been scientifically documented in more than 450 animal species. The claim that such behavior is "unnatural" is simply untrue, as Bruce Bagemihl details in his superb overview, *Biological Exuberance*. "From the Southeastern Blueberry Bee of the United States to more than 130 different bird species worldwide," he writes, "the 'birds and bees,' literally, are queer."[41]

* * *

One side in the fairness ordinance debate was grounded in the findings of recent scientific research. What about the other? Clearly, it was grounded in ancient scripture. At least, that's how it felt to many who spoke against the proposed ordinance. It's right there in the Bible, after all, in wisdom recorded two thousand years ago: "Do not lie with a man as one lies with a woman; that is detestable."[42] Where's the wiggle room in that?

But let's take a closer look. The Bible contains six verses, like the one above from the Book of Leviticus, that appear to censure homosexuality—although scholars debate the meaning of these passages, wrangling over questions like whether or not the original Hebrew and Greek words actually referred to sexual behavior. By contrast, more than two thousand verses focus upon the poor, the rich, and social injustice.[43] Christ himself, who spoke eloquently about those same issues, left not a single word about homosexuality. Queer sex, fair to say, is not a point of scriptural emphasis. The Bible also contains dozens of decrees that are treated even by fundamentalist Christians as flexible, even optional. Breaking with scripture, men trim their sideburns and women pray with uncovered heads. Bastards are allowed to enter church—as are males with genital injuries and women who have recently given birth. Gardens and fields are planted with more than one type of crop. Unmarried young women with torn hymens are permitted to live; no one stones them to death.[44] As with the verses on homosexuality, many of these rules are only mentioned quickly. But not always: scripture—including the word of Christ—repeatedly and unambiguously inveighs against divorce. And yet evangelical Christians end their marriages at higher rates than Americans who profess no religion.[45]

Wielding the Bible against queer sexuality relies upon a move that historian Randall Balmer, himself an evangelical, calls "selective literalism."[46] One set of verses is emphasized and treated as gospel truth at the same time that thousands of other passages are quickly passed over or interpreted flexibly. But here's the key: this lopsided reading did not arise spontaneously. It's not like thousands of Christian congregations all over the country independently decided to focus upon the same six supposedly anti-homosexual verses. The Bible may be ancient, but this particular instance of selective literalism is not. It is, simply put, a creation of the billionaire-serving mass-media industry created by Roger Ailes and Paul Weyrich and their many collaborators.

Which is to say, this particular use of scripture is a twenty-first-century capitalist product. Widespread alarm about "the homosexual agenda" is largely a script designed by highly paid urban executives and screenwriters, performed and recorded in places like Fox News' recently unveiled thirty-million-dollar Manhattan studio. A theatrical set designed by an elite architecture firm, the studio is crammed with cutting-edge technology, including monitors embedded in the floor and a hanging "video chandelier" sculpted from curving LED screens.[47] To reach viewers in Bear Lick Valley, engineered anxiety about the "gay threat to marriage," masquerading as old-fashioned moral rectitude, is literally beamed into space. A truck-sized robot, circling in geosynchronous orbit twenty-two thousand miles above the equator, then catches that beam and shines it back down, like the light of heaven, upon every hill and holler of Appalachia.[48]

Turns out, both sides in this debate are equally modern.

But why, it is fair to ask, would billionaires care about human sexuality? The answer is simple: they don't. While they vary from one individual to the next in their beliefs about queerness, they don't have any specific position on it as a group—matters such as sexuality have little effect on their investment portfolios. But as long as the rest of us keep fussing over what our neighbor does in her bedroom, we're likely to overlook issues that the billionaire class *does* care about, such as wages, environmental regulations, and tax policy. We're also likely to spend less time studying the hundreds of Bible verses that condemn greed, materialism, and excessive wealth. As famed evangelical pastor Billy Graham remarked, "The hard right has no interest in religion except to manipulate it."[49]

The stoking of debate on matters where it would not otherwise persist is a standard strategy of the oligarch-serving media. Our public discourse is crammed with "debates" in which one "side" is backed by data and the other "side" by dollars. The list includes inflated disputes about global warming, evolutionary biology, immigration, tax policy, gun regulation, and human sexuality; not long ago, it included similar disputes about whether humans were causing acid rain, whether pesticides were harmful to wildlife, whether sugar was a health food, and even about whether or not tobacco smoke made people sick. In each of these debates, one side represented the hard-won consensus of scholars and scientists, while the other side was simply the creation of pundits, lobbyists, think tanks, and hired-gun television and courtroom "experts."[50]

Consider, for example, the intense fear in the contemporary United States of Islamic terrorists. In a recent national survey of what people are most afraid of, terrorists came in second—a fear that translates into votes for far-right politicians, support for a militant foreign policy, and hundreds of billions of dollars in pork-barrel military contracts for companies like Lockheed Martin, Haliburton, and the Carlyle Group.[51] But this fear is mostly empty hype. In the last decade, Muslim terrorists have killed about six people per year on US soil. To put that in perspective, far more Americans are fatally shot by toddlers.[52] Soda pop, to give another comparison, kills nearly twenty-five thousand per year. And yet, which gets whispered about on the airplane? The brown-skinned guy with the beard and turban, or the snack cart full of Coke and Pepsi products?[53]

If we assume the homophobia displayed at the fairness ordinance debate is a kind of relic, rooted in the past and sustained by isolation, we are also likely to assume it will fade with the passage of time. Comparable suppositions are easy to make about related forms of fear and judgment, such as racism and xenophobia and misogyny. But as long as bigotry remains politically useful, powerful and well-funded modern institutions will apply the most advanced available technology to its continued manufacture—and it won't go away.

*   *   *

To create one of these fake debates, you have to take a set of concepts that have been carefully braided into the warp and woof of established knowledge and rip them out. You have to pretend, for example, that evolutionary biology does not form the core of the same biological science that explains cancer, that keeps a premature infant alive, that eradicates smallpox. You have to rage against the idea that the universe is fifteen billion years old—but stay silent on the stellar origins of the iron circulating in your veins. You have to act like global warming is just some theory, while carefully ignoring the twin calamity of ocean acidification, also caused by carbon dioxide emissions and already helping extinguish coral reefs around the world. You have to take, in short, one of our most amazing and important creations—the fabric of scientific explanation—and vandalize it.

For Ann Duncan, the woodshed-building therapist, with her active reading habit, this crude vandalism is laughably obvious. Is this because she's read the current scholarship on global warming, *and* evolutionary biology, *and* tax policy, *and* market deregulation, and so on and on? Of course not. But she has read, on her own and in college, many books and articles within both the natural and social sciences. She has a feel for how science works and a sense of the basic findings of modern scholarship. She can easily spot the difference between real scientific ideas and the tattered caricatures, torn from their context, that are belittled on Fox News and Capitol Hill and from the pulpit. Indeed, she's studied enough to understand that television is a dangerous drug and, like many bohemians, refuses to own one.

Equally important is the fact that Ann lives in a place deeply segregated by educational experience. At a typical bohemian gathering in Bear Lick—a garden party, for example—most adults are college educated and avid readers. Not everyone at such a gathering has picked up a recent book or article on a current issue like global warming—but one person will have, say, checked out from the public library a copy of *Six Degrees: Our Future on a Hotter Planet*. A couple of others will have passed around Bill McKibben's famous article about "Global Warming's Terrifying New Math." Some other attendee teaches a college ecology class, another works as a forest ranger, and yet another does outreach for a local environmental organization. Everyone knows, personally, working scientists and published authors. Through both individual reading and social connection with other readers, this is a group relatively familiar with scientific ideas, and they collectively stabilize for each other a certain world view.

Here's an important caveat: although it represents an incredibly powerful toolkit, literate intellectuality does not solve all problems. We can find obese bohemians, alcoholic professors, racist bookworms, and intellectuals who abuse their spouses—as well as non-readers who suffer no such af-flictions. Among Bear Lick bohemians, there is notable susceptibility to written pseudoscience, particularly when it has the trappings of genuine scholarship—like the books of Carlos Castaneda, or the proponents of blood-type diets.[54] Nor is there absolute segregation in Bear Lick between readers and non-readers; there are bohemian homesteaders who seldom open a book and country homesteaders who devour them. Everything I describe here is a tendency, not an unbreakable rule. Nonetheless, despite individual exceptions, these are astonishingly robust social patterns.

One common explanation for this sort of segregation is that it's driven by class snobbery. Perhaps folks with more book learning look down their noses at everyone else. Perhaps they think ballet is better than boxing, that a professor is a more important kind of person than a waitress, that income is primarily a map of value rather than power. Despite being baseless and juvenile, such arrogance is important—much of the culture of aristocrats, both today and in the past, is essentially just ritualized showing off.[55]

But snobbery is not what drives a wedge between people like Ann Duncan and Delia Howell. Without any condescension, it is still difficult to form close relationships across major differences in literate education. Consider the journey a first-generation Berea College student typically undergoes. She moves away from home and suddenly finds herself read-ing *Bury My Heart at Wounded Knee* and sharing a dorm room with a young Muslim woman from Senegal. She reads *When They Call You a Terrorist*, and weeps. She writes a paper on *The Beak of the Finch* and lives for a summer in Michoacán. Every time she visits her family, she discovers talking with them has become more difficult. The revelations of the past several years, she learns, are impossible to convey in dinner-table banter. Her thoughts have become alien to those she loves. Like Ann, she laughs at the fake debates blaring from the television in the living room. She realizes, with a sense of both liberation and loss, that even if she moved back, she can never go home again.[56]

Delia doesn't laugh at the fake debates. For all her intelligence and grit, she didn't somehow bootstrap herself, against all odds, into powerful literacy. It's not that she's only read a third as many nonfiction books as

Ann—with the exception of the Bible, she hasn't read any. Because of segregation, she encounters few who have. She will probably never have a conversation at a social gathering with a scientist or an author. No one will hand her a copy of *The Beak of the Finch*. No one will show her the Goodreads app on their phone. No one will invite her on a date to the bookstore, nor share a beautiful passage with her while they cuddle and read. As the fairness ordinance debate unfolded, Delia didn't consider recent research on human sexual diversity and then carefully reject it. She had no idea it existed.[57] This is the central condition that underlies the creation of fake debates: they only work because so many millions of people in the United States lack the basic means of intellectual self-defense.

Over the past several centuries, scientists and scholars have woven, strand by strand, a vast tapestry of interlacing knowledge—a fabric of description and explanation that is our most profound work of art, an invaluable heirloom of hard-won collective insight. It allows us to touch, with our thought, the astonishing and intricate patterns of the cosmos from which we sprang. It provides elegant answers to questions that otherwise would lie forever in the realm of the occult: why do we grow old and frail and eventually stop living? Why does sickness sometimes pass, like a vile rumor, from one person to another? What is sex, really, and why does it exist?[58] It even provides answers to questions we otherwise would never know to ask: why are there so few craters on the surface of Jupiter's moon, Europa? Why did the dinosaurs go extinct? Why do our mitochondria contain their own little genomes?[59]

Aside from love and care, this heirloom of knowledge is perhaps the most important thing we can share with one another.[60] As the creation of hundreds of thousands of men and women, all over the world, it belongs to no one; indeed, the more people grasp it, the greater it grows. Like language itself, it is a basic part of our heritage as human beings. It is—or should be—something Delia possesses no less than anyone else. But when we fail to nourish public education and create humane jobs, we leave millions of compatriots systematically deprived of this heritage. We leave them not just bereft of schoolroom facts, but bereft of beautiful and important explanations. We leave them marooned in a universe that appears more inscrutable, more unpredictable, and more frightening than it ought to be. But more than that: we leave them alone in the room with epistemological predators like Roger Ailes.

*   *   *

And that's why Boyd and Joseph never shared a beer around the fire. That's why the class divisions we *feel* are less about the unfair distribution of money and more about the unfair distribution of literate education.

This maldistribution of resources, which is the defining feature of socioeconomic class, is now largely a product of the ownership architecture of capitalism. But to really understand it, we must recall that the longer-term story of Appalachia is all about *colonization*—wave after wave of colonization. We must remember that Kentucky, in its present incarnation, was born 250 years ago when colonial authorities removed surviving Native peoples to open the land to Euro-American control. This first act of colonization was followed immediately by another, when men like Judge Henderson and Green Clay pried that same land from the grasp of poor whites and clutched it into vast feudal estates. A hundred years after that, at the end of the 1800s, corporations entered the mountain South to extract coal. This extraction was necessarily twofold: the black stone had to be taken from the earth and labor had to be taken from the inhabitants.[61]

Today, another century later, the means to prodigal wealth and power is still exploitation—and as long as that remains true, colonization will abide, continually morphing into new forms, such as the algorithmic maximization of shareholder value currently dominant. Like a slave plantation or a coal company, the car parts manufacturer Jigoku is a colonizing force, an institution designed for the extraction of Appalachian labor and wealth. Wal-Mart is a similar sort of thing, as is PepsiCo and McDonald's and Tyson Foods and Fifth Third Bank and Phillip Morris and Purdue Pharma.

All this exploitation and appropriation is much easier if people fail to fight back. The vulnerability of the colonized is, in many ways, *the* critical resource—more important to the colonizer than a fat seam of coal, more important than ivory or gold or virgin timber. Colonization is committed in frontiers, and a frontier, remember, is not usually a place without people. It's a people without power. So whole industries arise to cultivate that critical resource of powerlessness. To manipulate what people think. To confuse and demoralize. To engineer prejudice and fear. To disparage activism and deform faith.

As we have seen, in a place like Bear Lick these manipulations are made possible in part by widespread lack of powerful literacy. Thus, the colonization of Appalachia doesn't just take the form of an exhausted man, black death rattling in his lungs, limping from the mine shaft at the day's end. It's not just factories and fast-food joints taking advantage of non-union labor. It's an English teacher slumped on her couch in the evening, overwhelmed with too many students and too many required tests, trying to summon the energy to prepare the next day's lessons. It's a home with a satellite dish, but no books. It's a community arguing about things that are already known, like the diversity of healthy human sexuality, while their labor is extracted and their wealth hauled away.

The forms of colonization I've described in this chapter and the last are not old-fashioned. They're contemporary, cutting-edge, and technologically sophisticated. They form—to use this word in a slightly different way—a frontier. A frontier in the sense of something at the current limit, at the furthest boundary of possibility. In other words, eastern Kentucky does not represent, as is commonly assumed, the past. It's not backward, leftover, a place where modern change failed to happen. Quite the contrary. It's a place where certain kinds of modern change were more fully unleashed. Appalachian poverty isn't what we see when we look over our shoulders—unless we correct course, it's what we see when we look ahead, into the future.

At one end of this colonization, as always, you find concentrated wealth. This is not in doubt; it has been chronicled in a thousand books.[62] Nor is it abstract. You can take a road trip and see for yourself. Head to Palm Beach, the US city with the highest proportion of what's known as "passive income"—income not from labor, but from aristocratic ownership.[63] Stroll down Worth Avenue, a couple of miles north of Mar-a-Lago. There's the empowering education that Boyd Garrett should have had as a boy, swinging as a cluster of emeralds around some socialite's immaculate wrist. There's all the hours Delia Howell didn't get to hold her children, boldly displayed in the storefront windows of Worth Avenue Yachts.

What do you find at the other end of this colonization? You find the same thing as in all colonies: a devastated society.

*　*　*

One cold December night around Boyd's firepit, Steve Lewis and Jared Bowen started swapping drunken insults. Steve was Delia's man, and Bonnie—Delia's teen daughter—was Jared's woman. Steve had been spending more time with Delia and less in his tiny house, which meant he and Jared were crammed in that small trailer like two tomcats in a cage. With the vodka going around, their verbal jabs soon became real jabs. The other men scrambled to their feet and pulled the lawn chairs out of the way, leaving an open space. No one intervened; best to let the fellas get it out of their system. Steve, nearly thirty years older than Jared, soon took a punch to the temple that dropped him to his knees. Jared stood above him, feet planted wide, and rained haymakers on his face—left, right, left, right. He launched each swing with a workmanlike grunt. Steve toppled backward into the fire, and Jared leapt forward, grabbed him by the shirt, and dragged him out—then propped him back on his knees and landed a few more roundhouses on his already-swelling face.

The next day, bitter and embarrassed, Steve hid in the woods across the road with a shotgun, and peppered Jared's car with buckshot when he drove up. "Yep," said Boyd, "Stevie laywaid [sic] him." About a week after that, Delia came home early from a Saturday shift that was shorter than expected, and caught Bonnie and Steve making out on the couch. The sight of her boyfriend, half-naked on the sofa with her daughter, was like poison. She turned without a word, got in her car, drove to her cousin's house where the twins were spending the day, and stayed there.

Bonnie and Steve took that as a chance to shack up in Delia's trailer. Boyd didn't care for it one bit, and fussed at Steve whenever he emerged—but what are you gonna do? The honeymoon, however, was short. I drove by one afternoon and was startled to see police cruisers and fire trucks crowding the yard. In eastern Kentucky, when cops and firefighters show up in equal numbers, it usually means one thing: meth lab. A mess of buckets and dirty tubing and flammable chemicals, a meth lab is both illegal and prone to explode. After the cops hauled Steve and Bonnie off to the county jail—known as the Madison Radisson—Bonnie's jilted boyfriend Jared saw an opportunity to balance the scales. Hauling a jerry can of gasoline, he snuck up to Delia's empty trailer after dark and lit it like a barrel of trash. The blackened remains smoldered for days, filling the holler with a stench of charred plastic. Everything Delia owned, except her car and the clothes she'd been wearing when she left, was turned to ash.

Most working-class people in Bear Lick don't cook meth, sleep with their mom's boyfriend, or commit arson. There are plenty who never even drink or curse. Mostly, they hold it together, balanced on that narrow path. But even if they don't lose their footing, their brother does—or their daughter, their aunt, their best friend. All around, just a stumble or two away, calamities await: unemployment, eviction, medical bills, bankruptcy, drug addiction, domestic abuse, teen pregnancy. Each one appears as a small, isolated, family-sized tragedy; each is actually rooted in the larger tragedy of a class society, in the manifold dispossessions and injuries that are the inevitable shadow cast by massive concentrations of wealth.

To see how ordinary and widespread such stories are in eastern Kentucky, let's leave behind the ruins of Delia's trailer, and drop in on a different set of people. I live on a working-class street on the edge of Berea, twelve miles from Bear Lick. It's two blocks long, running from the railroad tracks at one end to a junkyard at the other, with the first foothills of the Appalachians rising in rumpled green just beyond that. Mostly, it's a quiet street—a double row of little one-story houses, clad in white vinyl or brick. Occasionally a tractor drives by, or a rider on horseback clatters along the asphalt. A few kids circle on bikes in the afternoons; at night, the blue glow of televisions peeks through curtains. It doesn't look overtly impoverished or precarious.

But look closer. The house beside mine was abandoned in 2008, when the family that bought it lost their jobs. It sat empty for years, moldering, sagging, gathering trash and graffiti. A shirtless man, skinny torso wrapped in tats, goes door to door, trying to sell a weed-eater for cash. He looks forty; he's probably twenty-five. There's a homeless camp beside the railroad tracks, and occasionally a family sleeps in their car in front of an empty lot. Down the street, a young woman sits on her porch deep into the night, chain-smoking and hoping to score some pills—or whatever else comes along. The houses are rented one month and empty the next, as people scramble from debt to debt. One night, three doors down, our neighbor leaves his duplex in the middle of the night and climbs into the driver's seat of his car. He's worked in a factory six and seven days a week, year after year after year. He lifts a pistol and shoots himself in the head. In the morning, his woman finds his body, and the whole neighborhood wakes to her screams. "My baby!" Her anguish fills the sky. "My baby! Oh *God*, my *baby!*"

The Yurok and Hoopa Reservations, where the other half of my family lives, are more than two thousand miles away, on the opposite end of the continent. A different set of people, yet again. They have a whole different history, different ethnicities, even a different landscape covered by different plants. But the waves of colonization? The stripping of resources? The back-breaking poverty that isn't just an empty wallet, but comes at you in every facet of life? All that is eerily similar. I've seen gallon cookie jars packed with meth, fifths of schnapps chugged like water, coke parties that ended in beatings. I know people who stumbled drunk into the road and got killed, and people who drove drunk and did the killing. Too many young men wind up in prison; too many young women find themselves raising babies alone. One of my brothers has a dent in his forehead and a glass eye from a savage attack; another bled to death on an apartment floor after his friend stabbed him during some argument over drugs.

I wish I was telling tall tales. I'm not. I'm leaving most of it out. I wish that hard living was just a Bear Lick thing, or an Appalachian thing, or a Reservation thing. It's not. Life is hard anyway, and then poverty makes it harder—and not just in Appalachia. It's the same in Milwaukee. In El Paso. In Kansas farm towns. In Baltimore. In the Ozarks. In Baton Rouge. In Spokane. These are stories from Appalachia, but they're not really stories about Appalachia.

They're stories about America.

*　*　*

When Jared Bowen burned Delia's home, he also burned Boyd's three-legged Chihuahua, Monster, who was caught sleeping under the wrong trailer. After Monster died, Boyd drove over to Monty's, bought several gallons of vodka, drove back to his trailer, and locked the door. The lawn chairs sat empty around the cold firepit. One morning, Delia came to check on her brother. She didn't want "nothin' to do with the place," but she hadn't heard from Boyd and he wasn't answering the phone. He didn't answer when she knocked, either; didn't answer when she hollered. She had to force the door with her hip. She found him in his tiny bedroom, in the frigid dark, curtains drawn tight. He was leaning against the mattress, tangled in covers, bent like he was tying his shoe. As he died, he must have tried to claw his way from the bed. "They couldn't even unbend him," Delia said; the fire in the woodstove had gone out, and his body was frozen.

Less than a week later, Delia and Boyd's little brother Willie drove up in his pickup in the small of the night. He walked to the trailer in the shadows, wraith-like, lugging his toolbox. He started by pulling the wiring from the walls, leaving ragged holes in place of electrical outlets. Wisps of fiberglass insulation floated in the air. He crawled under the trailer and yanked the rest of the wiring from beneath the floor. He ripped the air conditioner out of Boyd's bedroom window without bothering to unscrew it first; the fragile aluminum frame twisted and tore, leaving a gaping opening like an eye socket. The fridge was too big to drag to the truck by himself, so he rolled it away from the wall and gutted it, cutting out the wiring, the fan motor, and the compressor.

When the harvest was done, Willie drove away, leaving behind a second ruined trailer. But there was enough copper wire in the back of his truck to pay for a shopping spree. What did he get? Run-of-the-mill OxyContin pills? Dirty heroin? Or something really dreamy, like fentanyl patches? Fentanyl, a synthetic opioid fifty times stronger than morphine, is supposed to be reserved for things like breakthrough cancer pain. Whatever he got hold of, Willie broke through. Not two weeks after Boyd drank himself to death, Willie overdosed, and joined his older brother beneath the winter ground.

PART III

Homesteading as Resistance

8 Don't Need Their Coal

My son Finn and I walk beside a winding stream at the bottom of a narrow, wooded valley. It's the weekend of Valentine's Day, and the air hints of spring. Patches of daffodil, not quite in bloom, green the forest floor—one final trace of a long-abandoned cabin site. The stream, quick with February rain, tumbles over a stony bed full of geodes and fossils and knee-high waterfalls.

Earlier in the day, we helped clean the wreckage of Boyd's trailer, and I stepped on a scrap of lumber barbed with nails. One stabbed through my shoe and bit deep into the ball of my foot. Now I limp gingerly along the path. Weighed by that devastating scene, I keep asking myself, what can we do about this curse of class and exploitation? Since the dawn of civilization, five thousand years ago, people have toiled and struggled beneath oligarchy and macro-parasitism; these ills now girdle the planet.[1] They seem insoluble. If kings are overthrown, robber barons arise; when robber barons are pulled down, dictators take their place. No matter how hard we push the boulder up the hill, sooner or later it escapes our grasp, and rolls back to the bottom.

Before long, Finn and I overhear the exclamations of children running in the forest and catch the spice of woodsmoke on the breeze. Turning a bend in the trail, we glimpse, through the trees, a tiny shack—just four cedar posts supporting a roof of rusty tin. The shack has no walls; old windows stacked along one side serve as a wind break. A stovepipe juts above the tin, wisps of smoke tangling in the clear air. Cody Shulyer sits on a makeshift bench inside this hut, in front of a squat stove improvised from concrete block and firebrick, mortared with clay scooped from the creek bank. He tosses a friendly wave, then languidly feeds a piece of wood to the fire. On the hillside above, his two boys, armed with stick rifles, shout and scamper, their passage leaving churned wakes in the leaf litter.

As Finn and I join Cody beside the fire, we see the real business behind this picturesque shack: set into the rectangular top of the stove, two stainless steel cafeteria pans billow with steam. One pan holds what looks like simmering water, but the second pan, more directly over the flame, roils with beautiful amber fluid. My mouth waters at that unmistakable color: maple syrup. As soon as he learns what it is, Finn sticks his tongue into the steam cloud, trying to lick sweetness from the air. A blue plastic barrel leans against one of the cedar posts, and Cody stands to ladle fresh clear sap from its open mouth into the first cafeteria pan, then uses the ladle to check the consistency of the thickening sap in the second.

As Finn runs off to hunt for a stick gun and join the battle, I tell Cody about the drama that led to Boyd's death. He is saddened but unsurprised. He grew up mostly in the back end of Bear Lick, attending the underfunded rural schools he told me about earlier, on the drive to Lexington to sell mushrooms. After earning an English degree from Eastern Kentucky University, he found a low-level management job with one of the smaller factories in Richmond. With his combination of practical homesteader know-how and fluent literacy, he ended up with more and more responsibility, and ultimately spent ten years managing the place, before quitting to become a part-time mushroom farmer. When he described capitalist corporations as rogue artificial intelligences, he spoke as a witness. He is witness also to the sufferings that ensue. The failures of education. The hard living. They used a temp agency at his factory, he says, not just to cut costs, but also because it's "hard to find people who can just show up for work on time." It's the agency's responsibility to send another temp worker when one goes missing, strung out on pills, beaten by a boyfriend, sobering up in jail—or single, alone, caring for a sick child.

Finn and friend tasting the maple cloud

While Cody stokes the fire, we launch into a wide-ranging conversation about these knotted social problems. About the depressing headlines, overflowing with grift and martial posturing and calibrated xenophobia. About the poison of money in politics. About advertising and the siren song of consumption. About mountaintop-removal mining and climate change. Global warming isn't easy to see everywhere yet—by that time, it will be far too late—but, like polar bears and coral reefs and salmon, maple trees are a sensitive barometer of climate. Over the past few years, sugar content in US maples has dropped precipitously.[2] "This is probably one of the last winters I'll be able to make syrup," Cody tells me. He stirs the sap, sending clouds of steam swirling into the sunlight.

I feel troubled and hopeless. My foot throbs around the nail puncture, and I worry it might grow infected. But there is no way to clean a wound so deep.

* * *

We fall silent. The boys take a break from cavorting through the woods to sit in front of the firebox and roast hotdogs on sticks. Cody fills a mug with steaming sap and passes it around. Cool sap fresh from the tree tastes remarkably like water, with just a suggestion of maple sweetness. But this, hot from the pan and about halfway to syrup, is one of the most delightful things I've ever tasted. If I were Cody, I'd be tempted to stop, pour that nectar in jars, and call it a job well done.

Cody breaks the silence with a laugh. "We didn't *solve* any problems," he says, "but we sure did a hell of a job *enumerating* them." His words snap me from morbid reverie. They remind me that, in some wonderful turn of fortune, I teach in a department at Berea College called Peace and Social Justice Studies. That discipline began in the mid-1900s after two world wars forcibly revealed a terrible and reckless imbalance: we had harnessed science and scholarship more fully to the work of killing than to the work of peace. We had solved daunting technological problems yet struggled with basic questions of fairness. We pried death from the hidden heart of the atom, but, like toddlers, failed to resolve conflict without shoving and hitting. We filled the very sky with murder but could not fathom how to care for each other. The discipline of peace and social justice was created to help redress this imbalance.

One of many things I've learned from this discipline is that our view of activism is distorted. In one popular version, offered on the silver screen, social movements are created by extraordinary souls like Mohandas Gandhi and Martin Luther King Jr.—in which case all we need to do is just sit back and await a savior. In another version, mass movements are seen as spontaneous eruptions of outrage and desperation. Neither view is accurate. At this point, with thousands of prior social movements to learn from, we know that effective campaigns, like the civil rights movement, are created not by charismatic leaders, but by the hard work of thousands of ordinary people, many of them women—folks like Rosa Parks and Septima Clark and Daisy Bates. We know nonviolence is better than violence, not just for moral reasons, but because it *works*. We know even the most brutal regimes derive power from the consent of the governed, and activists have invented hundreds of tactics, direct and indirect, for revoking that consent. And we know that while the road is long, walking it doesn't have to be a slog: tyrants fear laughter as well as bullets, and a dance party stops traffic as surely as a march.[3]

But—you may well ask—if movements are so well studied and so powerful, why do we still have so many problems? Why hasn't activism transformed the world? The answer is straightforward: it already has. But these transformations are hard to see, and that's why Cody and I lost sight of them as we wandered amid the frightening headlines. But try this: look down, right now. Chances are, there is a floor beneath you, and hidden beneath that floor is a foundation. Can you see the sweat and skill that built that foundation? Even as it lifts you, this labor is overlooked. In the same way, we stand upon a foundation of invisible activism—and that's a more accurate metaphor than Sisyphus's boulder rolling endlessly back to the bottom of the hill. We live in a society shaped and reshaped by social movement. Women can now vote and own property and run for office. Weekends and social security are no longer socialist fantasies. It is illegal to own another person, make a child work in a factory, or burn an astronomer for explaining starlight. There is still much injustice, but these are profound triumphs, and it does not help to forget them.

So, what can we do about class and exploitation? About the modern aristocracy? About Delia Howell, bowed beneath more than her share of the labor, bereft of her share of the fruit? In some ways, the answer is simple. We keep organizing. We keep protesting. We keep marching. We build upon the foundation laid by those who came before. But we must also recognize that intentional, progressive social change takes many forms. It's not just marching but setting up a local time bank. Developing a restorative justice program at your high school. Empowering women—or stepping back while they empower themselves. It's going to the courthouse with your proud queer love and exercising the right to wed. It's taking time to sit with a child and read her a good book.

In fact, even as Cody and I griped, was he not engaged in a kind of activism? I have argued that back-to-the-landers are activists, that Craig Williams was an activist not just when he marched, but also when he plowed. As Cody ladles sap from one pan to the next, am I not witnessing an act of intentional social change?

That's a comforting thought. But it has problems. For example, how could homesteading do anything to reform dominant political and economic institutions? How could it do anything to tackle the problems of capitalism and class? After all, the factory that Cody used to manage hums along fine without him. Fox News still shines from the heavens. Overworked teachers remain overworked. The capitalist algorithm continues its ruinous calculation. Perhaps Cody is making the world a bit sweeter—but sooner or later, don't you have to deal with electoral politics, with corporations, with the Koch brothers? Activism may come in many forms, but isn't this a stretch?

If I claim that contemporary homesteading is activism, I beg a basic question. It's the question at the heart of this chapter, and it's one of those that's easy to ask but difficult to answer: does homesteading *work*?

In some ways, the answer is *no*. Homesteading, as a form of activism, has real limitations. Even in eastern Kentucky, where land is relatively cheap, many folks can't afford even a small parcel—and even if they can, an onerous job may leave little time and energy for subsistence work. (Although the same could be said of other forms of activism, all of which require time and effort.) If you're a person of color or openly queer, the prospect of living in rural Kentucky, with its undercurrents of racism and bigotry, may not feel especially liberating. But the biggest limitation is the one noted above: homesteading does little to change the social structures of capitalist plutocracy. In fact, coal companies in eastern Kentucky a century ago gave prizes for the "best garden grown by a miner's family"—the more food people produced for themselves, the lower the wage they could survive upon.[4] If ten million people in the United States engaged in a coordinated labor strike, the billionaire class would have a serious problem on their hands. But if that same ten million headed off into the mountains and forests to try their hand at self-provisioning? Wouldn't plutocrats just gaze down from their private jets, and laugh?

That's the short answer. The long answer is more complex, and we'll spend this chapter exploring it. For one thing, many homesteaders aren't trying to change the system, they're trying to step partway out of it— and we should probably measure the success of homesteading primarily against the goals held by homesteaders themselves. For another, while homesteading might not *directly* change mainstream social structures, it sure changes people's lives, and does so in unexpected and important ways. In thinking about this question, I recall that when I take college students to visit homesteads, most of them are blown away. They feel they've encountered something profound, a space that offers a new vantage on life's parameters and possibilities.

I am inclined to trust them.

*   *   *

Regardless of what anyone else thinks, many Bear Lick back-to-the-landers consider homesteading to be a form of activism and resistance. As a form of activism, however, homesteading is unusual. For one thing, people don't see it as an answer to one or two particular problems; they see it as an answer to almost any problem they can imagine. Back-to-the-landers conclude that building a house and growing vegetables might be a way to avoid getting stuck in a crappy job—but it might also allow a more balanced mix of physical and mental labor. It may provide a healthier space for your children *and* reduce your carbon footprint. Perhaps you can step closer to the divine at the same time you prepare for society's imminent collapse. Homesteading is seen not just as activism, but a remarkably protean form of it, a kind of resistance against all things.

This is different from most forms of activism. A protest, for instance, usually targets specific policies: dismantle nuclear bombs, don't invade Iraq, stop police brutality. A big protest can be an electrifying experience for participants, but even the most impassioned demonstration soon subsides, everyone carpools home, and normal life resumes. Other common activist strategies are similar. Even labor strikes, crucial as they are, usually aim at incremental changes in the workplace, and come and go like a summer rain. Homesteading, by contrast, feels like a long-term response—not a deviation from the norm, but a new norm. Not merely an action, but a different way of *being*.[5]

This multitude of homesteading goals forms a major challenge in answering the question, does it work? Does it work for *which* goal? Escaping the rat race or saving the planet? Raising well-rounded children or spiritual awakening? And it's not like homesteaders compartmentalize these goals; no one says, "I'm 40 percent resisting capitalism and 20 percent getting closer to nature." Diverse purposes flow and blend, in thought and deed, into a complex whole.

Another challenge is that some goals are highly subjective. Almost every homesteader I know voices religious or spiritual aspirations—but how would you determine whether homesteading is an effective means of realizing such aspirations? Does prayer work better on a mountaintop? Are pokeweed and poison ivy conducive to enlightenment? Is there less sin in a melon patch than on a street corner? I'm not sure those are answerable questions.[6]

There's a third challenge in addressing this question about homesteading's efficacy. Not only do Bear Lick homesteaders pursue a bunch of goals, but each goal comes in two main flavors, country and bohemian. We are so deeply shaped by mainstream social processes that we don't see the same problems and threats as those in the other group. Do you homeschool your children so they can read less science, or more? Do you reject television because it shows too much skin, or too much bigotry? Do you avoid driving because oil is the mark of the beast, or because it causes global warming? Back-to-the-landers, as I noted in the introduction, are indelibly marked by the system they dream of escaping.

Take, for example, one important homesteading goal: preparing for the apocalypse. In the United States, it's not just sign-wearing eccentrics who believe "the end is nigh"—one recent survey found a quarter of the population thinks the world will end in their lifetime.[7] The idea of imminent collapse is near-universal among both groups of Bear Lick homesteaders. (This does not mean they're hunkered underground counting shotgun shells and cans of spam; they generally see normal homesteading activities, such as growing food and living off the grid, as appropriate preparation.) There are similarities: both sides see so many potential calamities—economic, military, environmental, moral—that they blend into an ill-defined smog of foreboding. Because these fears concern the future, which is inherently unknowable, both sides struggle to debunk apocalyptic theories, and storylines proliferate beyond evidence and reason.

Beyond these similarities, however, people imagine wildly different cataclysms. Many country homesteaders believe this is the end time, when Christ returns to Earth. Even secular events, like ozone depletion or trade wars, may be wrapped in overtly religious interpretation. For Nathan Hamilton, the recession of 2008 was not merely an economic or political phenomenon, but a biblical one. "Prophecy all down through time has predicted it to come," he told me, citing the King James Bible. "I believe we're gonna suffer. We've lived way too delicious. And it can't last forever. Everything has a cycle and I believe our cycle's running toward the end."

For bohemians, by contrast, the myriad collapses sort mainly into two categories. One category is based on solid scholarship and linked to empirical evidence and reasonable extrapolation. This category is full of calamities that keep scientists and scholars awake at night, such as global warming unleashing methane from the seafloor, egomaniacs unleashing nuclear war, and corporations unleashing job-killing automata. It also includes devastations that are unlikely but possible, such as a pandemic of airborne Ebola, an asteroid impact, or the eruption of the Yellowstone caldera.

As I mentioned in the previous chapter, some bohemian homesteaders are susceptible to pseudoscience—especially when draped with trappings of scholarship like a PhD after the author's name, specialized vocabulary, and a hefty bibliography. The second category thus contains a different set of catastrophes: toxic chemtrails and black helicopters and alien invasions; Mother Earth behaving like an infected organism and eradicating us; a celestial collision with a rogue planet known as Nibiru—named, perhaps overenthusiastically, in advance of its detection. A few years ago, some bohemians worried the world would end in 2012, when the ancient Mayan calendar supposedly completed its final cycle. This led to a small influx of new homesteaders into Berea and Bear Lick; word on the street is that the area is one of a few exceptional sites around the globe protected by an "energy vortex."[8]

This is astonishing: most homesteaders live under the working assumption that society will collapse. Not eventually, in some science-fiction future, but tomorrow. Or next year. These beliefs strike me as ironic, given that human life, in many measurable ways, has never been better. But every time I start to chuckle, I remember that during childhood I was aware, as a mundane fact, that my family might be blasted to cinders and ash at any moment by a nuclear strike. Or I recall that society did partially collapse during the Great Depression, and Appalachian families during that time fled the cities for the mountains. Or I note that we're well into the sixth mass extinction in the history of the planet, this one caused by us. And if mass extinction doesn't count as some sort of world-ending event, I don't know what does.

For now, the point is that prepping for apocalypse is one of the most common and urgent goals for homesteaders. But how would you measure homesteading's effectiveness at meeting that goal? Do you nuke Bear Lick and see who survives? And how would you deal with the fact that while one family prepares for ecological dislocation, their neighbors are preparing for that rapturous moment when the faithful follow Jesus through the sky?

Luckily, despite the huge array of goals homesteaders hold dear, and despite the subjective or prospective nature of some of those goals, one aspect of homesteading serves as a keystone: it has to be economically viable, or it can hardly serve as a means of resistance against *anything*, let alone against everything. Back-to-the-landers don't have to achieve absolute self-sufficiency, but if a homestead is simply an inefficient drain of effort and money, then it's just a resource-intensive hobby, like water skiing. You're driving to a bedroom in the woods every evening after work, but little has changed. You can't even spend more time with your kids, let alone survive a second Great Depression. You're engaged in what scholars have dubbed "rural amenity consumption," which may be pleasant—but it's no answer to major social problems.

To begin answering this chapter's central question—does homesteading work?—we have to tackle a second question first: is homesteading economically viable? And that question, as we'll see over the next four sections, generates interesting answers—even without dropping any nukes.

* * *

Consider a jar of Cody's maple syrup. It's beautiful. Held in sunlight, it shines like liquid gemstone, chestnut and gold in perfect balance. The flavor is flawless. To fill a dozen quarts, Cody got to pass several days in the woods, feeling winter unfold into spring, watching woodsmoke map the curling breeze. His labor created a delightful and relaxing scene; it certainly helped my peace of mind during a difficult time. But did it make sense *economically?*

Problem is, each jar consumed a ridiculous amount of labor. Collecting and boiling sap took so many hours that Cody and his family probably ate more food while doing the job than the job produced. That amber treasure, for all its loveliness, may represent a net loss of nutrition. This returns us to Adam Smith's argument, in *The Wealth of Nations*, that the main determinant of material wealth is the productivity of labor. Unjust distribution creates poverty amid wealth, of course—but setting that aside for a moment, if people labor long but produce little, they will inevitably be poor.

This is why many economists find it self-evident that homesteading is no longer economically viable. Compared with modern industrial production, subsistence seems a reckless waste of labor. Consider not just maple syrup, but agriculture more broadly. A contemporary combine harvester, like a John Deere S690, with a sixteen-row head, can pick and shuck and de-cob over ten football fields' worth of corn in a single hour. That's one hundred thousand pounds of grain processed in sixty minutes.[9] How much dry corn could you and I harvest, by hand, in that same hour? The difference is jaw dropping.

Case closed? Is homesteading, for all its aesthetic appeal, an economic dead end? As with so many ideas, this one is worth a closer look. Let's examine four lines of evidence that suggest a different conclusion.

The first is that subsistence continues to play a major role even for non-homesteading families. Most of us spend many hours each week preparing meals, scrubbing pans, doing laundry, getting the kids ready for school, and picking Legos from between our toes. Indeed, when economists finally noticed and measured household labor, they found that it comprised something like a third of the total economic activity in the United States.

Which makes you wonder: if subsistence production is inefficient, why is it still so common? Partly this is because, for many household tasks, the subsistence version is actually *more* labor efficient than the market alternative. If I read to Finn at night for forty minutes, that's forty minutes of labor. If I hired someone to read to him, it would, for one thing, be a little weird. But it would also take longer than forty minutes, because of what economists refer to as "transaction costs." We'd have to spend time arranging the schedule and negotiating payment, the reader would have to drive or walk to our house, I'd have to make sure I had cash in my wallet, and so on. Unless you hire a live-in maid or butler, similar inefficiencies would occur with outsourcing many household chores, from washing dishes to changing diapers to putting away laundry. For most families, it just doesn't make sense, economic or interpersonal, to tackle such activities by paying someone else to do them.

A second line of evidence is that subsistence today is not the same as hundreds of years ago—or even fifty years ago. It's been industrialized. We ease domestic chores with modern tools and products: coffeemakers, microwaves, water heaters, trash bags, vacuum cleaners, lawn mowers. We use machines, in other words, to make household labor more productive, and that's the essence of industry. A contemporary Bear Lick homestead is no different; it abounds with labor-saving machines and machine-made products. If a homesteader tills at all, she probably uses a gas-powered rototiller. She germinates seeds in plastic trays and guards them from frost with sheets of polyethylene. Cody Shulyer and his wife irrigate their garden naturally from a spring-fed pond—but using vinyl garden hoses to create the siphon. Some still preserve fruits and vegetables through canning, like Caleb Hayward's family in the 1930s, but many use an easier method: they put the extra harvest in a freezer. Even Cody's maple syrup relies upon industrial tools: the metal taps he drove into the trees, the cafeteria pans for boiling the sap, the Ball jars—manufactured by an aerospace firm—that held the final product. (You may ask, of course, if it's so industrialized, does it still count as subsistence? That's an excellent question; we'll tackle it in the next section.)

At the same time that subsistence has been partly industrialized, commercial production retains elements of handcrafting. Which brings us to the third line of evidence: building houses. As we have seen, homesteaders tend to construct smaller dwellings, which offer, among other virtues, economy of both effort and finance. In terms of cost, owner-built homes are more than competitive with market housing. But what about the *labor* efficiency of owner-built homes?

Most commercial homes are still built on site, by hand. Concrete blocks and bricks are laid one at a time. Walls are assembled from individual studs. Siding is puzzled together, cut by cut and board by board. These are the same methods employed by homesteaders. Homesteaders also use many of the same tools as professional crews—concrete mixers and circular saws and impact drivers. In short, there is little difference between the construction technologies used in a typical owner-built home and in a commercially built one. Unless a homesteading family makes a major construction mistake or chooses some impractical "alternative" house design, the difference in labor per square foot is not dramatic. For one of the largest objects in our lives, a home, it's not clear the commercial version saves much work.

Okay. Perhaps owner-built homes rival commercial ones in terms of labor and cost. But let's return to this section's opening questions: what about that jar of maple syrup? What about the corn? Given the insane labor productivity of certain industrial crops, it's easy to assume a back-yard garden cannot compete. For crops like field corn that can be seeded, cultivated, harvested, processed, and stored using large-scale machinery, that may be the case. However—and here's the fourth line of evidence—as any gardener knows, each crop is different. What about harvesting, say, a fresh tomato? For the present—until the coming AI-based labor force matures—a tomato bought at Berea's Wal-Mart is picked in the same manner as one grown in a garden: by someone's fingers.[10] But then it's loaded onto a truck, driven to a processing center, unloaded, loaded onto another truck, driven from California to Kentucky, unloaded, parked in a storeroom, trundled through the store and placed on a shelf, picked by a customer, bagged, loaded in the car, unloaded, carried into the house, and then finally eaten. That poor tomato hasn't been picked—it's been picked and re-picked and picked yet again. A tomato in your backyard? Walk outside, pick it, eat it. If you want to be less efficient with your labor, carry it inside and slice it onto an omelet. Like many crops beloved of gardeners, that homegrown tomato contains far less labor, and far more flavor, than the commercial version.

So, can homesteading compete, in terms of that crucial metric of labor productivity? It depends. If you're not careful, you may find yourself working long hours without much to show, like when I tried to build an underground house by hand as a naïve teenager. However, if you pick projects with care, and do the reading, and consult experienced friends and neighbors, then contemporary rural subsistence can indeed compete with mainstream production, at least for certain goods and services.

Before the Industrial Revolution, labor efficiency was perhaps the most pressing economic concern. No longer. We may never have the luxury of ignoring it, but it's not the only efficiency that matters, even from a hard-headed economic perspective. We can—and should—measure the performance of something like agriculture in many ways: not just calorie of food per hour of human effort, but "pounds of soil eroded per calorie," or "pounds of CO_2 emitted per calorie" or "grams of pesticide ingested per calorie." For many of these other measures, local, diversified gardens and farms perform better than conventional agriculture.[11]

Ultimately, the most important economic concern is that when we produce a good, we also produce particular kinds of people and particular kinds of society. Slavery, for example, achieved high labor productivity—but at what cost? It damaged those who were enchained and deranged those who chained them. On the line at Jigoku, car parts are produced with fanatical efficiency, but the impact upon workers is horrendous. What if, as anthropologist James C. Scott suggests, instead of focusing on labor productivity—or profit, or shareholder value, or other narrow criteria—we focus on gross *human* product?[12] What if we looked at the full range of impacts and benefits of a given economic activity? Does the work increase the well-being and knowledge of those who perform it? Does it promote community, equality, and democracy? Seen through this wider, more humane lens, homesteading appears even more viable. When Cody and his family built the maple syrup shack, they weren't just trading labor for dollars. They were raising their own skills and capacities at the same time they raised the roof. When his sons helped construct the masonry stove, they also constructed a classroom. When they invited others to join, they fostered community and mutuality. Ultimately, they weren't just making syrup. They were making healthy, confident, independent people.

* * *

Rolling a big sawlog by hand is difficult at best. So Nathan Hamilton and I each wield a logging tool called a "cant hook"—a stout wooden handle, four feet long and thick as my arm, with a twelve-inch metal hook dangling from the business end. I lay mine across the cedar log we're rolling into place, set the hook deep into the bark, and lever the handle upward. The heavy, ten-foot-long section of trunk slowly steamrolls the forest floor. With a grunt, I shove the handle overhead as Nathan readies his hook. Turn by turn, we roll the log until it bumps against two others, their fat ends pointing the same direction like an oversized bouquet.

Even though it's a cool day in mid-March, I wipe sweat from my eyebrows. We're working deep in a holler, about twenty feet above a creek, on a wide bench of clay that follows the stream out of sight in both directions. Eastern red cedar crowds the bench, thriving in the heavy soil that daunts other plants; between larger cedars, the undergrowth is mostly just smaller cedars. This is our third day of logging. After Nathan selects a batch of trees, we drop them, trim the branches, cut the trunks to length, and roll the sawlogs into bundles of two or three, depending on size. That's just the beginning of the job, however—the nearest road is a half-mile away, uphill, through dense forest.

That's why Nathan brought his team of horses. Gigantic sibling mares, they stand harnessed shoulder to shoulder, cords of muscle rising and falling beneath their chestnut flanks. Once a set of logs is ready, Nathan backs the sisters into position. Draped in tackle, they have trouble seeing behind themselves, and back clumsily, massive hooves churning the clay. Nathan screams and curses, jumping like a wild man and swatting them with his straw hat. I was shocked at first. Nathan is mild-mannered and loves horses. But they each outweigh him by nearly a ton and possess their own ideas about what they would rather be doing. Part of his job, I realize, is to be the bigger grouch.

Throughout history, small-scale farmers have freely mixed subsistence and barter and wage labor and market production; the bounds between different types of economic activity were porous and flexible. This job is no exception. The land belongs to a friend, and Nathan is logging in exchange for a portion of the cedars. He will set aside part of his share for posts and mill the rest into lumber. Most of those boards he'll use to extend the porch around his grandmother's cabin, but he'll sell or trade any leftover.

Once the mares have backed up, Nathan wraps a heavy chain around one end of the logs, and off they go. It's not a Zen-like chore. These ladies aren't taking a woodland stroll—they're lunging against the weight, breath sharp and heavy, four thousand pounds of steaming beast. Divots of muck and moss arc through the air. A groove is already worn into the forest floor, but still the logs buck and jump as they skid up the hill. Nathan trots alongside, reins held loosely in one hand. On smoother stretches he jumps upon a log and rides, legs wide, knees bent, surfing the mountain. But lose your balance on this wave, your ankle snaps like a toothpick.

It makes an old-fashioned tableau: Nathan, disappearing into the sun-flecked forest in hat and suspenders, dark beard-tip blown back over one shoulder. Rendered in black and white, it would be a hard scene to date. But while Nathan drags one set of logs, my job is to prepare the next by limbing and sectioning them—and I'm not using some rustic implement. I'm using one of Nathan's big orange Husqvarnas. As he jogs away, I crank the saw and go to work. Like any single-stroke engine, chainsaws can be fussy and cantankerous, and you have to keep the chain sharp. But a well-tuned saw, with its restless, grumbling voracity, is a wonder. It weighs as much as a plump Yorkshire terrier but devours ecosystems. It's like a hologram of the Industrial Revolution, a part that contains the whole; using the chainsaw as starting point, you could write the history of modernity. As I cut, pink sawdust fountains and piles around my boots, the perfume of the wood mixes with hydrocarbon stench—and the old-fashioned tableau is shattered.

But that's okay. Nathan isn't logging with horses because of how it *looks*. He isn't trying to be picturesque or put on a performance. He's using horses because they are the best tool for the job; snaking sawlogs with heavy machinery would take *more* time, not less. Before we even started cutting lumber, we'd have to cut a road. Using horses isn't just labor-efficient, it's also better for the environment. Logging machinery costs a lot: a skidder, which is a kind of tractor that does the same job as Nathan's horses, can set you back a hundred grand. Once you've spent that kind of cash, you have to take all the trees you can get.

Nathan, by contrast, doesn't want the maximum number of cedars. He's trying to make a porch, not a profit. And because horses are relatively cheap—a single skidder tire costs more than the annual upkeep of a draft horse—he can afford to take only what he needs.[13] He carefully chooses a subset of the larger trees, leaving behind a mostly intact forest. His mares churn the forest floor and the logs cut a channel in the ground—but compared with the wounds of a bulldozed logging road and acres of stripped land, these are like briar scratches. They will soon heal.

Subsistence can be surprisingly labor-efficient—in this case, even using old-fashioned methods. But what about that Husqvarna? What about the truck and trailer Nathan used to haul his horses? What about the bandsaw he'll use to mill the lumber? Like so much of subsistence—like economic production in general—even horse logging has been partially industrialized. But not just industrialized: the chainsaw, the pickup, and the sawmill are *capitalist* products. Husqvarna, for instance, is a publicly traded, profit-maximizing transnational corporation. Subsistence, we find, has been colonized by capitalism. Which raises the obvious question: is it really subsistence if you're using a capitalist chainsaw?

Contemporary subsistence in Bear Lick is, in many ways, dependent upon capitalist products. Not just chainsaws, but most store-bought tools and inputs: tin roofing, double-glazed windows, wiring, solar panels, shovels, electric pumps, tape measures, fencing, garden hoses, and so on and on. But that's only part of what's happening. When Nathan uses a capitalist chainsaw in a subsistence project, it's an example of what scholars call the "articulation of modes of production." A "mode of production" is one way of categorizing economic activity, with a focus on the relationships between the people involved in that activity.[14] For instance, if the people working to create a product, like cedar boards, are the same ones who will use those boards, that's the subsistence mode of production. If, by contrast, the workers were paid to produce cedar boards by a business owner, who then sold the boards to consumers on a market, that would be the capitalist mode of production. And if Nathan produces cedar boards using his own tools and labor, and then sells them to a customer, that's the "petty bourgeois" mode of production—or, as we call it today, small business. These different modes "articulate" when they overlap and interact; articulate here means "form a joint," rather than "speak clearly."

Modes of production form joints all the time. The capitalist iPhone is packed with components developed under the state socialist mode of production. Our state-socialist public school in Berea is full of textbooks printed by capitalist publishing houses, and the school nursing staff is employed by a nonprofit corporation. We have, in other words, a "mixed economy" in which different kinds of productive activity and different kinds of institutions interface and work together.

But there's something easy to overlook about the articulation of modes of production: no single mode is dominant. When we see the chainsaw, it's easy to conclude that homesteaders are piggybacking upon capitalism. But recall, subsistence still makes up a huge part of the economy. Every morning, when workers arrive at a Husqvarna factory to build chainsaws, they have been clothed and fed and bathed—and born and raised and educated—to a surprising extent through subsistence labor inside the home.

If this is hard to see, it's because our view of the economy has been warped. We have a long history of noticing paid, official labor more than the unpaid and the unofficial. Of attending to traditionally male domains and overlooking those of women. We focus upon the flow of dollars and profit more than upon the lives of workers and the flow of well-being. That's how the economy looks from the perspective of a macro-parasite, obsessed with grabbing wealth. It is, to steal a phrase from geographer James Blaut, part of a colonizer's model of the world.[15] But it's a view the rest of us should resist. Because we could, with equal validity, look at capitalism and ask: is it really capitalism, when it's piggybacking upon subsistence?

Homesteading, while it cannot produce an airplane or a printing press, is not, and may never be, economically outmoded. It can be surprisingly efficient, and can produce intangible goods that corporations neglect: lives balanced between mind and body; a healthier environment for children; food and homes and other goods with reduced elements of exploitation and autocracy. It creates opportunities for meaningful, engaging, non-alienating labor—and does so at a time when the mainstream economy's need for labor may soon plummet, owing to artificial intelligence and automation. It seems homesteaders are right: a turn to subsistence can indeed serve, for some of the goals they imagine, as an effective form of activism and resistance.

Before we move on to consider two environmental goals—living closer to nature and being more sustainable—there remains one more economic aspect of homesteading to examine. But this aspect does not involve something back-to-the-landers make or build or do. It involves something they try *not* to do.

* * *

On a Bear Lick ridgetop, as dusk gathers the shadows, a small home glows with firelight. Inside, Levi Patton pours steaming water into a couple of pottery mugs. The scent of fresh peppermint mingles with that of woodsmoke. It's the last week of April and still cool enough for tea. In his late sixties, Levi remains fit and slim, with buzzed grey hair, a freshly shaven jaw, and reading glasses that frame a winking smile. He's not a professor—he's one of the few bohemians without a college degree—but he is a published author and could stroll into a university classroom, pick up the chalk, and no one would bat an eye.

His guest, Jessica Elston, is conducting an interview for a Berea College course I'm teaching on back-to-the-land movements. Jessica grew up in rural Alabama, outside Birmingham, but had not heard of back-to-the-landers before our class. Funny, quick-witted, and relaxed, she's a skilled interviewer. While Levi stirs a spoon of honey into each mug, she sets a digital recorder on the round, knee-high Japanese table at which they will sit.

Levi was born in New England in 1946, he tells Jessica once they're settled, right at the beginning of the postwar spike in births that created the baby boomers. His family moved frequently as his father—regional salesman for a pudding company—climbed the middle rungs of the corporate ladder. Levi grew up in suburbs all over the Northeast at a time when suburbia was still more aspiration than punchline. He attended college for one year, but there was, he says, "a sense of revolutionary change in the air. Like suddenly going from Tony Bennett to Jimi Hendrix." Along with many of his peers, he dropped out. "That was pretty exciting times," he chuckles. "A hundred-and-fifty thousand freaks living in the streets of Boston."

Over the next few years he traveled constantly and worked occasionally, doing manual labor across the United States. "I worked a lot of factories—a bra factory, a valentine box factory—but I'd only work for a couple of weeks. It's like, 'let's work in a ping-pong paddle factory and see how they make ping-pong paddles.' I cut tobacco, hauled hay, painted houses. You know, unload a railroad cart full of hundred-pound sacks of flour all day."

He was trying to avoid the rat race that ensnared his parents. "This looks like a trap," he tells Jessica. "You're gonna be doin' the same shit over and over again for forty years and you're gonna be essentially asleep. You won't get the kind of stimulation you need. A lot of people were figuring, 'How can I get enough money to get by without getting stuck in a crap job?' So people had different strategies. But a lot of it came down to keeping your expenses low."

Before long, he helped form a commune in the hills of Tennessee, where he met his wife, Elena Scott, who is out visiting friends at the moment. "Part of that back-to-the-land thing," he says, "was a way to minimize your bills." They started by building an eight-by-twelve cabin. "It was funky," he laughs, "but it was, like, free." It was an eye-opener, he said, realizing you could live that cheaply. Like Craig Williams, they faced a steep learning curve; they also tried to garden in the shade. "I didn't know shit. It's incredible how useless an eighteen-year-old kid comin' out of the American suburbs is." But he and Elena stuck with it—and it worked.

"Like with housing," he continues. "For twenty thousand dollars I can get 80 percent of what I'm gonna get for three hundred thousand. It's about diminishing returns. The difference between havin' no sink and one sink is big. The difference between havin' one sink and two is less. The difference between havin' two and three is nothing. And the difference between havin' four and five is just another sink to clean."

Jessica's nodding. "Yeah, that's interesting." She's had thoughts like this before, but Levi lays them out with the fluency of long reflection.

One year, in the middle of winter, Levi hitchhiked from Boston to Central America. The contrast with consumption-oriented life in the United States was stark. "It totally blew my mind," he says. "You go into places like rural Nicaragua, people are sitting on little stumps or log ends or something like that. Kids crawling all over the place, everybody's havin' a good time. It might not be any electricity, but it's like—everybody's fine, everybody's cool. And then you're here in the US and it's like 'Oh, I'm so embarrassed my saucer doesn't match my thing.'"

They share a quiet moment, sipping tea.

"People get strung-out on convenience and it's very seductive," Levi concludes. "You can drive your car that's gonna start right up and it's got twelve cupholders. Yeah. But then thirty years later you're thinking, 'I got no stories. I got no good stories.'"

*   *   *

Levi's words point to something fundamental: without frugality, homesteading hardly counts as activism, even if you're serious about subsistence. If you build your own house and grow your own food but spend a ton of money, you'll still be yoked to the mainstream economy. You won't have accomplished much except an expensive hobby and a longer commute. So, don't buy excess stuff. How hard can that be?

It's really hard.

There are many reasons. Some products, as we've seen, are difficult to live without, like eyeglasses. Some things we buy are bigger or nicer or more expensive than we want, but our choice is constrained. New cars, for example, are glutted with gadgetry. You can no longer find a recent model with manual windows or key-operated locks; they all feature not only twelve cupholders but heated seats and moonroofs and more computer circuits than the entire Apollo space program. Houses are likewise bloated. The first thousand square feet or so is a home, but the remainder is primarily a debtors' prison with bars of drywall and a warden named Wells Fargo.

Even setting aside such problems, it's hard not to spend on things we don't really need—and getting harder. In *The Overspent American,* Juliet Schor tracks the way mass-media advertising and programming expose everyone to affluent lifestyles. Over time, the average person's list of material requirements and aspirations has swollen to include swimming pools and garages and name-brand shoes. Affluent individuals report feeling poor on $100,000 a year.[16] We are no longer keeping up with the Joneses next door, she notes, but with the effortlessly well-off families modeled on TV.

Some people do succumb to this spell, but when I read about it, my immediate response is, "I don't do that!" I guard against unwarranted expense; I don't own a TV, clothes dryer, or dishwasher. On the rare occasion I find myself watching a commercial, I feel insulted; the manipulation is so crude. But my scoffing dismissal is unimpressive—most of us, Schor writes, are "not conscious of being motivated" by things like advertising or social status.[17] My denial woefully underestimates the power of consumerism. Like a taste for junk food, consumer desire worms deep inside, even when we are on guard; our consumption is driven by an elaborate meshwork of intimate and potent emotions.

Let me offer two personal examples to illustrate the unspoken compulsion of such emotions. The toilet bowl in my house is crusted inside with brown mineral scaling. This crust doesn't affect the function or cleanliness of the toilet—but it looks like poop stains. If guests are coming, I'm gripped by a sudden urge to "fix" it, which would mean wasting money either on some toxic cleaning product or a new toilet. I'm embarrassed, as Levi put it, that "my saucer doesn't match my thing." And several years ago, I went to the dentist with a rotten front tooth. Instead of having it pulled, which is cheaper, I paid a thousand bucks for a root canal and crown. Why? Either way the tooth is dead. Either way, I'm the same person. I would simply feel unattractive with a gap in my smile. We are often driven to excess spending less through acquisitiveness or greed and more through powerful feelings like shame. Try to seriously curtail your consumption, and your brain will squirm with profound-seeming anxieties.

What about people with low income? Aren't they frugal whether they like it or not? For most of history, yes, the poor were frugal by default. But recall that people aren't generally poor because they don't work—they're poor because their work is someone else's wealth. And so is their debt. Over the past several decades, the banking industry has aggressively developed ways to lend money to those with limited income, and to ensure they pay. And pay. And keep paying. Indeed, credit card companies and payday lenders make little profit from those who pay bills on time: the real windfall is pried from those wracked by fees and interest because they *can't* pay. With this proliferation of easy credit, avoiding excess spending is no longer a challenge just for those with discretionary income.

Bear Lick homesteaders generally understand that frugality, in the contemporary United States, represents a basic form of self-defense. It is a vital ingredient in the back-to-the-land project, and many tackle it like any other subsistence task: with a vigorous sense of purpose, forethought and research, support from family and friends, and practice. Frugality is a refrain in the stories homesteaders tell. "It was kind of my way of saying, look, 'I really don't need you motherfuckers,'" Craig Williams said about squatting in a backwoods shack after the end of the Vietnam War. "I can come out here with a little walking stick and a horse and say, 'fuck you, I don't need you.' Alright? And I think that was something I needed to do on the heels of what I had been through. I guess now if I had to, I could be like, 'I've done it—I've lived without Wal-Mart.'"

Cody Shulyer quit his job and transitioned to homesteading after reading a book called *Un-Jobbing: The Adult Liberation Handbook*. He and his wife Joyce now live comfortably on about $25,000 a year. "I think things have gotten really backwards," he told me, "when people are willing to give up their community to pursue a career or a job. I think there's something inherently flawed in that. People too caught up in the need to have more stuff, basically." They don't even buy health insurance. "I did for years," he said, "and a lot of good it did me when I had a medical situation. They found ways not to pay. It was very clear afterward that the insurance companies are made up of two groups of employees: one selling policies and one figuring out how not to pay."

Nathan Hamilton also spoke of the dangers of consumerism. "People trade their life to money and they're not happy," he said. "You gotta be smart enough to know not to do that. There was a lady told me one time, 'Well, if you played the lottery you might win it.' I said 'Why in the hell would I want to win it?' It would destroy my life! I would probably die on drugs or something. I don't need none of that money. Cause it ain't liable to make you happy—it's liable to make you sad."

Some homesteaders are more skilled at frugality than others. But when people combine practiced subsistence with serious frugality, the effects are astonishing. They loosen the imperious grip of wage labor and debt, and recenter their lives in activities that promise growth and meaning, rather than mere remuneration. It was through a mix of self-provisioning and cheap living that Virginia Webb weathered the difficult early years of developing a livelihood as a potter. She is not alone: Bear Lick is full of potters and weavers and jewelers and musicians and painters who are able to make a living through art because their monetary needs are modest. It's no accident that Berea is both a hotbed of back-to-the-land activity and the self-proclaimed "arts and crafts capital of Kentucky."[18] Ann Duncan's combination of carpentry and frugality allowed her to attend graduate school without taking loans. "Valuable work," she said, "is not necessarily work you get paid for." Another bohemian homesteader, a licensed massage therapist, was able to drop from five workdays per week to three, and spent much of that reclaimed time with her daughter and son.

Ultimately, if you're not chained to the paycheck, you can simply walk away from an intolerable job. Nathan told a story about building wooden fences for a man who was harsh with the young helper Nathan had brought along. "I sort of got tired of it directly. I said, 'Bob Brewer, I am going to tell you something. I'm as independent as hell. And don't you ever think I'm not.' And he goes, 'How are you independent?' I said, "Cause I got a cellar full of food and a smokehouse full of meat, and I don't need your damn money.'"

Back in the little home on the ridgetop, Levi and Jessica finish their tea. Levi stands up from the low table, steps over to the plywood kitchen counter, and reaches for a plastic gallon jug of spring water. A blue-tailed skink, perched on the handle, zips away into the shadows. "Agricultural productivity increased twelvefold here in the last forty years," he says as he refills the teapot. "A guy forty years ago took a full forty-hour work week to produce what a farmer now produces in three-and-a-half hours."

"That's insane," Jessica replies.

"There was a huge increase in productivity, but we took it all as cash. We didn't take any of it as free time. Politicians always say, 'I'm gonna create jobs, I'm gonna create jobs.' It's like give us Friday off, man. Time to hang out with your kids or learn to play the guitar or whatever."

Jessica laughs. "I know, right?"

Levi sits back on the floor, across the table from Jessica, and nestles the teapot into the edge of the open campfire burning beside them in the center of the living room. Smoke twines above their heads, flowing up to an opening in the ceiling. Levi and Elena have a lovely home, but it's not a house. It's a tipi. It takes them a day to set up; less to take down. They start by digging a firepit and perimeter drains, then they raise the homemade poles one at a time, stacking them into a pyramid; the tarp rides up with the final pole. They lay down a plastic tarp, unfold blankets atop that, and install the ozan, a cloth liner that controls the flow of air and rain. Finally, they set up two fifteen-watt solar panels outside to charge their phones and the laptop that Levi writes upon. The whole rig cost about a thousand bucks. They spend so little on ordinary expenses that their money is available for the extraordinary. In a few months, they will roll up their home and head to the tropics for the winter to work with children in Honduras—and they have no shortage of excellent stories.

"Well," Jessica says, "we're pretty much done. I can turn this recorder off and we can just talk."

Levi smiles. "Now I can say all the good stuff!"

*   *   *

High above Bear Lick Creek, a shallow cave in the white cliff-face watches over forest and field. Rectangles of corn and hay quilt the valley far below; ranch houses and mobile homes and barns, made tiny by distance, lie scattered like thrown dice. An arching chamber fifty feet wide, twenty feet deep, and fifteen feet tall at the highest point, the cave has a flat floor of hard-packed clay and scalloped rock. Pale cauliflower heads of rough min-eral adorn the vaulted roof. To one side, a spring pours from a waist-high fissure in the back wall, flowing across the floor and over a short ledge to tumble down the wooded mountainside. To the other side stands a simple iron bedframe. Barely large enough to hold a small adult, it looks like something scavenged from a spartan dorm room a century ago. The rails are welded together by accretions of rust and spanned by an improvised weave of bailing wire. A song of falling water fills the grotto, and a warm May wind bends round the cliff, rustling the forest leaves outside. But these sounds seem to stand beyond time. They do not break the silence.

This cave is just one of hundreds in Bear Lick. A thick layer of lime-stone rises around the valley, forming a pocked and fissured upland that geologists call "karst." The hills are tunneled, pitted, and carved. Streams disappear into dark holes, only to emerge suddenly a mile later from some crevice. Farmers take care, lest their tractor tire finds a new sinkhole hid-den beneath the hay. It's this limestone, dissolved into the tap water, that deposits embarrassing crusts inside my toilet.

Bear Lick's karst landscape

Presently, the silence is broken. Ruth Hamilton, wearing a long brown dress, gunny sack slung over one shoulder, labors up the steep slope below the cave. She picks her way carefully across the forest floor, jumbled with leaves and roots, deliberately placing each foot. Sharp taps of a walking stick syncopate her steps. It's a breathless climb, even for young legs, and Ruth is in her eighties. She pauses to catch her wind. When she reaches the base of the cliff, she climbs with familiarity over the rock lip into the cave, sets her sack upon the wire bed, and kneels to wash her face and drink from the cold spring. Then she stands and fetches a tiny Bible from where it was secreted in a crack near the ceiling. This bower of unhewn stone is part of the higher ground that called Ruth back to the mountains from Dayton. It is a place of solitude, prayer, and vision. She will live here for several days—but long before then, she will find that silence has returned.

* * *

Ruth's pilgrimage exemplifies a common goal of both country and bohemian homesteaders: to live closer to nature. But isn't this one of those subjective goals, like spiritual awakening, that we set aside at the beginning of the chapter? Indeed, most homesteaders consider interaction with nature to be a spiritual act; the two are not separate. As with prayer upon a mountaintop, the effectiveness of homesteading in this case is hard to assess. Does "getting back to nature" work? How would you measure such a thing?

From a certain angle, the whole idea seems like hippie-dippie foolishness. In Bear Lick, living close to nature includes gnats dying on your eyeball, chiggers feasting upon your crotch, and ticks drooling bacteria into your veins. Humans throughout history have often needed nothing so much as a bit of distance from the great outdoors. Drowning in a tsunami or gagging to death on volcanic ash both count as intimate encounters with Mother Nature. Malaria still kills almost a million a year. And no matter how awe-inspiring or sacred, you still can't eat scenery.

Any attempt to touch the wild is also rendered difficult given that wilderness, in the usual sense of the word, no longer exists.[19] Scientists have shown that no place remains untouched by human hands; that touch, rather, has been repeated and often ungentle. Even the remotest patch of Appalachian forest has been reshaped as deeply as any farm field. Once-dominant species like chestnuts and Colombian mammoths have been subtracted; newly dominant ones like honeysuckle and wooly adelgid have been added. From decades of fire suppression, deadfall clots the understory; logging and plowing have thinned the soil and withered the streams.[20]

But just because something is hard to measure doesn't mean it's trivial or silly. Not everything that counts can be counted.[21] Wilderness, in the sense of virgin nature, unsullied by humankind, is indeed a thing of the past—and yet there is clearly a difference between the fabricated interior of a building and even the most docile outdoor space, such as a suburban lawn. Despite our impacts, outdoor spaces remain essentially untamed. Even that lawn is alive in ways a bedroom is not—full of organisms only superficially understood and temporarily under control. Abandon a suburban parcel for a year and it becomes clear the lawn was but a barely contained explosion of non-human life. In one sense, there is no more wilderness; in another, we are engulfed by it every time we venture beyond the synthetic bounds of our vehicles and domiciles.

Living in a rural area by itself does not guarantee more time outside. Most Bear Lick homes sport the full suite of contemporary sensual enticements: five hundred channels of satellite TV, Xboxes, internet porn, air conditioning, ice-cold beverages, La-Z-Boy recliners. Homesteading, however, will reliably send you out the door to interact with wind and stone, rain and root. As with many aspects of homesteading, there is a learning curve, and this one can be particularly intense, fraught with uncertainty and fear. Any notion that nature has been domesticated will vanish well before you have survived your first night sleeping alone outside. "When I first moved out here," said a homesteader named Ryan Crist, "I was bugged out by a lot of things. Just the shadows of the fire, and the noises that you've never heard before. The pine borers. Little things that you just never heard 'cause you lived in the city your whole life. Now people come out and are freaked out by a wasp. You gotta learn to live with things. It is definitely something that you acquire over time. And it's beautiful. It's harmony."

As a matter of daily routine, many homestead chores require working closely with other living things. The sensations are vibrant, unforgettable, even sublime. Transplanting tomato seedlings in the morning, dark leaves bejeweled with sunlight and dew, the soil cool and soft between your fingers. Squatting in a creek to tug a heavy rock loose, mindful of hidden snakes; standing slowly, stone hugged to your chest, mindful now of the silent internal conversation of joint and sinew, of the angles and limits of the body. You grip the rooster behind the shoulders, trapping his wings, hints of warm skin beneath deep-layered feathers; his avian head is somehow both darting and still. When you slice his throat, the blade grates upon spine, and the sudden flash of crimson, though expected, is startling. Pausing upon the hillside to brush aside dry leaves, revealing the bright sunset fluting of a chanterelle; the rising smell is like fresh apricots. Steam warm in your nostrils, you stick your tongue into a cloud of maple syrup.

Being outside is not just a matter of chores and production, but also of play and celebration and ceremony. Of bonfires and stargazing, of dreams in a cave, of bathing beneath the cold drumming blast of a waterfall. Caleb Hayward once sipped coffee on his porch and watched a black snake, thinking it was alone, leaping clumsily after a butterfly. Levi and Elena, cuddled in their blankets, grinned themselves to sleep as flying squirrels scuttled up and down the tipi poles above their heads. When Ann Duncan was building her tiny home, she buried a phone line in the dirt and mounted an old-fashioned phone on a tree. "I'd answer, 'Ann's tent!'" She'd sit and talk as deer and grouse and pileated woodpeckers passed by. "Wildcats just walking down the drive, like it's no big deal, you know." Such stories are seen as a basic part of life well-lived. "How can you be okay," one homesteader asked, "living your whole life and never dancing in the moonlight naked?"

Meanwhile, the majority of us sit inside, surrounded by drywall and upholstery and paint. This isn't just a subjective condition—it's one of the most profound and unprecedented shifts in human life in the past ten thousand years, and it is imminently objective and measurable. Researchers have begun assessing the effects of our physical inactivity and isolation, and their findings aren't reassuring. When we imprison animals in a zoo, even a luxurious one, they are sickened by "diseases of captivity." Their minds collapse into neurosis—like Gus, "the bipolar polar bear," swimming figure-eights forever in his pool. Without freedom of movement and the exercise it entails, the dorsal fins of captive killer whales sag and slump. This is what we have done to ourselves. Buildings seldom left might as well be cages. A soft couch becomes a kind of body cast, weakening even as it soothes. "Our unquenchable desire to be comfortable has debilitated us," writes kinesiologist Katy Bowman. "Ironic, as there is nothing comfortable about being debilitated."[22]

The time we spend sedentary is astonishing. Kids today log something like six hours a day looking at screens, and almost none outside. They are, as one scholar wrote, on a kind of "house arrest." Surveys find that eight-year-olds can identify *Pokémon* characters but not "common neighborhood flora and fauna, such as local oak trees."[23] I encounter this imbalance when I take Berea College students, fresh from their pixilated childhoods, on camping trips. Some are experienced, but many have never lit a fire, peed outside, or eaten directly from a plant. They have never woken with morning dew frosting their eyelashes, jumped into a river, or slipped an egg from beneath a chicken. They have spent their lives inside houses but never truly explored their home. They are like astronauts, seeing Earth only through portholes.

Adults fare little better. Nearly a third of us are obese, and while junk-food addiction plays a crucial role, this is also a consequence of poor "movement nutrition."[24] One recent study tracked the actual movements of twenty-six hundred people with accelerometers, instead of relying on the usual method of self-reportage. The researchers specifically measured the frequency of "vigorous exercise"—by which they meant any movement that would make your heart pound and your sweat pour, that would make you breathe like you're not in hibernation. They were shocked by what they found. Obese men averaged less than four hours of intense exercise *per year;* obese women, less than a single hour. "They're living their lives," said lead author Edward Archer, "from one chair to another."[25] The health consequences of our sequestered lives aren't limited to weight gain—our bodies and minds are comprehensively impacted. Rates of depression, anxiety, and hyperactivity skyrocket. Our eyesight suffers. Our bones demineralize. The microbial ecosystems that populate our skin and digestive tract dwindle and grow unbalanced; partly as a result, our immune systems go haywire, leading to rising rates of auto-immune malfunctions such as asthma, arthritis, and irritable bowel syndrome.[26]

With wilderness, as in any relationship, we must strike a balance of intimacy and retreat. Finding that balance requires skill and knowledge; you don't just leap from the couch and suddenly run to the untamed mountaintop. Which means that when a child understands how to navigate different varieties of remote control or breakfast cereal but not different varieties of landscape, something has been lost that cannot be immediately replaced. More and more, we need people who know how to live beyond buttons and screens, to serve as exemplars and inspiration. We need guides with deep practice of being in the wild. We need those who have dwelled, untamed, upon the mountaintop.

As dusk falls across Bear Lick, Ruth pulls a blanket from her gunny sack and unrolls it onto the bailing wire mesh that webs the rusted bedframe. Near the lip of the cave, she has built a small fire of fallen branches. The golden flames dance, trancelike; warm light fills the shallow room. From where she sits, she can watch a thousand solar systems wheel in a never-ending gyre. She imagines that she looks not up into the sky, but down. She hangs from the belly of the earth, dangled above bottomless void. Nothing stands between her skin and naked eternity. In this place, the true measure of distance is manifest: Ruth has not come closer to nature. She *is* nature, and always has been.

* * *

From Virginia Webb's porch, I can see for miles. Blue sky sweeps overhead, unbroken save for the piercing brand of the noonday sun high above. Below, Virginia's homestead steps down the long hill toward the valley floor. Along the grassy slope beneath the house, a dozen people, spattered with clay, cut a shallow pit into the ground with shovels. They're digging a small irrigation pond—the perfect labor-intensive job for a June work party. Along one edge of the growing dimple, where groundwater seeps, four or five children engineer a tiny pond of their own. Below the rising dam, long garden rows, mounded with midsummer crops, curve around the contour of the hill, each one bookended with fruit trees that wade in a living mulch of marigolds and comfrey. Below that, Virginia's wood-fired kiln stands beneath a tin roof in the middle of a gravel turnaround. A second work crew, led by Virginia's new partner, Lauren Shelton, installs additional rafters along one side, extending the kiln roof to enclose an open-air kitchen.

One of Virginia's goals in creating this homestead is not just to live closer to nature, but to reduce her impact upon it. Bohemian back-to-the-landers in the sixties were driven partly by ecological concerns, and in the decades since, that impetus has redoubled. With good reason: the number of human-caused environmental problems is staggering. Habitats are chopped, by freeway and field, into wounded fragments. Plastic microfibers shed, through our washing machines, into rivers and oceans, where they will outlast both Parthenon and Pentagon. Industrial farms leak fertilizer into those same aquatic ecosystems, creating vast deoxygenated graveyards upon the sea floor; the mouth of the Mississippi, once a fount of life, now disgorges death. An invasive fungus, hitchhiking on boats and boots, wipes out frogs, another slaughters bats, and we fashion, loss by loss, a planet of rats and jellyfish. And that's just a handful of environmental issues, a tiny sample from an interminable list. It's hard to keep them from merging into that apocalyptic fog that haunts homesteaders' minds.

People imagine so many goals for homesteading, as I noted earlier, that it's a challenge to answer the question, does it work? Within this one subsidiary goal—living sustainably—we find, as in the fractal repetitions of a snowflake, a smaller version of that same challenge. There are hundreds of environmental problems, and no approach can address them all; a behavior or strategy that alleviates one may exacerbate another. A green manuring technique that improves the soil, for example, may require non-native vetch and rye. A hydroelectric dam cuts carbon emissions but destroys habitat. Because of such trade-offs, a full assessment of the environmental efficacy of contemporary homesteading would require hundreds of pages. Let me instead offer, in this section and the next, two observations about homesteading as environmental practice.

Global warming is the biggest environmental problem, so for the moment let's focus on that. Homesteading is capable of supporting, as we have seen, profound changes in people's lives at the individual and family level. But in combating global warming, personal change won't suffice; reducing the level of greenhouse gases in the atmosphere requires *systemic* change. It requires installing different technologies on the far side of our buttons, so that as we bumble through our routines—peering into refrigerators and stomping gas pedals—energy arrives from a wind farm rather than an inferno of fossil carbon. There is no way around it: this is a vast, collective endeavor. It's not impossible, but it would take an effort roughly on par with that expended in World War II. We need to care about the planet, in other words, with the same fervor we cared about firebombing Dresden and Tokyo.

Even if ten million Americans retreated to the woods and reduced their connection to the mainstream economy, would it make much difference against such a problem? They'd still pump gasoline into their Fords and Toyotas. Politicians would still get paid to pretend global warming is fake news. Oil companies would still book their crude reserves as future profit. We've encountered here again that problem from the beginning of the chapter: homesteading does little to change the social structures of capitalist plutocracy.

As with every other aspect of homesteading, however, this is worth a closer look. Let's consider one major category of energy use: heating and cooling homes, which currently accounts for nearly a quarter of fossil fuel demand in the United States.[27] There are smarter ways to keep a house comfortable than burning lumps of coal. Several of the best methods can be seen right here in Virginia's straw-bale cabin. The simplest is that her house is smaller than usual—but that's just a start. The floor, built of tamped earth over polystyrene insulation, serves as "thermal mass," storing heat in the winter and cold in the summer. The house uses passive solar: windows clustered in the south wall beneath a carefully angled overhang admit light in December, when the sun is low in the sky, and block it now, in June, when the sun is high. The thick straw bales insulate far better than a typical stud wall stuffed with fiberglass. Virginia also built a "rocket mass heater" against the back wall, a masonry stove that burns wood with astonishing efficiency; the long flue runs through a heavy earthen bench that soaks up heat, and when the gases finally exit the chimney, they're neither smoky nor hot. Through combining such techniques, Virginia has created a home that essentially heats and cools itself. A bit of scrap lumber sees her through the frost, and even in the longest days of summer she needs no electricity to cool the air.

As a teenager in the late 1980s, I didn't become interested in the back-to-the-land movement, as stereotype might suggest, because I longed to live in a commune and smoke pot all day. I became interested partly because back-to-the-landers were dead serious about experimenting with "appropriate technologies" like the ones in Virginia's house. At that time, few others were. There were a handful of university programs and a smattering of architects—but mostly, if you wanted to see appropriate technology in action in the United States, you had to find a homesteader. Now, thirty years later, some of these methods are finally catching on. In progressive, affluent enclaves like Boston and San Francisco, green building has become normal. New homes boast environmentally friendly features like improved insulation, solar panels, and rainwater capture. But in most places, like Kentucky, the home construction industry carries on

A passive solar home

as if environmental crises didn't exist, failing even to apply passive solar principles. The energy of the winter sun—which could be harvested for free with mere forethought—is squandered.

This brings us to my first observation about homesteading and sustainability: back-to-the-landers play an essential role as stewards of appropriate technology. They develop and test practical alternatives, import them from other countries, and form an incubator market for novel technologies. Some serve as educators, hosting tours and school field trips, writing articles and books. They play this role not just for energy-efficient home design, but for a wide range of technologies: no-till farming, companion planting, and integrated pest management. Mulching and composting and vermiculture. Rammed earth and cob building techniques. Solar water heaters and photovoltaics. Gray-water recycling and composting toilets.

I have focused on bohemians in this section because they're explicitly concerned with technologies that support environmental amelioration. But country homesteaders have played a similar role with a slightly different set of techniques. Nathan Hamilton's cabin is also off-grid, disconnected from oil wells and coal mines. He and others like him have kept alive horse logging and blacksmithing, root cellars and smoke-curing. They've preserved, by handing seeds down across generations, unique varieties of beans and tomatoes and other important landraces. They are, in other words, the contemporary editors of a rich encyclopedia of vital knowledge.

The impact of innovators and stewards and educators is measured not by their numbers, but by the importance of the knowledge they create and sustain. In this role, small groups have powerful effects. Fewer than one in a hundred individuals is a doctor. Fewer than one in a thousand buildings is a public library. Does that mean doctors and libraries have little impact? Recently, Finn and I watched a trumpeter swan float with supple grace down the Yellowstone River. Along with the rest of the Americas, swans were subject to violent colonization; after an orgy of overharvest, these majestic waterfowl nearly vanished. By the 1930s, millions of years of hard-earned and irreplaceable information about how to be a swan was preserved only in the bodies of a couple thousand survivors. But from that small reserve, the population has recovered;

trumpeter swans no longer stand upon the brink. In the preservation of knowledge, that's how it goes—the difference between persistence and oblivion is often the difference between a few, and none.

*   *   *

The second observation about homesteading and sustainability is best conveyed with a story. Years ago, I drove with two friends deep into the Sonoran Desert in southern Arizona. The Sonoran is our iconic desert, a place where coyotes chase roadrunners and saguaro cacti stand sentinel, arms lifted in perpetual salute. It is insanely hot, fatally harsh, and one of the most beautiful places I have ever been. We followed the endless dirt road beneath a blast-furnace sky, past desiccated arroyos and the red-tipped branches of ocotillo. After miles of dust, washboard ripples rattling the teeth inside our heads, we parked near a clump of cottonwoods at the foot of a gentle hill. An ordinary three-strand barbed-wire fence, like you might find around a cow pasture, ran nearby—the only marker, at that time, of the international border. A hundred yards to the south, trucks growled along Mexico's Highway 2.

Hidden behind a screen of pale desert shrubs lay a small pond, fed by a steady flow of spring water—one of the only true oases in North America. Officially named Quitobaquito, it has been known far longer by the Tohono O'odham tribe as *A'al Waipia*. Part of Organ Pipe Cactus National Monument, the oasis is protected from people. The National Park Service purchased it in the 1940s and removed the small settlement there, returning the place to wilderness. We found, beneath the cottonwoods, an unspoiled sanctuary abounding with turtles and fish and birds. Especially birds—ornithologists have recorded more than thirty species that rely upon the spring.[28]

But what my eyes saw was not true. To see, I had to read. Later that trip, I picked up a book called *The Desert Smells Like Rain*, Gary Paul Nabhan's lyrical exploration of the sophisticated methods the Tohono O'odham use to farm the desert. I learned there is a sister oasis, *Ki:towak*, forty miles across the barbed wire into Mexico. Ki:towak has not been protected by government and, at the time of Nabhan's writing, an elderly Indian man still lived there.

That elder did what people have done at these oases for millennia. He cleaned debris from the stream to keep it flowing. He planted willows and squashes and watermelons and beans. Wild greens found a home in his fields. "He has dug fig and pomegranate shoots from the base of ancient, abundantly bearing trees," Nabhan wrote, "and transplanted them out to the more open areas in the orchard where they can thrive."[29] Animals were drawn to this horticultural abundance, including more than sixty species of birds—twice as many as at the "protected" site of A'al Waipia. When the Park Service removed people from A'al Waipia, in other words, it did not become wilder.

It began to die.

The point is not that all things modern are bad and all things ancient good; premodern humans authored their share of environmental woe. The point is this: almost eclipsed from view by tales of environmental devastation are countless stories of humans figuring out how to sustain the ecological systems they depend upon. Cultural ecologist Robert Netting, in his classic book *Smallholders, Householders,* describes peasant farming systems across the world—from Switzerland to Mexico to Nigeria—that remained stable for thousands of years. In the Amazon jungle, scientists have discovered great swaths of uncharacteristically rich soil, called *terra preta,* which turned out to have been generated by pre-Conquest farmers. The rainforest itself, appearing wild, is actually enriched in fruit trees through thousands of years of human tending; one researcher described it as "among the finest works of art on the planet." In California, Native peoples managed a complex array of natural resources for millennia, and the "natural" abundance marveled at by Euro-American colonists was partly their product.[30]

Living closer to nature can be healthy for people. But when done with care, the relationship does not have to be one-sided. Our lives do not inevitably fall as a curse upon the land. Look again at Virginia's homestead. It's neither pristine nor unchanged; as a site of labor and production, it's been heavily modified. Nonetheless, those modifications are exemplary. Virginia has gently recontoured the surface so that rainwater, instead of rushing down the hillside, meanders and percolates. The hand-dug pond will provide both new wildlife habitat and a reserve of drinking water during drought. She has built rich garden loam from shale and clay, through a careful rotation of cover crops and green manure. She has created a mosaic of field and forest that together supports more biodiversity than either alone. The fruit trees she planted will outlive her, offering sustenance to both human and non-human for generations.

If we visited Virginia's homestead a century from now, we would find a place with enhanced capacity to support life. We would find, in other words, a kind of oasis. But, like Ki:towak and A'al Waipia, this oasis was not created by nature alone. It is a *peopled* oasis, and it represents something the Earth, drifting alone in the infinite sterility of space, desperately needs: humans and nature joined in symbiosis.

* * *

I leave the aerie of Virginia's porch and walk past the crew digging the pond, down to the outhouse. A board-and-batten closet perched beside the garden, it's plain on the outside but intricate within. The walls are crowded with information; postcards and photos from Virginia's travels overlap with magazine clippings and posters of wild mushrooms and heirloom tomatoes. From the toilet lid—set atop a five-gallon bucket—a bumper-sticker reminds me that "Compost Happens." Once seated, I can peek through the door and glimpse, above waving corn tassels, the winding valley below—or better yet, leave the door open and enjoy the view unbarred.

There are, of course, piles of books and magazines. From the bottom of one stack, I carefully wriggle, in a kind of bookworm Jenga, an oversized, rag-eared volume. The cover is matte-black save for an image of the crescent Earth and the title in big white letters: *The Last Whole Earth Catalog.* Many books have been written about sixties counterculture, but this, winner of the National Book Award in 1972, captures the vibe like no other. The language is vibrant, uncensored, and refreshingly informal. "We are a bunch of amateurs," the editors write. "The judgements in the reviews are wholly sincere. They are also only partially informed, often biased, very often wishful thinking, occasionally a temporary enthusiasm. Many are simply hasty. I wouldn't rely on them too far."[31] Divided

Outhouse library

into sections like Land Use, Shelter, Nomadics, and Desperate Ecology Action, it's 450 pages of product reviews covering an astonishing array of goods—from pamphlets on raising goats to spear-fishing equipment—with overarching themes of self-sufficiency and appropriate technology. It's the Sears Catalog for those trying to escape the consumerist world built by things like the Sears Catalog.

The *Whole Earth Catalog* is also a testament to the inherent nerdiness of the bohemian back-to-the-land movement.[32] The first forty pages offer little but books, and not just groovy reveries about dropping acid with dolphins. It's a formidable list, packed with classics of science and history and critical thought. You'll find Richard Feynman on physics, Eugene Odum on ecology, and D'Arcy Thompson on biological shapes and forms. World historian William McNeill is listed alongside political philosopher Hannah Arendt and anthropologist Claude Lévi-Strauss. There are masterpieces of environmentalism like *Silent Spring, A Sand*

County Almanac, and *The Long-Legged House.* It's heavy on men and somewhat dated, but if you had read a tenth of these in the 1970s you would have covered a better curriculum than in most universities.

Tucked into the corners of the *Catalog's* pages is a full-length novel, *Divine Right's Trip,* by Kentucky author Gurney Norman. It's the story of an Appalachian kid, DR, struggling with that sense of uselessness that burdens modern American youth. He drives aimlessly around the West with his partner, Estelle, in a filthy VW bus. It's not a flattering portrait; DR's life is not one you'd wish upon a friend. Lost in a psychedelic fugue, he can't even recall how long he's been with Estelle. "The only things he measured were miles and micrograms," Norman notes, "and even then he had little use for precision."[33] But in the end, DR stumbles onto solid ground by returning to the mountains of Kentucky, where he begins caring for his family's neglected homestead and finding, for the first time, labor with purpose and meaning. Flipping through the *Catalog,* there in Virginia's shitter in those same mountains, is a recursive experience, like finding yourself inside one of those spiraling M. C. Escher prints: the outhouse contains the catalog, which contains the story of the outhouse.

But the experience also raises painful questions. One problem we've explored is the way people are divorced from powerful literacy, how this allows manufactured divisions to be driven through our communities, how it leaves us vulnerable to colonization and exploitation. Homesteading can be effective in so many ways. But does it help with scholastic dispossession? Does it promote literacy and intellectual engagement?

That's a tough question. The quick answer, just like at the beginning of the chapter, is *no.* Mostly, to promote literacy, we have to build better schools. But I'm suspicious of the quick answer. So, I asked Virginia. She is, after all, a hick and a hippie. She's a bookish redneck lesbian Appalachian pagan with a master's degree and a southern drawl. Her answer was that several generations ago, her people weren't caught up in reactionary politics. "They were mountain people, they ran moonshine," she said. "They were a liberal people, they were very counterculture, they were connected." In her view, when folks left the mountains for factories and shopping centers and push-button life, they lost their radical edge and intellectual independence. "If they hadn't all gone north," she concluded, "I would just be one of everybody else."

Several people told me that same thing. They didn't mean Bear Lick had no bigotry or racism or religious fundamentalism before the economic boom of World War II. They meant that when millions of Appalachians traded subsistence farming for wage labor, their children often wound up doubly dispossessed. They weren't given access to meaningful scholarly knowledge, and they lost access to meaningful practical knowledge. They meant that the anti-intellectualism common today is not a leftover—it's a contemporary product. An eighteen-year-old from Bear Lick who has never read a book didn't arrive from the past in a time machine. He endured twelve years in school, spent ten thousand hours staring at screens, and attended little churches that have been retrofitted into the political machinations of billionaires. He is not disconnected from modernity: he's fully connected, but in ways that render him scholastically helpless. He's got a head full of pop-culture nonsense, but he's nearly bereft of knowledge that matters. He's trying to become a man, but all he's got to work with is an Xbox, a baseball bat, and a case of beer.[34]

The country folks who returned to homesteading—or never left it— while still largely disconnected from book learning, are nonetheless deeply connected with useful knowledge. They are, to use a phrase from earlier, practical intellectuals. Raising pigs and replacing clutches and building cabins won't give you the same knowledge as reading *The Beak of the Finch* or *Dark Money* or *The Color Purple*, but it keeps you curious and engaged. It fosters intellectual self-confidence, critical thinking, and communication skills. The Hamiltons, with their rejection of schooling and television and politicized churches, with their refusal to be hooked into modernity in debilitating ways, are far more learned and intellectually open than many of their rural neighbors. This is what Virginia meant: the cultural distance is less, ironically, between bohemian homesteaders and more "old-fashioned" folks like the Hamiltons.

As I flip through the *Last Whole Earth Catalog,* reading about how to hop freight trains and sand-cast aluminum, I realize I've made a mistake. I should have invited Delia Howell to this work party. There are plenty of country folks here, such as Virginia herself, or her partner Lauren, a doctoral student at the University of Kentucky who grew up in the back end of a holler. But they're all bohemians, which is why I didn't think of Delia. Plus, she disappeared after Boyd drank himself to death, and I don't know how to get in touch with her. But I still should have tracked her down and asked her to come. What was I afraid of? That she'd offend people with some racist joke? That she'd be bothered by the unabashedly liberal talk? I should have invited her anyway, cultural schism be damned. Perhaps it would have been difficult. But we don't get through difficult things without trying. Without stumbling. Like it says right here in the *Catalog:* "We're generally down on Utopian thinking around here, holding to a more evolutionary fiasco-by-fiasco approach to perfection."[35]

* * *

I emerge from the outhouse to find that the pond has been dug. Puddled water traces a brown oval in the bottom, below a waist-high dam of fresh clay. Most of the pond crew has shifted to the garden. In the grass at the edge of the raised beds, a half-dozen people pull folded cardboard boxes—dumpster-dived at a furniture store—from a big stack. They unfold the boxes, ripping off tape and plucking staples, then lay the sheets flat on the grass, overlapped like shingles. A pair of work-partiers shovel horse manure from Virginia's truck bed onto the cardboard; atop that, they'll scatter a heavy layer of straw. Within a couple of months, chewed and churned by the restless life of the soil, grass and cardboard will be gone, and these new beds ready for an autumn cover crop.

A smaller crew moves slowly through the garden, harvesting. I find Virginia kneeling beside an uncovered bed—mulch piled to one side—plucking blue potatoes from the black earth. The tubers, small and irregular and dark, are difficult to spot. As I help her sort spud from clod, I ponder. Does homesteading work? Does it accomplish the goals back-to-the-landers hold dear? As we have seen, they turn to rural subsistence for so many reasons it's impossible to give one simple answer. But at this point, we can say that, much of the time, in many ways, the answer is *yes*. Homesteading can work.

But it can also fail.

What if you fall from a ladder while building your dream house and wake in the ER with a broken spine? Or discover the house costs too much in cash or labor, and wind up with a half-built mess you can't even sell? What happens when homesteading devours your marriage? What if land is expensive, your vision of autonomy endlessly deferred by mortgage payments? What if you can't afford land, period? What about those with demanding and inflexible jobs, who have no energy left for hammering and weeding? What happens as the decades pile and bend you with frailty? What if your father is a petty tyrant, his back-to-the-land shtick just a means to dominate and abuse in bucolic isolation?

Without making anything up, we could criticize homesteading until we've convinced ourselves it's pointless. We could dredge up a story of failure for every success, an ambiguity for every improvement. That would be a mistake. As I squat in the dirt, hunting tubers, I am reminded of exercise. Truly, exercise is rife with drawbacks and risk. You can injure your back. It can be expensive. How are you supposed to work all day and still muster energy for running or swimming? It's even trickier to exercise if you're elderly, ill, or disabled. Weight rooms can stink of toxic, preening masculinity. There are so many problems with exercise, in fact, we could easily persuade ourselves it's not worth doing. Might as well live from one chair to another. But this would be a lopsided, overly aggressive argument—assembled from truth, yet still untrue. Despite pitfalls and complications, exercise is, in fact, astonishingly effective. Without vigorous physical activity, as we have seen, our bodies fall apart; with it, we age slower, move faster, remember more, worry less.

Virginia piles our harvest into a big wicker basket and moves to the adjoining bed. She strips armfuls of mulch, revealing little red potatoes snuggled in clusters between the straw and the dirt, like hidden treasure. In the bed we're leaving behind, I spy a few renegade purple fingerlings— but Virginia says if we leave them, they'll sprout next spring without replanting. I stand for a moment, letting blood flow back through my legs. In the meadow below the garden, children warm up the volleyball court with a clumsy game of dodgeball, tripping over their own giggles.

People who exercise know the downsides better than anyone. But few say, "I wish I hadn't done it. It made my life worse." It's the same with homesteading. I've talked with hundreds of back-to-the-landers, and all endured difficulties and setbacks. Some have been hurt. Many homesteaded for a few years then shifted away. Everyone has tried projects that failed. But I cannot recall a single person who said, "I wish I hadn't done it. It made my life worse." Instead, they say things like Cody, as he stirred the thickening sap. "It might be the most important thing I accomplish in my life—creating a place that is semi-independent from the machine." Or Nathan, straight to the point. "What I've got," he said, "money don't buy it."

Virginia and I sift the soil with our fingers, feeling for the smooth plumpness of buried spuds. It occurs to me that I should ask what she thinks about homesteading—is it an effective form of resistance?

She answers without hesitation. "Yes. It's one thing to be standing up on a soap box and then go home and turn on your cable. You know what I'm saying?" She laughs. "I don't want to be that person."

Virginia's sweetheart, Lauren, comes strolling along the garden row toward us, legs brushing leaf and blossom; startled grasshoppers buzz through the air. In the crook of one arm, she carries a basket brimming with harvest—a jumble of zebra tomatoes and green beans and yellow squash, lustrous in the sun. Virginia stands, lifting her own laden basket. "It's my chosen form," she says, "so of course I would think it's the utmost form of resistance."

As Lauren arrives, they reach out and clasp hands. Two hundred feet below us, Bear Lick Creek nestles deep in the green valley it carved around itself. Above, upon the grassy hilltop, summer light flashes from the gable window of Virginia's little straw-bale home. They're about to walk up there to start preparing a big pot of vegetable soup for the evening's potluck meal. But Virginia pauses a moment to finish her thought.

"It's the same thing Gandhi did," she tells me. "You don't need what they are offering. Stop needing it. Don't need their TV. Don't need their coal." She smiles, still holding Lauren's fingers gently with her own. "Then you're in control."

Epilogue
Without a Chief

During part of my time as a graduate student at Berkeley, I lived in a huge, rambling house called Kingman Hall. Built in 1914 as a fraternity, it had four stories, twenty-five bedrooms, a creek-side patio, and a rooftop deck looking over the bay to where San Francisco's skyscrapers carded the fog like raw wool. The frat chapter was disbanded in 1964 and the building became known, for a while, as Toad Hall, half boardinghouse, half commune—the kind of place where Ken Kesey and David Crosby would drop by to score drugs.[1] When I lived there, Kingman was home to fifty students, mostly undergrads; in my mid-thirties, I was the village elder. The vibe was, shall we say, boisterous. Resident artists had colored every surface with graffiti and murals and poetry, some of it magnificent. A vast amoeboid table, big enough for everyone and usually wanting a good scrub, curved around the dining hall. A prominent bulletin board encouraged safe sex in frank language—"finger fucking feels a lot better with a latex glove"—while a glass fishbowl below brimmed with free condoms and packets of lube. They'd throw all-night parties with themes and costumes and bands, wrestle seminude in strawberry Jell-O, inhale whippets by the case from rinsed-out five-gallon soymilk bags. I went downstairs to make breakfast one morning and found the restaurant-sized kitchen crammed with balloons. No one knew how they got there.

Beneath the zany exuberance, the students were serious. They were studious and intellectual, witty but earnest. They debated authors and ideas. They traveled en masse to local protests. They skillfully dismantled norms of gender and race. And they didn't rent Kingman Hall—they owned it. Since 1977, it's been part of the Berkeley Student Cooperative, a nonprofit consumer co-op, started during the Great Depression, that provides housing to thirteen hundred students in twenty different buildings.[2] Like a credit union, the cooperative is owned by the members, which in this case are the residents. Our monthly payments covered upkeep, but not profit; there was no landlord. Rather, we were our own landlords. As a result, a shared room cost, when I was there, about four hundred a month—perhaps two-thirds of what you'd pay for "market" rent. The individual co-op houses also purchased groceries together, in bulk, at wholesale prices. That same monthly fee covered not only housing, but food.

Most of the time, Kingman was moderately filthy. Sometimes it was chaotic. People occasionally fussed and fumed. But it wasn't a free-for-all commune; there was order behind the clutter and noise. Residents gathered for weekly house meetings, deliberating and voting. Everyone held a designated labor position—five hours per week of cleaning bathrooms or washing pots or sorting groceries. Breakfast and lunch were do-it-yourself, but every evening two residents cooked, as their labor for that week, supper for the entire house.

Kingman represented a form of democratic socialism, and it worked better than capitalism. Remember James Scott's idea of gross human product—of looking at the full range of impacts and benefits of a given economic activity? Compared with a normal rental situation in an apartment or dorm, Kingman's gross human product was off the charts. It was a living critique of the economic isolation and subjugation so many families endure, rent-racked or mortgaged to the teeth and overly confined inside a nuclear unit with only one other adult. To me and many others, Kingman felt like entering a liberated territory.

As a form of activism and resistance, homesteading is not like a march, sit-in, or protest rally. Nor is it a paper model, a pipe dream, tomorrow's perfection. Like Kingman Hall, a homestead is a living critique, an alternative model you enter and experience with your whole body. Liberated spaces, even if they're atypical, are vital; indeed, they are vital precisely when they are *not* typical. Like the Highlander Center in Tennessee—one of the few places where blacks and whites in the segregated South could talk and laugh and dance, unafraid, together—such spaces demonstrate, in an immediate, palpable, non-abstract way, that there are different ways of being. After spending time at Highlander, or Kingman Hall, or on Virginia Webb's homestead, the mainstream world feels crimped with narrow folly.

But if homesteads serve as an alternative model, what are they a model of?

* * *

Most modes of production have been around for a while and have old names. Hunting and gathering. Feudalism. Capitalism. Socialism. Homesteading has been around longer than capitalism or state socialism, but it's not quite clear, as a mode of production, what to call it.[3] I have generally referred to it here as "subsistence," which is the proper term when an individual or family provides something for themselves. But what about the voluntary exchanges that occur *between* homesteading households—the work parties and labor trades and bartering and pooling and sharing? If we're being precise, that's not subsistence. For a long time, I scratched my head in vain. Shouldn't we have a good word for this kind of informal economic reciprocity?

We do, but it's been so vandalized and distorted it has nearly been lost: *anarchism.* For most of my adult life, that word made me picture a skinny twenty-year-old in a balaclava, hurling a paving brick through the window of a Starbucks. But smashing shop windows isn't anarchism. It's a protest strategy, and usually one of dubious merit. Or the word brought to mind the *Mad Max* movies, full of leather and blood and chaos. But those films don't depict anarchy, either. They're about dysfunctional and violent dictatorship, of which we already enjoy a surfeit. Or it makes me think of a glib, well-dressed white dude arguing that government is tyranny and we should tear it down and let markets solve all our problems. That's still not an anarchist—that's a so-called libertarian, who somehow

overlooks the fact that capitalist corporations are also powerful autocra-
cies, and that the rules governing markets are made by the powerful.

So what *does* the word anarchy mean? Translating from the Greek, it
means, literally, "without a chief." The first person to popularize the term,
a nineteenth-century French printer and writer named Pierre-Joseph
Proudhon, used it to name all those things people do together with no
one in charge, when some project or activity is a genuine group effort.
There are still social rules and norms, of course, but no rigid chains of
command, no formal demarcations of authority. There might be a facilita-
tor, but there's no boss. Without a boss, no one's a subordinate; those two
positions exist only as a pair. Anarchy, as James Scott writes, is "cooperation without hierarchy or state rule." Or anthropologist David Graber:
"Anarchists are simply people who believe human beings are capable of
behaving in a reasonable fashion without having to be forced to."

It is, in short, order without power.[4]

This may sound idealistic and far-fetched. Everywhere we look, we find
bosses and ranks, commands and compliance. Corporations, which are
ubiquitous, are in many ways the antithesis of anarchy. So are government bureaucracies; both are attempts to create predictable, formally channeled, top-down authority. At a glance, it would appear that Proudhon's
anarchism resides only in the pages of utopian novels or in some distant,
Elysian prehistory. But remember, subsistence production also appears to
be a thing of the past—until we look closer and realize it's still common
and widespread. Are there anarchist moments in the contemporary world?
Can we find ordered human activity without formal hierarchy?

In fact, anarchy is all around us, all the time—but without a name, it
remains largely invisible. It slips unheeded from our perception. Consider,
for example, a pick-up game of basketball at the local park. It is, like any
other game of basketball, highly ordered; even the competition represents,
ironically, not disagreement or strife, but a kind of complex agreement.
Still, no one is in charge. There's no referee. There's no overpaid commis-
sioner of pickup basketball, no millionaire coaches, no zillionaire owners.
The players make the game together.

Or consider human language. Who created language, originally? Was
there a central committee? Grammar czars who invented and distributed

the first rules of syntax? No. Languages are a pick-up game, created as they are spoken. Grammarians come later and, like play-by-play announcers, generally report what has already happened on the court. For example, the *Oxford American Dictionary* now contains the word *buttload*. Did authorities decree its inclusion? No. It took a buttload of us, working together in spontaneous irreverent coordination.

Anarchy happens even in the most regimented places. Assembly lines are designed, in part, to diminish the human element of production, to extinguish any need for skill, imagination, or initiative. But at a place like Jigoku, the line runs smoothly largely because of the complex dance performed by the workers. When Delia kneels to fix a machine, others seamlessly fill her place. When the painting process malfunctions, their practiced eyes catch it; they're the ones who stop the line. These coordinated actions are not designed by engineers or written in policy; they're a creation of people working together. Jigoku could run just fine without many of the senior executives—or *any* of the absentee shareholders—but it couldn't run without anarchy.

As social psychologist James Brown observed, "In order to achieve the goals of the organisation workers must often violate orders, resort to their own techniques of doing things, and disregard lines of authority. Without this kind of systematic sabotage much work could not be done." In a fantastic illustration of this principle, workers sometimes engage in what's known as a "work-to-rule" strike or a "rule-book slowdown."[5] In response to a grievance, they start doing everything *exactly by the book*. They follow every imposed procedure, obey every last directive, toe every line. They shut down the complex organic dance, the tacit shortcuts, the bottom-up collaboration.

And the workplace is crippled.

Indeed, the more autocratic a workplace is, the more susceptible it is to such disruption. "The more likely it is to be parasitic," James Scott notes, "on informal processes that the formal scheme does not recognize and without which it could not continue to exist."[6] Just as capitalism piggybacks upon subsistence, autocracy piggybacks upon anarchy.

Cooperation without hierarchy is everywhere. In the flea market beside the country store. In our choosing of romantic partners. In the play of unsupervised children. In the creation of blues and jazz. At Quaker services, where anyone can speak. In the informal conversations among fellow students that guide people through graduate school. In Europe, there's a movement to remove traffic lights and road signs because traffic flows more safely; apparently, when we can't lean on a formal armature of control, we sit up, pay attention, and drive with more intelligence. Visiting Mexico City once, I stayed with a family in a neighborhood, Santo Domingo, that looked like any other neighborhood, with streets and sidewalks and nice homes. But it began in a massive illegal land rush in the dead of night in 1971, and was developed, bit by bit, over the following decades, by the labor and collaboration of the residents. In the words of British author Colin Ward, anarchism is "far from being a speculative vision of a future society." Rather, it's "a description of a mode of human experience of everyday life, which operates side-by-side with, and in spite of, the dominant authoritarian trends of our society."[7]

Anarchism has been overlooked for many reasons. Although they ultimately depend upon it, neither governments nor corporations are fans. They prefer things measured, recorded, and tracked. They're addicted to homogenization and predictability and legibility—they need children with interchangeable test numbers, beef with bar codes, obedience to the plan, everything visible from the center. The ideal social space for an autocratic organization is the kitchen in a McDonald's, each second monitored, every item tallied, an autocratic harmony with everything (supposedly) determined from headquarters.

Another reason anarchism has been dismissed is that many of its master performers have been marginalized peoples—those for whom formal order and institutionalized power are largely oppressive. The same people, in other words, that mainstream culture has historically dismissed as backward and ignorant. Sophisticated anarchic practices were invented by "savage" Native Americans, who shocked the colonists of New England by their insistence on granting an individual respect—or not—according to his behavior rather than his social rank. By "ignorant and lazy" black slaves, who built robust underground systems of mutual support inside one of the most viciously tyrannical societies ever known. By dispossessed third-world squatters—often portrayed as a kind of human overburden—who built for themselves, in the teeth of official opposition, entire neighborhoods to call home. To really learn about anarchism, we have to go to the margins and the edges, to rejected places and silenced peoples, and listen to those whom society begs us to ignore.

* * *

The United States is supposedly a democracy.[8] The United States is so democratic, the story goes, that we export democracy around the planet, and tyrants shrivel in the beacon-flame of our freedom. What this actually means, in practice, is that every two years—if you're diligent like that—you head to a school or firehouse or church, scrawl your marks on a ballot or tap a computer screen, and go home. It's not much harder, or all that different, than scratching that silver coating off a lottery ticket. It doesn't take much reflection to realize this is thin gruel. It does not represent real participation in the making of important decisions—which is a major reason most folks don't bother. (But let's be clear: having the right to vote is way better than *not* having the right to vote. Just ask Caligula. Of course, democracy is not just a mark on a ballot—but every time you *don't* mark that ballot, a Koch brother marks it for you.[9])

The myth that the United States is a democracy, even if we see through it, still shapes our thinking. It keeps our eye on elections, which are just one small element of democratic governance. More subtly, it steers our attention to the national scale, which is so vast it's essentially an abstraction. We forget to pay attention to how decision-making is handled in the small-scale, concrete settings where we actually live. I was at a community gathering in Berkeley once, with about thirty people in a room, all different ages. The speaker, John Hurst, a scholar of popular education, asked us to raise our hand if the high school we attended was democratically run. "In other words," he clarified, "did everyone in the classroom work together to figure out what they should study and how?" A couple of hands went up. Not mine; I never experienced a classroom like that. Then he asked about our church experience. A couple of hands, again. Then he asked about workplaces, and families. He went through each major institutional setting in which we spend our hours and asked point-blank if they were democratic. Many of us never raised our hand a single time.

This exercise demonstrates, in a down-to-earth way, that while we talk democracy, we often walk autocracy. The exercise also steers our eye away from mere ballots and back to the actual character and challenge of democracy. When you were stuck in a classroom and the teacher was wasting everyone's time, did you raise your hand and say so? Why not? When the preacher said something hypocritical or nonsensical from the pulpit, did you stand to point it out? Why not?

Fundamentally, democracy requires the creation of truly egalitarian relationships—but this is really hard. Breaking autocracy means breaking decorum. It means talking back to those with power. And we really struggle with that. In high school, I tried to speak against a teacher's abusive authority a couple of times, and I was really bad at it. I was so nervous, I had to stop in the middle of sentences to catch my breath. My voice quavered and my hands shook. All the carefully rehearsed arguments fell from my memory like pebbles into a muddy river. Instead of serving as a healthy counterweight to the teacher's unearned power, my trembling protest probably just reinforced it, serving as a cautionary tale to the other kids in the room.

We don't tend to think of democracy as being comprised of difficult emotional work, but it is. We also don't tend to think of emotions as something that require training, but they do. They are a set of complex and difficult skills improved through careful practice. Indeed, they're arguably the single most important thing that we *can* improve through practice. In writing this book, for example, the main challenges I faced weren't intellectual or practical. The main challenge was my *feelings*. How do I write even when I'm exhausted, stressed out, or sad? How do I write despite the choir inside chanting that my ideas are all secondhand or foolish? How do I keep writing when my dearest desire is to do anything else—wash dishes, fill out tax returns, visit the dentist? I learned to set these feelings aside, but it didn't take a day or a week or a month. It took years of practice. That's what maturity is in a nutshell: emotional competence achieved through sustained practice.

Realizing that democracy is, above all, a set of honed interpersonal skills changes everything. Democracy shifts from a matter of episodic voting, or some abstract notion best left to philosophers, to a competence that anyone may acquire over time. We all know what practice looks like, at least for activities like sports or music. Most importantly, practice isn't something you do once in a while. You don't master the clarinet by picking it up once every four years. You don't get better at calculus by pulling an all-night cram session three times a semester. Practice must be a part of ordinary life. It's what you do, almost every day. It's who you are. It's how you be.

At the moment, we don't get enough practice at democracy. That's why I wasn't good at talking back to my teacher: I lacked practice. So let us return, one last time, to the work party at Virginia's hillside homestead, where something astonishing happened. Complicated projects were efficiently completed—a pond was dug, a roof was built, garden beds extended—even though no one was in charge. Virginia and Lauren served as facilitators, but there were no bosses. No one got paid more than anyone else; no one got paid at all. Nobody did the dirty work while someone else "managed" them. There was no rulebook, no syllabus, no statutes, no officials. No profit was maximized; nothing was marketed. It was just people getting shit done. It was living democracy—and living democracy, turns out, looks a whole lot like anarchy.

There were real challenges. It's not like there were zero differences in status. Some participants were gregarious and quick-witted and made everyone laugh. Others were shy and self-effacing. Some liked to pontificate and show off their knowledge; others sulked if they were misunderstood. There were little flows of power and charisma, little violations of the egalitarian mode. But these aren't reasons to abandon democracy—they are reasons why it requires practice. It's like the pick-up game of basketball at the park: when the participants have experience, they don't collapse if one of the players is hard to deal with. They don't snatch their ball and go home. They handle it like grown-ups and use their words.

Am I saying we should get rid of governments and corporations? No. We need them. Being cynical, we need government just to keep worse government at bay; we need presidents to preclude dictators. Being hopeful, we need government because it is capable of accomplishing beautiful things, like easing the lives of elders and limiting the power of the rich and supporting scientific discovery and ending slavery. We need corporations because some products can't be made except by huge organizations. But if these formal institutions are going to function well, they must be deeply democratic. To ensure that, we desperately need more practice at the difficult interpersonal skills of democracy. This is one reason liberated spaces like Kingman Hall or the Highlander Center or Virginia's homestead are so important: they are the gymnasia of democracy. They are where people may practice that endangered art of creating informal but high-functioning egalitarian social structures. Like I said earlier, when Cody and his family built their maple syrup shack together, they weren't just raising walls, but crafting richer, fuller versions of themselves. And a crucial part of that growth is learning, with each other, how to live without a chief.

Notes

Introduction

1. Indeed, because it has to do with class differences, some version of the hick-hippie distinction runs through other subsistence-pursuing groups, such as African Americans and Native Americans.

2. Branagh, *Thor*.

Chapter 1. You Can See Other People's Poop

1. This and other oral history interviews were done under the guidance of the Institutional Review Board protocols of the University of California, Berkeley and Berea College. Transcriptions and permission forms or narratives are in the office of the author at Berea College.

2. The term "American" refers to anyone from North, Central, or South America, but I will use it occasionally as shorthand for people from the United States. Also, *everyone* speaks with an accent; what we hear as "neutral" or "unaccented" is just the socially dominant accent.

3. Brown, *Back to the Land*, 229.

4. Green, "Where Tiny Houses."

5. "Mountain men" from Bowles et al., *Understanding Capitalism*, 148; "beads and sandals" from Lavigne, "A Real Tough." Lavigne quote from 1984, but typical of the genre.

6. Wolf, *Peasants*.

7. Ironmonger, "Counting Outputs"; Madrick, "Why Mainstream Economists."

8. Halperin, *The Livelihood of Kin*.

Chapter 2. A Buzzel about Kantuck

1. Appalachian Regional Commission, "Map."

2. Couto, "Appalachia," 3. Also Shapiro, *Appalachia on Our Mind;* Batteau, *Invention of Appalachia.*

3. This is a condensed version of events taken from Hatcher, "Appalachians and Little Tennessee River," and Reece and Krupa, *Embattled Wilderness.*

4. Morgan, *Boone,* 99.

5. Bourne, *Narratives,* 3.

6. "Catch" some people from Bourne, *Narratives,* 3; "collars and chains," 108; "killed them all," 20.

7. Ibid., 14.

8. Ibid., 112.

9. Crosby, *Ecological Imperialism,* 131.

10. Mann, *1491,* 109.

11. Ibid., 122.

12. Ryen, "Cherokee," 181.

13. The flu pandemic of 1918 may have been close in absolute numbers, but not in terms of percentage of global population.

14. Mann, *1491,* 360.

15. Billings and Blee, *Road,* 34.

16. There are arguments about where Boone first saw the Bluegrass, but detailed accounts place him within the area I'm calling Bear Lick. See Renner, "Daniel Boone's Station Camp."

17. Ellis et al., *Madison County,* 2. Note that there is some uncertainty about the provenance of the "walls" at Indian Fort Mountain.

18. Mann, *1491,* 362.

19. Jones, "Scotch-Irish."

20. Kincaid, *Wilderness Road.*

21. "Strongly built" from Morgan, *Boone,* 441; buckskin and hair, 139.

22. Billings and Blee, *Road to Poverty,* 35.

23. Morgan, *Boone,* 284.

24. Ibid., 178.

25. Billings and Blee, *Road to Poverty,* 37; "chain and compass" from Morgan, *Boone,* 282.

26. Morgan, *Boone,* 198.

27. Ibid., 185.

28. Ellis et al., *Madison County,* 12.

29. Morgan, *Boone,* 282.

30. Billings and Blee, *Road to Poverty,* 37.

31. Virginia General Assembly, *Special Grant.*

32. Dunaway, *First American Frontier,* 57; Billings and Blee, *Road to Poverty,* 43.

33. Ellis et al., *Madison County,* 43.

34. Brechin, *Imperial San Francisco.*

35. Some of these resource grabs are known to the reading public, such as the battle over "net neutrality." But rainfall? See, for example, Finnegan, "Leasing."

36. Kentucky Historical Society, "Index for Old Kentucky."

37. "Historical Census Browser."

38. Ibid. The number of slaves reported in the entirety of Jackson County in 1860 was *seven*.

39. Channing, *Kentucky*, 43.

40. The term "macro-parasite" is from McNeill, *Plagues and Peoples*. Overall, however, the approach to class here is grounded in the work of scholars like Michael Burawoy, Andrew Sayer, and especially Erik Olin Wright.

Chapter 3. You Can't Eat Scenery

1. Ellis et al., *Madison County*.

2. Fairlie, "A Short History"; Thompson, *Whigs and Hunters*.

3. Collective ownership and management have been common around the world; see, e.g., Ostrom, *Governing the Commons*.

4. I am giving a simplistic sketch of British enclosures and "clearances" here, which suffices for present purposes—but note that the fuller history is complex, geographically differentiated, and still an area of scholarly debate.

5. More, *Utopia*, 33.

6. Block and Hostettler, *Hanging in the Balance*, 21.

7. Marx, *Capital*, 272.

8. Jefferson, *Notes*, 165.

9. Berry, *Bringing It*, 34.

10. Thoreau, *Walden*, 29.

11. Ibid., 346.

12. Allebaugh, "Disputanta Oral History Collection." In 1978 a student at Berea College, Terry Allebaugh, conducted a series of wonderful interviews with rural elders in Rockcastle County, which is part of the area included in this book. The majority of interviewees were born in the late 1800s or early 1900s, and the interviews represent an invaluable historical source.

13. Brown, *Beech Creek*, 4.

14. My phrasing is cheeky, but this is an important point. Some scholars argue that peasant farmers have children in part as a strategy for producing a labor supply and as a source of security in later years. I am skeptical that having large families was a labor strategy; if it was, people would have adjusted family size according to circumstance. Families with smaller parcels would have fewer children, for instance—but such intentional curtailments seldom occurred. There is a simpler, if less happy, explanation for why people had so many children: women didn't have power over their own sexuality and their own procreation.

15. Centers for Disease Control, "Achievements in Public Health."

16. "Historical Census Browser."

17. Allebaugh, "Disputanta."

18. Groundhog oil from Allebaugh, "Disputanta"; "ailments or deformities" from Ellis et al., *Madison County*, 308; "3,798 out of 4,980," 323.

19. Allebaugh, "Disputanta."

20. Ibid.

21. Biographical details from "Richard W. Sears"; cover quote from 1898–1930 Sears Catalog.

22. Catalog details from Sears Catalog No. 104, printed in 1897; see "Consumer Guide." Circulation numbers from 1898–1930 Sears Catalog.

23. Sewing machines from Latson, "The Invention"; condom survey from Collier, *Humble Little Condom*, 174; radio from Smith, "Radio."

24. Appalachian scholars have noted that during the first decades of white settlement in eastern Kentucky, people were not notably poor; the argument has been made that they became poor over time (e.g., Billings and Blee's excellent book, *The Road to Poverty*). But it's crucial to keep track of *relative* versus *absolute* poverty. As population grew and farm size shrank, it's possible that some families experienced an absolute reduction in income—but even if they didn't, they lost ground relative to rising living standards in other parts of the United States, and they knew it.

25. Thoreau, *Walden*, 345.

26. Schiavo and Salvucci, *Iroquois Wars I*, 102.

27. Strawberry farming in Spence, "Annual Report"; "blackberries" from Ellis et al., *Madison County*, 327

28. Quotes from Allen, Shearer, and Abney all from Allebaugh, "Disputanta."

29. Patterson, *Century of Forestry*, 3; edited slightly for flow. See also Davis, *Where There Are Mountains*.

30. Smith, *Wealth of Nations*, 11.

31. Pin factory stat from Pratten, "Manufacture of Pins"; "threshing machine" from Arrington, "Industry and Economy"; rice from Netting, *Smallholders*, 138.

32. Henry Ford doubling wage from Nilsson, "Why Did Henry Ford"; "stabilize the workforce" from Cwiek, "The Middle Class."

33. Ridley, *Evolution of Everything*, 96.

34. Berry, *Southern Migrants*, 39.

35. Production numbers from Drummond, "Keeping Watch." Employment: US Bureau of the Census, "Bicentennial Edition," Part 2, Chapter D, Labor, Series D 1–10.

36. Jackson County lost 40 percent from Berry, *Southern Migrants*, 110. Ultimately, something like twenty-three million people left the mountains—one of the largest migrations in human history.

37. Eller, *Uneven Ground*, 49.

38. Bureau of Labor Statistics, "Quarterly Census."

39. Children worked to death: Engels, *Condition*; Marx, *Capital*, chapter 10. The "satanic mills" phrase is famous, but it's from William Blake, not Marx.

40. A major theme in this chapter is the idea that people had to be pried from the land in order for capitalism to grow. In many cases, to be sure, forceful removal of farmers is absolutely what happened, both in the past and today; it's easy to then assume forced removal happened *everywhere*. Within Appalachian Studies, there have been debates about how mountain labor was made available to capitalists. Some

earlier works, taking a romantic view of pre-modern life in the mountains, implied that people were forced from the land as part of the process of becoming coalminers or factory workers (e.g., Eller, *Miners, Millhands, and Mountaineers*). But in later works, there is recognition that mountain life, albeit rich and wonderful in many ways, was poor and hard, and that people left of their own accord when other economic opportunities became available. Chad Berry and Wilma Dunaway, for example, make no bones about this. Eller's recent book, *Uneven Ground*, loses the romantic streak.

41. Berry, *Southern Migrants*, 7.

42. Pronounced ôrōwī, which is the Yurok word for "dove." Through my stepfather, Merk, I have a number of stepsisters and stepbrothers, but Orowi is my half-sister, born when I was seventeen.

43. Baumann, "Changes."

44. Frost, *Poetry of Robert Frost*, 363.

45. Or, these days, to own the factory's debt. The extraction of wealth through ownership has become increasingly abstract and baroque; much of it happens today through "finance." Still, the fundamental dynamics are similar: wealth derives ultimately from labor, and ownership of the means of production—however abstracted, securitized, and derivated—is the way exploitation is accomplished.

Chapter 4. Never Seen So Much Hair in Your Life

1. Virginia's experience jibes with recent research on the beneficial psychological effects of mushrooms; see, e.g., Hoffman, "A Dose."

2. Considering how big the post-sixties counterculture back-to-the-land movement was—and continues to be—the corpus of scholarly research is surprisingly thin. Within Appalachian studies, this particular back-to-the-land movement appears sometimes in works focused on other things; e.g., Beaver, *Rural Community*. But works that focus upon it are unusual; they include Black, "Kentucky Garden"; Salstrom, "Neonatives"; Seaton, *Hippie Homesteaders*; and Turman-Deal, "We Were an Oddity." For the United States as a whole, there are plenty of memoirs and how-to books, which represent, of course, valuable writing. But in terms of formal scholarship, there is a similar dearth. Notable works include Boal et al., *West of Eden*; Brown, *Back to the Land*; Daloz, *We Are As Gods*; Fels, *Buying the Farm*; Gould, *At Home in Nature*; Jacob, *New Pioneers*; Miller, *The 60s Communes*; and Slonecker, *A New Dawn*.

3. Morford, "The Hippies Were Right!"

4. "Electric Kool-Aid" from Kates, "Yuppies"; "moon-faced" from Hitchens, "Where Aquarius."

5. Watts, *1968*.

6. In 2008 I read every newspaper article I could find—more than two hundred—on the hippie back-to-the-land movement, both contemporary and historical.

7. Johnson, "Excesses Blamed." I heard the same conversations among former rural communards at a conference at UC Berkeley in 2004.

8. Niman, *People of the Rainbow,* 32.

9. Jacob, *New Pioneers,* xi. Although Jacob also found many people who wanted to engage in homesteading, but found themselves fully tied, by mortgages and other bills, to wage labor.

10. Brown, *Back to the Land,* 3.

11. Ibid.

12. Gandhi, *Autobiography.*

13. Woodcock and Avakumović, *Peter Kropotkin.*

14. Fairlie, "A Short History." These original Diggers inspired the name of the 1960s group.

15. Brown, *Back to the Land,* 3.

16. For brevity, I have condensed Craig's early experience in Kentucky; he actually lived in communal situations on three different properties.

17. Average house size from US Department of Commerce, "2015 Characteristics." House price in May 2017 from "Median and Average Sales Price."

18. The Pew Charitable Trusts, "Household Expenditures."

19. In many parts of the United States, especially urban areas, owner-built homes may clash with building codes and zoning rules. Such rules, intended to ensure safety and minimal standards, inadvertently prevent the use of non-standard building techniques and often outlaw tiny homes. In Bear Lick, however, such rules are, for now, generally looser.

20. Miller, *Hippies and American Values,* 4.

21. Memoirs comprise one of the largest sets of contemporary books about the back-to-the-land movement. A disproportionate number of these are stories of wild communes, e.g., Coyote, *Sleeping;* Mungo, *Total Loss;* Price, *Huerfano.*

22. Evans, *Nerve.*

23. Ibid. The quote is a famous one, attributed to Saul Alinsky.

24. Breines, *Community and Organization.*

25. Mendel-Reyes, *Reclaiming Democracy,* xxv.

26. Tarrow, *Power in Movement.*

27. Seaton describes a similar dynamic in *Hippie Homesteaders,* 8–9.

28. The word "fakelore" is from Niman, *People of the Rainbow.* For Castaneda, see, e.g., Marshall, "Dark Legacy."

29. "Census Explorer."

30. Among adults over twenty-five in the United States, in the year 2015, only 32.5 percent had a college degree or more, although the percentage has been rising steadily for decades; US Census Bureau, "CPS Historical Time Series Tables."

31. Gould, *At Home in Nature,* 25.

32. The distinction is explored by Walter Ong in his seminal work, *Orality and Literacy.*

Chapter 5. Ain't Nothin' in Them Books

1. Ranked 45th: "Common Core of Data." A third of the funding: Hoyt, *An Evaluation.*

2. I am concerned mostly with the schooling experienced by people who are now adults, so the emphasis here is on what school was like a generation or two ago. (If you go back farther than that, the basic institutional structure was different: small rural counties in eastern Kentucky had dozens of one-room schools scattered all over; a school had to be within walking distance, or a child couldn't attend. Each tiny school had tremendous autonomy, both for better and worse.) The portrait drawn in this chapter may not be fair if applied to classrooms today. That being said, I've had more than a hundred Berea College students—fresh out of secondary school—respond to drafts of this chapter, and they generally report that it accurately captures their overall experience.

3. Finn, *Literacy with an Attitude*, 37.

4. The International Bank for Reconstruction and Development, *World Development Report*, 293.

5. E.g., Anyon, *Social Class*; Finn, *Literacy with an Attitude*; Sieber, *Politics*; Weis, *Working Class*; Willis, *Learning to Labor*.

6. Finn, *Literacy with an Attitude*, 10.

7. Weis, *Working Class*, 86; edited slightly for readability.

8. Finn, *Literacy with an Attitude*, 71.

9. Ibid., 4.

10. Ibid., 59.

11. Wolf, *Proust and the Squid*, 141.

12. Ibid., 136.

13. The idea of school generating an "oppositional identity" is drawn from the work of John Ogbu.

14. 31 percent: Dillon, "Literacy Falls"; "do not have the skills" from Bradshaw et al., *Reading at Risk*, 15; "One in ten" from The Associated Press and Ipsos Public Affairs, "One in Four." The numbers have shifted little since these surveys were conducted; see, e.g., Crain, "Why We Don't Read."

15. "Are Too Many Students."

16. These two skill sets—literate intellectuality and practical intellectuality—do not have to be mutually exclusive. There is some opportunity cost between them, in that the more time an individual spends engaged in a certain kind of task, the less time there is to practice other tasks. Nonetheless, the often sharp differentiation between those possessed of practical skills and those possessed of scholastic skills is more a product of current social processes than an inherent trade-off in human life.

17. Dean, "Scientific Savvy."

18. I am not implying that powerful literacy is simply a birthright, that Dylan Graves automatically turned into a well-educated adult. Unlike wealth and status, education doesn't pass to a child regardless of the level of effort on her part. Fluent literacy and book learning are difficult achievements requiring thousands of hours of practice. But high-quality schooling, by demonstrating that the life of the mind is vibrant and meaningful, makes it far more likely that a young person will engage in that necessary practice. Dylan worked hard for his college degree. But Caleb Hayward, let us note, worked even harder—and his labor barely covered the bills.

19. Lareau, *Unequal Childhoods.*

20. Hart and Risley, "Early Catastrophe."

21. Most country homesteaders lack the kind of expanded vocabulary produced by reading and growing up among other readers. Many of them, however, as participants in a vigorous oral culture, are skilled users of verbal language; a capacious lexicon isn't necessary to elegant self-expression.

22. Finn, *Literacy with an Attitude;* Heath, *Ways with Words;* Howell, *Hard Living;* Lareau, *Unequal Childhoods;* Rubin, *Worlds of Pain;* Willis, *Learning to Labor.*

23. Allebaugh, "Disputanta."

24. Stevens, "Dr. Spock's Baby."

25. Smith, "The Case Against Spanking."

Chapter 6. I Haven't Felt My Hands in Years

1. Estep, "Not Enough Jobs."

2. For the time being, factory-type jobs are an inevitable part of material affluence. But a new economic era is coming—and soon—where repetitive jobs will be done by AI-powered machines. Whether this produces mass unemployment and poverty or general prosperity is a political question; practically speaking, it could produce either. Also, the phrase "a world lit only by fire" is taken from the book of that title by William Manchester.

3. While I am calling for shorter hours, many part-time workers want the opposite, and many factory workers wouldn't want their hours reduced. But let's keep in mind what's really going on: people want longer hours because they're trying to pay their bills, not because they just love stocking shelves and racking parts. If workers made living wages, they wouldn't clamor for more and more and more hours.

4. Kelly, *Divine Right,* 2.

5. Stock markets do have some important economic functions; just imagine not being able to sell a company at all. But at present, useful functions are swamped by their role as a billionaire's roulette table, one at which the rest of us, should we be afforded a seat at all, are known as "dumb money."

6. Kelly, *Divine Right.* Note that from a conservative perspective—where people are supposed to be paid in proportion to their contribution—capitalism ought to be anathema.

7. Jordan, "Washington Monthly."

8. People at the college are aware that income generated by the endowment bears a high human and ecological price. A few years ago, a group of students organized and pressured the administration to invest in ways that don't contradict the college's humanitarian mission. The college responded, after debate and study, by placing a hundred million dollars—nearly 10 percent of the endowment—into what's called an ESG fund (for Environment, Social, and Governance). That money is used to buy ownership in companies that treat their workers better and have relatively good environmental and management practices. This is a huge step in the right direction. But let's be clear: it leaves the basic ownership architecture of capitalism intact. This

isn't a failure of imagination or political nerve on the part of the college. Under our current economic system, investment is extractive ownership, and no single person or institution can fix that. It's a society-level problem.

9. Kurtzleben, "While Trump Touts."

10. I am, to some extent, avoiding Marxist language. Nothing against Marx per se; much of our best thinking about capitalism comes from the Marxist tradition. At the same time, that tradition has been vilified from outside, and on the inside often gets caught up in debates about doctrine and terminology. Fresh wording is welcome.

11. See, e.g., Alperovitz, *What Then*, 108.

12. I am not implying that increasing industrial output, in this case of cars, is an unalloyed good. Even if business owners treat workers fairly, there are major social and environmental downsides, such as sprawling settlement patterns and global warming. But note that making products *less efficiently* isn't generally the best way to deal with such issues.

13. E.g. Reynolds, *Taking the High Road*.

14. Motavalli, "Zero Factory Waste."

15. "Mercedes Innovation." Some safety improvements, such as seatbelts, were not adopted by the auto industry because of market competition, but by pressure from activists like Ralph Nader.

16. Hirschmann, *Branding Masculinity*.

17. "30–40 times" from Selin, "One of the Biggest"; other companies cheated: Schlanger, "It's Not Just Volkswagen."

18. Gilbert, "Why Tesla"; Silver-Greenberg and Gebeloff, "Arbitration Everywhere."

19. For good accessible treatments of the costs of runaway shops, see William Adler's book *Mollie's Job* and the excellent article by Dan Baum, "The Man Who Took."

20. Cobb, *Selling of the South*.

21. There is an important implication here: to some extent, wages are low because a portion of the wealth that workers produce is given to shareholders, in the form of dividends—or taken by overpaid executives. That's a zero-sum game. But some corporate labor strategies are designed to weaken workers politically, *even at the cost of production*. That's not a zero-sum game: it's a negative-sum game. Dividend payments themselves don't account fully for the bad treatment of workers.

22. Elliott, "World's Eight Richest."

23. Schor, "(Even More) Overworked American," 10–11; things have not improved since 2000.

24. For an overview of these policy scams, see Hacker and Pierson, *Winner-Take-All Politics*.

25. So-called tulip poplar is related to magnolias and not actually a poplar species; in Bear Lick, however, it is just called "poplar."

26. Bui, "50 Years." In 2017 public-sector workers were unionized at 34.4 percent while private-sector union density was a paltry 6.5 percent; Bureau of Labor Statistics, "Union Members Summary."

27. Sayer and Walker, *New Social Economy*.

28. Raskin, "Nancy Pelosi." Many scholars have noted the work that this "TINA" stance—There is No Alternative—does in buttressing capitalism and neoliberalism.

29. I say "largely non-capitalist" because contemporary homesteaders, of course, rely upon products of capitalist companies, such as chainsaws and tin roofing. This is a point we will return to in chapter 8.

30. "Quick Facts About Nonprofits." Note that while nonprofits avoid the problem of absentee owners, they don't always avoid that of overpowerful and overpaid executives.

31. *Oxford Dictionaries,* "socialism," accessed July 24, 2018, https://en.oxford dictionaries.com/definition/socialism.

32. Mazzucato, *Entrepreneurial State;* Ellis, "Sam Hurst."

33. Zhang, "Ranked." Am I saying government-owned companies necessarily treat their workers better? Nope. (Although in the US, government jobs are much more likely to be unionized.) The point is that the claim that government is always incompetent at production is bunk.

34. Etehad and Kim, "U.S. Spends More"; Anderson et al., "It's the Prices."

35. Harkinson, "How the Nation's Only."

36. Mitchell, "How One State Escaped."

37. Moskowitz, "Chattanooga."

38. Another critique of state socialism is that you can have public ownership or market competition, but not both. That's not true. Convinced of the bracing effects of competition? Then create a publicly owned business in each sector to compete with for-profit ones. On the one hand, if capitalist firms are so lean and mean, what do they have to fear? On the other hand, if the city of Chattanooga can produce internet at five times the speed for half the cost, why shouldn't we experiment more with government production? Could it really be worse than Jigoku? See, e.g., Schnurer, "When government competes."

39. Deller et al., "Research on the Economic Impact," 2.

40. Zirin, "Those Non-Profit Packers."

41. Deller et al., "Research," 47.

42. "Credit Union Data and Statistics."

43. National Center for Employee Ownership, "A Statistical Profile."

44. Okonite uses what is known as an ESOP—an Employee Stock Ownership Plan. This is, by far, the most common form of worker-ownership in the United States, ranging from companies that retain a predominantly capitalist ownership architecture while sharing a small percentage of stock with employees, to companies like Okonite with 100 percent employee ownership. There are other notable ESOPs in Kentucky, such as DC Elevator in Lexington and Houchens Industries, based in Bowling Green. See also Reece, "Cleveland Model."

45. There has been a fair bit of writing and research on market socialism, but given its importance, we need more. Some of the best in-depth treatments include: Alperovitz, *What Then Must We Do;* Curl, *For All the People;* Kelly, *Owning Our Future;* Nembhard, *Collective Courage;* Pencavel, *Worker Participation;* Restakis, *Humanizing the Economy;* Wolff, *Democracy at Work.*

46. Pérotin, "What do we really know."

47. You might wonder, if worker co-ops compete so well, why aren't there more of them? Partly it's because people don't know about them, partly that they're hard to set up, and partly because they don't enjoy the policy and financial support given to capitalist firms.

48. For an excellent one-stop resource on a diverse range of economic alternatives, check out the website community-wealth.org, created by a nonprofit called Democracy Collaborative. For fascinating research on minimum income, see Lapowsky, "Free Money"; participatory municipal budgeting: Fung and Wright, *Deepening Democracy*; peer-to-peer solar electric trading: Lacey, "Drift is a new startup"; co-operative wind farms: Kelly, *Owning Our Future*, 108.

49. Hanisch, "The Personal is Political."

50. White, "Escaping Poverty."

51. There are two main ways to explain poverty in the modern world, where the problem is not that we struggle to produce enough stuff. One set of theories claims there is something wrong with how society is set up—with the basic "structures" of the economy and politics and so on. The other set of theories claim there is something wrong with poor people. Among scholars, "structural" approaches are more widely embraced, partly because they're supported by evidence, and partly because the other set of approaches—sometimes called "culture of poverty" theories—has generally been a cesspool of racist and ethnocentric bunk, like "black people are lazy," "Appalachians are ignorant," and "Indians are drunks." I agree with scholars that structural causes of poverty are dominant. However, to understand how poverty works, we can't ignore the fact that structural forces work partly by hurting and limiting people, and that existing social structures are stabilized by these injuries. If you leave that part out, your analysis is incomplete. Not only that, but this incomplete analysis is less persuasive to those who need it most, working-class people for whom the most *visible* causes of poverty—in their own lives and the lives of those around them—*appear* to be personal failures like drug use or laziness or deadbeat fathers. If you want folks to understand the structural aspects, you can't begin the conversation by pretending these "behavioral" aspects don't exist. But if you did want to identify a "culture of poverty"—a set of beliefs and behaviors that actively create poverty—don't look at the poor. Look at the rich.

52. Let us not forget, though, that compared to an industrial worker in the United States in the nineteenth and early twentieth centuries, Delia is partially shielded by an array of important New Deal–type government programs such as Social Security, unemployment insurance, school lunch programs, and so on.

Chapter 7. Hard Living

1. Oreskes and Conway, *Merchants of Doubt*.

2. Isaacs and Schroeder, "Class."

3. Creating logical and consistent categories of class is hard, and you don't end up with a simple, easy-to-remember taxonomy. In the real world, there are too many hybrid positions, like, say, a woman who owns and runs a bookstore that hires a couple of wage laborers. Is she capitalist, or proletarian? For most purposes, loose

definitions of class are good enough, as long as we keep our eye on the core elements of power and exploitation. Probably the best scholar to consult if you want careful thinking about how to define class is the sociologist Erik Olin Wright.

4. Note that people aren't short of calories per se; they're short of *nutrition*. For a good overview of crop subsidies and diet, see Fields, "Fat of the Land."

5. It's unusual to have a class where *no one* knows how to read nutrition labels; usually there are a handful of students who can do so.

6. The FDA has moved to update serving sizes to better reflect what people actually eat, but at the time of writing, the proposed new rules have yet to take effect.

7. Bittman, "Is Junk Food"; emphasis mine.

8. One reason poor people eat junk food is that they are more likely to live in areas without grocery stores and they are less likely to have reliable transportation. Such "food deserts" are common in rural Appalachia, as well as in areas of concentrated poverty in cities and on Indian reservations. On the Hoopa Reservation, where I write this note, the local grocery store was closed for several years, and the only place to buy food was the gas station.

9. Obesity rate in Bear Lick area based on research by Jill Day at the University of Kentucky.

10. Khazan, "Kentucky is Home."

11. Cigarettes: Jha et al., "21st Century Hazards"; years of school: Kolata, "A Surprising Secret"; MacKenzie, "More Education."

12. Lemieux et al., "Emissions." It's ironic that many locals worked hard to prevent a nerve gas incinerator at the Blue Grass Army Depot (see chapter 4), while at the same time other locals nonchalantly spew similar chemicals into the air.

13. Rock et al., "Cigarette Smoking."

14. Barclay, "Mountain Dew Mouth"; Otto, *Teeth*.

15. It's illegal in Kentucky to burn trash, but this is not a well-enforced law, partly because it's culturally accepted. Cops will drive right by a dozen deadly burn barrels on their way to bust someone for growing a pot plant in their yard or sleeping under a bridge.

16. King began writing clandestinely, but eventually was allowed paper to finish. King, "Letter from a Birmingham Jail."

17. Statute: Unlawful discrimination by employers, KRS § 344.040 (1966). Some LGBTQ workers in Kentucky, such as public employees, are protected by specific policies, but as of this writing there is no statewide protection.

18. Initially, as I understand, what was proposed was not a "fairness ordinance" per se, but a municipal Human Rights Commission empowered to deal with discrimination based on, among other things, sexual orientation. It was a fairness ordinance by other means, so to speak.

19. The invocation of Darwinian ideas as an argument against homosexuality doesn't fly for a whole bunch of reasons. Briefly, note that an organism can propagate its genes not only by directly reproducing but also by helping relatives reproduce, as is the case with ants, bees, ravens, wolves, and so on.

20. "Election Results."

21. Sherman, *Loudest Voice*, xvi.

22. Lynch, "The Average American."

23. Kubey and Csikszentmihalyi, "Television Addiction."

24. Thus, Marshall McLuhan's famous phrase, "the medium is the message."

25. Cunningham and Stanovich, "What Reading Does." Edited slightly for flow.

26. McFarland, "Master Deceivers."

27. Sherman, *Loudest Voice*, 76. Edited slightly for flow.

28. Ibid., 40.

29. Tate, "Another Ailes Legacy."

30. Dickinson, "How Roger Ailes Built."

31. Such manipulation is as old as plutocracy itself. In the United States, the manipulation of mass opinion used to be accomplished by newspapers—see, for example, William Randolph Hearst and the Spanish American War. Radio has long been used in the same way, as has the postal service and direct mailing. Roger Ailes didn't invent electoral dirty tricks and propaganda; rather, he adapted such techniques to new media technologies.

32. See, e.g., Mayer, *Dark Money*.

33. Roberts, "Russia Targeted"; Robb, "Pizzagate." These efforts targeted—and will continue to target—both conservative and liberal voters, but operatives found it harder to foist falsehoods on liberal audiences, which tend to be better educated; according to research, "Conservatives retweeted Russian trolls about 31 times more often than liberals" (Stewart, "Study").

34. Smith, "Show, Don't Tell."

35. Roach, *Bonk*, 12.

36. Around the world and throughout history, different peoples, classes, families, and individuals have varied in the degree to which they repressed knowledge about sex and reproduction, versus open and frank communication. That being said, prudery and silence and shame were, and still are, globally common.

37. Milar, "The myth buster."

38. "Perverts Called Government Peril"; Johnson, *Lavender Scare*.

39. Minton, *Departing from Deviance*, 228.

40. The phrase "emancipatory science" is from Minton, *Departing from Deviance*. Gregory Herek, a psychology professor at UC Davis and expert on anti-gay prejudice, has an excellent overview of the literature on his website, "Facts About Homosexuality and Child Molestation." See also Gartrell et al., "Adolescents of the U.S."

41. Bagemihl, *Biological Exuberance*, 9.

42. Leviticus 18:22.

43. Wallis, "From a Shoebox."

44. Beards: Leviticus 19:27; uncovered heads: 1 Corinthians 11:5; bastards in church: Deuteronomy 23:2; genital injuries: Deuteronomy 23:1; post-partum: Leviticus 12:5; mixing crops: Leviticus 19:19; stoning non-virgins: Deuteronomy 22:20–21.

45. Glass and Levchak, "Red States, Blue States."

46. Balmer, *Thy Kingdom Come*, 9.

47. Stinson, "Check out Fox."

48. "DirecTV-14."

49. Michaels, "Billy Graham."

50. Many "expert witnesses" who help sustain these controversies are part of a small roster of hired guns with academic credentials who built careers from reciting pro-corporate talking points on one issue after another; see Oreskes and Conway, *Merchants of Doubt*.

51. Chapman University, "What do Americans Fear?"

52. Mosher and Gould, "How likely . . ."; Younge, "Trump Fears Terrorists."

53. Singh et al., "Estimated global."

54. For every level of literacy, there are associated literary hucksters. Ann Duncan is well-read enough that she's not vulnerable to Fox News–type nonsense, but she *is* vulnerable to legit-appearing pseudoscience. Inside the ivory tower, where people read professionally, works that might fool Ann, like *Mutant Message Down Under*, don't fly. But academics like me suffer our own variety of textual con, in the form of unwarranted idolization of the abstruse writing of fashionable social theorists.

55. Bourdieu, *Distinction*; Veblen, *Theory of the Leisure Class*.

56. Dews, *This Fine Place*; Ryan and Sackrey, *Strangers in Paradise*.

57. There is an irony here: the research demonstrating that homosexuality is healthy is part of the same corpus of scientific work that helps us understand how to prevent sexually transmitted diseases, sexual assault, teen pregnancies, and so on. In other words, the sexual literacy that would help you understand your gay neighbor or family member—or yourself—is also the single best means to prevent abortion. The main cause of abortion, after all, is not abortion clinics—it's unplanned pregnancies (Alterman and Zornick, "The Costs").

58. I have focused on natural science, but there are just as many wonderful insights from the social sciences. Quick answers: 1. Why do we age? It's easy to assume flesh just wears out over time. But that's not the answer, as you can see by noting that mouse bodies "wear out" in about three years, elephant bodies in sixty, and Greenland shark bodies in five hundred or more. To understand senescence, ask how long a given organism, like a mouse, would be likely to survive even if it didn't age; how long would it take, generally, for fatality through predation or disease or injury? There is little use for genetic adaptations that promote longevity past that point. 2. Why does sickness sometimes spread? We know now, of course, that infectious disease is caused by living things, and sickness is a side-effect of their reproductive strategies. But that knowledge is recent. 3. What is sex? The knee-jerk answer is that it's for reproduction. The real answer: not really, because asexual reproduction is twice as efficient as sexual reproduction (every member of the population can make copies of itself). There are multiple theories about the function of sex, many of which focus on the mixing of genomes to stay a step ahead of disease-causing organisms.

59. More quick answers: 1. Europa doesn't have craters because it's covered in a thick layer of ice; when struck by a meteorite, the cracked ice refreezes, leaving no crater. Underneath the ice lies a vast ocean, containing more water than all the oceans on Earth—and, perhaps, life. 2. Non-avian dinosaur species went extinct because

of an asteroid impact off the coast of the present-day Yucatan Peninsula. (Some survived: birds are dinosaurs.) This is common knowledge now—but not very long ago, people did not even know extinction was *possible*. 3. Our mitochondria have their own genomes because they arose through symbiosis, via the combination of two single-celled organisms.

60. Science has problems, of course. Like most everything else, it has a racist and sexist and ethnocentric history. It has played central roles in colonization and militarism. Because of such problems, some scholars grow extreme in their critiques; I have read work that claims science is just ideational imperialism and does nothing to provide a more accurate picture of the world (and other similar critiques). That's silly. Science, at root, is just the practice of using evidence and reason to improve ideas over time. Critics of science, to the extent they ground their work in evidence and reason, are doing science themselves. The best response to the various shortcomings of science is not to throw science out, but make it better.

61. There are many classic works on the history of Appalachia as an "internal colony." See, e.g., Eller, *Miners, Millhands, and Mountaineers;* Gaventa, *Power and Powerlessness.* The work of Helen Lewis was seminal in this regard; see Lewis et al., *Colonialism in Modern America.*

62. Notable recent works include Hacker and Pierson, *Winner-Take-All;* Kelly, *Divine Right;* Piketty, *Capital;* Reich, *Saving Capitalism;* Stiglitz, *The Price of Inequality;* Wolff, *Occupy the Economy.*

63. Del Giudice and Lu, "Palm Beach Boasts."

Chapter 8. Don't Need Their Coal

1. Small-scale "hunting and gathering" societies have their problems, but exploitation based upon class position was generally muted.

2. Brown, "Global Warming Pushes."

3. Movements made by many: Holsaert et al., *Hands on the Freedom Plow;* Fisher, *Fighting Back in Appalachia.* Activists have invented hundreds of tactics: Engler and Engler, *This is an Uprising;* Sharp, *Waging Nonviolent Struggle.* Nonviolence works: Chenoweth and Stephan, *Why Civil Resistance Works.* Doesn't have to be a slog: Popovic, *Blueprint for Revolution;* Boyd and Mitchell, *Beautiful Trouble.*

4. Salstrom, "Newer Appalachia," 92.

5. There have been protest actions that lasted long enough to generate this feeling of a "different way of being." The Montgomery bus boycott, for example, endured for more than a year and depended on community members supporting each other in profound ways. Recent US examples include the Occupy Wall Street encampment and, notably, the protest against the Dakota Access Pipeline at Standing Rock, which galvanized Native groups all over North America.

6. By noting the difficulty of "measuring the efficacy" of this aspect of homesteading, I do not mean to imply it is less important or that there is little to say about it. Indeed, it forms the central concern of Rebecca Gould's excellent history of the back-to-the-land movement in New England, *At Home in Nature.*

7. Hanlon, "22% of Americans."

8. In *Apocalypse 2012,* published in 2007, author Lawrence Joseph argued that Berea would be one of the safest places to weather the coming collapse. "Of all the sacred sites in the world," he wrote, "none embodies the sacred Mayan values of service to humanity and Mother Earth like the town of Berea" (231–32).

9. Edwards and Plastina, "Grain Harvesting." These numbers aren't for fresh sweet corn but for field corn, which is a feedstock for industrial food production. Of course, the labor productivity of a combine harvester looks better if we ignore, as I have here, the labor of manufacturing, fueling, and maintaining it.

10. Fresh tomatoes are still picked by hand; tomatoes destined for ketchup and other processed foods have been bred for durability and are harvested mechanically.

11. For example, cultural ecologist Robert Netting, in *Smallholders, Householders,* reports that a pound of peasant-grown Chinese rice contains far more labor than a pound of rice grown with combines in Louisiana. But that pound of peasant rice also consumed so much less fossil fuel that it cost less energy, overall, to produce.

12. Scott, *Two Cheers,* 67.

13. There is a level between horses and full-sized skidders: for a few hundred to several thousand dollars, you can purchase a "skidder attachment" for a tractor. But you still need a healthy tractor, which is expensive, and you still need to cut road access for the tractor.

14. There are many other ways of categorizing economic activity, each useful in its own right; they are not mutually exclusive. Others include "primary, secondary, and tertiary production," "market versus non-market activities," and "formal versus informal."

15. Blaut, *Colonizer's Model.*

16. Schor, *Overworked,* introduction.

17. Ibid., 19.

18. Seaton reports similar stories from West Virginia in her lovely recent work, *Hippie Homesteaders.*

19. Cronon, "The Trouble with Wilderness."

20. Every landscape has become, as scholars phrase it, *anthropogenic,* which means "human produced" or "human caused." The point is well-taken, but since humans modify landscapes rather than create them, a more accurate term might be anthro-po*formic*—"human shaped."

21. Cameron, *Informal Sociology,* 13.

22. "Gus the bipolar polar bear" from Smith, "Zoos Drive Animals Crazy"; killer whales from Bowman, *Move Your DNA,* chapter 1; "unquenchable desire," ibid., introduction.

23. Driessnack, "Children."

24. Bowman, *Move Your DNA.*

25. Quote from Dotinga, "Average." Study itself is Archer et al., "Validation of a novel protocol."

26. Depression and anxiety: Williams, "This is Your Brain"; eyesight: Filip, "Near-sightedness"; bones demineralize: Schoutens et al., "Effects of inactivity"; microbial

ecosystems: Yong, *I Contain*. Note that labels like "asthma" or "irritable bowel syndrome" denote entire categories of disorder, rather than specific diseases with specific etiologies; some types of asthma have an auto-immune component, while others do not.

27. MacKay, *Sustainable Energy*, 53.

28. Nabhan, *Desert*, chapter 7.

29. Ibid., 93. Figs and pomegranates are not native, but they have been in the Americas for hundreds of years.

30. Amazon soils is Mann, *1491*, 344–49; "finest work of art," Mann, 344. For California Indians see Anderson, *Tending the Wild*.

31. Brand, *Last Whole Earth Catalog*, 2.

32. The creator and editor, Stewart Brand, graduated from that elite prep school, Phillips Exeter, I described in chapter 5—the one that shows how a real classroom works.

33. Norman, *Divine Right's Trip*, 43.

34. I focus on young men in this passage because they're particularly hard hit by this double dispossession. They struggle to make a good life anymore through sheer masculine effort, and they're more estranged from the bookish-professional route than young women. At many colleges, the ratio of women to men is three to two—and in many cases, the only reason it's not worse is because of quiet affirmative action on behalf of male applicants.

35. Brand, *Last Whole Earth Catalog*, 27.

Epilogue

1. Thompson, "Berkeley Landmarks." After Toad Hall, it became the Living Love Center, a place of nude meditation.

2. It hasn't always been called the Berkeley Student Cooperative; members have voted to change the name several times over the years.

3. The "peasant mode of production" is sometimes used, which is not bad—but you won't hear that outside of academia.

4. This lovely phrase is generally attributed to Proudhon, although I have not been able to find it in his writings.

5. Scott, *Two Cheers for Anarchism*, 46.

6. Brown, *Social Psychology*, 145; Scott, *Two Cheers for Anarchism*, 45.

7. Scott, *Two Cheers for Anarchism*, xxi.

8. The claim that the United States is a democracy reliably prompts—in a classroom, on the internet—the counterclaim that the United States is "not a democracy, it's a republic." Since a republic is a type of democracy, this counterclaim is a head-scratcher.

9. In a clear demonstration that elections matter, elites in the contemporary United States are mounting, as I write, sophisticated and expensive multipronged efforts to prevent certain categories of people from voting, especially blacks and college students. They shut down polling centers in neighborhoods and regions where people

of color reside. They refuse to designate a national holiday for elections. They shout "voter fraud!" to justify imposing ID requirements. They set up official-sounding robocalls that target certain voters, "informing" them that the date of the election has changed or directing them to the wrong polling place. See Berman, *Give Us the Ballot.*

Bibliography

"1898–1930 Sears Catalog Covers." Chicagology. Accessed August 5, 2018. https://chicagology.com/business/sears/searscatalogs01/.

Adler, William. *Mollie's Job: A Story of Life and Work on the Global Assembly Line.* New York: Scribner, 2001.

Agnew, Eleanor. *Back from the Land: How Young Americans Went to Nature in the 1970s, and Why They Came Back.* Chicago: Ivan R. Dee, 2004.

Allebaugh, Terry. "Disputanta Oral History Collection," 1978. Berea College Special Collections.

Alperovitz, Gar. *What Then Must We Do?: Straight Talk about the Next American Revolution.* White River Junction, Vt.: Chelsea Green, 2013.

Alterman, Eric, and George Zornick. "The Costs of Enforced Sexual Ignorance." Center for American Progress, May 8, 2008.

Anderson, Gerard, Uwe Reinhardt, Peter Hussey, and Varduhi Petrosyan. "It's the Prices, Stupid: Why the United States is so Different From Other Countries." *Health Affairs* 22, no. 3 (May 1, 2003): 89–105.

Anderson, Kat. *Tending the Wild: Native American Knowledge and the Management of California's Natural Resources.* Berkeley: University of California Press, 2006.

Anyon, Jean. "Social Class and School Knowledge." *Curriculum Inquiry* 11, no. 1 (1981): 3–42.

Appalachian Regional Commission. "Map of the Appalachian Region." Accessed March 1, 2018. https://www.arc.gov/appalachian_region/mapofappalachia.asp.

Archer, Edward, Gregory Hand, James Hébert, Erica Lau, Xuewen Wang, Robin Shook, Raja Fayad, Carl Lavie, and Steven Blair. "Validation of a Novel Protocol for Calculating Estimated Energy Requirements and Average Daily Physical Activity Ratio for the US Population." *Mayo Clinic Proceedings* 88, no. 12 (December 1, 2013): 1398–1407.

"Are Too Many Students Going to College?" *Chronicle of Higher Education*, November 8, 2009.

Arrington, Benjamin. "Industry and Economy during the Civil War." In *The Civil War Remembered*. National Park Service, n.d. Accessed August 13, 2017.

The Associated Press and Ipsos Public Affairs. "One in Four Adults Read No Books Last Year," 2007. https://tinyurl.com/y4ytmdpj.

Bagemihl, Bruce. *Biological Exuberance: Animal Homosexuality and Natural Diversity*. New York: St. Martin's, 2000.

Balmer, Randall. *Thy Kingdom Come: How the Religious Right Distorts Faith and Threatens America*. New York: Basic Books, 2007.

Barclay, Eliza. "'Mountain Dew Mouth' Is Destroying Appalachia's Teeth, Critics Say." *National Public Radio*, September 19, 2013.

Batteau, Allen. *The Invention of Appalachia*. Tucson: University of Arizona Press, 1990.

Baum, Dan. "The Man Who Took My Job." *Rolling Stone*, April 27, 2000.

Baumann, Robert. "Changes in the Appalachian Wage Gap, 1970 to 2000." *Growth and Change* 37, no. 3 (September 1, 2006): 416–43.

Beaver, Patricia. *Rural Community in the Appalachian South*. Long Grove, Ill.: Waveland, 1992.

Berman, Ari. *Give Us the Ballot: The Modern Struggle for Voting Rights in America*. New York: Farrar, Straus and Giroux, 2015.

Berry, Chad. *Southern Migrants, Northern Exiles*. Urbana: University of Illinois Press, 2000.

Berry, Wendell. *Bringing It to the Table: On Farming and Food*. Berkeley, Calif.: Counterpoint, 2009.

Billings, Dwight, and Kathleen Blee. *The Road to Poverty: The Making of Wealth and Hardship in Appalachia*. New York: Cambridge University Press, 2000.

Bittman, Mark. "Is Junk Food Really Cheaper?" *New York Times*, September 24, 2011.

Black, Kate. "Kentucky Garden Stories: Planting Resistance." *Journal of Appalachian Studies* 16, no. 1 (2010): 122–30.

Blaut, James. *The Colonizer's Model of the World: Geographical Diffusionism and Eurocentric History*. New York: Guilford, 2012.

Block, Brian, and John Hostettler. *Hanging in the Balance: A History of the Abolition of Capital Punishment in Britain*. Sherfield-on-Loddon, U.K.: Waterside, 1997.

Boal, Iain, Janferie Stone, Michael Watts, and Cal Winslow, eds. *West of Eden: Communes and Utopia in Northern California*. Oakland, Calif.: PM Press, 2012.

Bourdieu, Pierre. *Distinction: A Social Critique of the Judgement of Taste*. Cambridge, Mass.: Harvard University Press, 1984.

Bourne, Edward Gaylord, ed. *Narratives of the Career of Hernando de Soto in the Conquest of Florida*. New York: A. S. Barnes, 1904.

Bowles, Samuel, Richard Edwards, and Frank Roosevelt. *Understanding Capitalism: Competition, Command, and Change*. New York: Oxford University Press, 2005.

Bowman, Katy. *Move Your DNA: Restore Your Health Through Natural Movement*. Sequim, Wash.: Propriometrics Press, 2017.

Boyd, Andrew, and Dave Oswald Mitchell. *Beautiful Trouble: A Toolbox for Revolution*. New York: OR Books, 2016.

Bradshaw, Tom, Bonnie Nichols, and Kelly Hill. "Reading At Risk: A Survey of Literary Reading in America." Washington, D.C.: National Endowment for the Arts, 2004.

Branagh, Kenneth. *Thor*. Paramount, 2011.

Brand, Stewart, ed. *The Last Whole Earth Catalog: Access to Tools*. Menlo Park, Calif.: Portola Institute, 1971.

Brechin, Gray. *Imperial San Francisco: Urban Power, Earthly Ruin*. Berkeley: University of California Press, 2006.

Breines, Wini. *Community and Organization in the New Left, 1962–1968: The Great Refusal*. New Brunswick, N.J.: Rutgers University Press, 1989.

Brown, Dona. *Back to the Land: The Enduring Dream of Self-Sufficiency in Modern America*. Madison: University of Wisconsin Press, 2011.

Brown, James. *Beech Creek: A Study of a Kentucky Mountain Neighborhood*. Berea, Ky.: Berea College Press, 1988.

Brown, James. *The Social Psychology of Industry*. New York: Penguin Books, 1961.

Brown, Sarah. "Global Warming Pushes Maple Trees, Syrup to the Brink." *National Geographic*, December 2, 2015.

Bui, Quoctrung. "50 Years of Shrinking Union Membership, In One Map." NPR.org, February 23, 2015.

Bureau of Labor Statistics. "Quarterly Census of Employment and Wages." Washington, D.C., 2012.

Bureau of Labor Statistics. "Union Members Summary," January 19, 2018. https://tinyurl.com/z5mm20a.

Cameron, William Bruce. *Informal Sociology: A Casual Introduction to Sociological Thinking*. New York: Random House, 1963.

Centers for Disease Control. "Achievements in Public Health, 1900–1999: Family Planning." *Morbidity and Mortality Weekly Report* 48, no. 47 (December 3, 1999).

Channing, Steven. *Kentucky: A Bicentennial History*. New York: Norton, 1977.

Chapman University. "What Do Americans Fear?" *ScienceDaily*, October 12, 2016.

Chenoweth, Erica, and Maria Stephan. *Why Civil Resistance Works: The Strategic Logic of Nonviolent Conflict*. New York: Columbia University Press, 2012.

"Cigarette Smoking Among Adults—United States, 2006." Accessed February 17, 2018. https://www.cdc.gov/mmwr/preview/mmwrhtml/mm5644a2.htm.

Cobb, James Charles. *The Selling of the South: The Southern Crusade for Industrial Development 1936–1990*. Urbana: University of Illinois Press, 1993.

Collier, Aine. *The Humble Little Condom: A History*. Amherst, N.Y.: Prometheus, 2007.

"Common Core of Data; Build a Table." National Center for Education Statistics; US Department of Education, 2012.

"Consumer Guide: Catalog No. 104." Chicago: Sears, Roebuck, 1897.

Couto, Richard. "Appalachia." In *Appalachia: Social Context Past and Present*, edited by Phillip Obermiller and Michael Maloney. Dubuque, Iowa: Kendall/Hunt, 2002.

Coyote, Peter. *Sleeping Where I Fall: A Chronicle*. Berkeley, Calif.: Counterpoint, 1999.

Crain, Caleb. "Why We Don't Read, Revisited." *New Yorker*, June 14, 2018.

"Credit Union Data and Statistics." Credit Union National Association. Accessed August 8, 2018. https://tinyurl.com/y6k9qpya.

Cronon, William, ed. "The Trouble with Wilderness." In *Uncommon Ground: Rethinking the Human Place in Nature*. New York: W. W. Norton, 1996.

Crosby, Alfred. *Ecological Imperialism: The Biological Expansion of Europe, 900–1900*. New York: Cambridge University Press, 2004.

Cunningham, Anne, and Keith Stanovich. "What Reading Does for the Mind." *American Educator* 22 (1998).

Curl, John. *For All the People: Uncovering the Hidden History of Cooperation, Cooperative Movements, and Communalism in America*. Oakland, Calif.: PM Press, 2012.

Cwiek, Sarah. "The Middle Class Took Off 100 Years Ago . . . Thanks To Henry Ford?" *All Things Considered*. NPR, January 27, 2014.

Daloz, Kate. *We Are as Gods: Back to the Land in the 1970s on the Quest for a New America*. New York: PublicAffairs, 2016.

Davis, Donald Edward. *Where There Are Mountains: An Environmental History of the Southern Appalachians*. Athens: University of Georgia Press, 2000.

Dean, Cornelia. "Scientific Savvy? In US, Not Much." *New York Times*, August 30, 2005.

Del Giudice, Vincent, and Wei Lu. "Palm Beach Boasts Trump's Mar-a-Lago, Most US Passive Income." *Bloomberg*, April 12, 2017.

Deller, Steven, Ann Hoyt, Brent Hueth, and Reka Sundaram-Stukel. "Research on the Economic Impact of Cooperatives." University of Wisconsin Center for Cooperatives, June 19, 2009.

Desmond, Matthew. *Evicted: Poverty and Profit in the American City*. New York: Crown, 2016.

Dews, C. L. *This Fine Place So Far from Home: Voices of Academics from the Working Class*. Philadelphia: Temple University Press, 2010.

Dickinson, Tim. "How Roger Ailes Built the Fox News Fear Factory." *Rolling Stone*, May 25, 2011.

Dillon, Sam. "Literacy Falls for Graduates from College, Testing Finds." *New York Times*, December 16, 2005.

"DirecTV-14—Spacecraft and Satellites." Accessed May 15, 2018. https://tinyurl.com/y5zy2wbs.

Dotinga, Randy. "Average Obese Woman Gets Just 1 Hour of Exercise a Year." *HealthDay*, February 20, 2014.

Draper, Lyman Copeland. *The Life of Daniel Boone*. Mechanicsburg, Pa.: Stackpole, 1998.

Driessnack, Martha. "Children and Nature-Deficit Disorder." *Journal for Specialists in Pediatric Nursing* 14, no. 1 (January 12, 2009): 73–75.

Drummond, Steve. "Keeping Watch on the Home Front." *Michigan Alumnus*, August 24, 2015.

Dunaway, Wilma A. *The First American Frontier: Transition to Capitalism in Southern Appalachia, 1700–1860*. Chapel Hill: University of North Carolina Press, 2000.

Dynarski, Susan. "For the Poor, the Graduation Gap Is Even Wider than the Enrollment Gap." *New York Times*, June 2, 2015.

Edwards, William, and Alejandro Plastina. "Grain Harvesting Equipment and Labor in Iowa." Iowa State University Extension and Outreach, June 2016.

"Election Results: Ballot Measures/Kentucky Amendment 1." CNN.com. Accessed July 14, 2018. https://tinyurl.com/y5lk48qd.

Eller, Ronald. *Miners, Millhands, and Mountaineers: Industrialization of the Appalachian South, 1880–1930*. Knoxville: University of Tennessee Press, 1982.

———. *Uneven Ground: Appalachia since 1945*. Lexington: University Press of Kentucky, 2008.

Elliott, Larry. "World's Eight Richest People Have Same Wealth as Poorest 50%." *Guardian*, January 16, 2017.

Ellis, Normandi. "Sam Hurst Touches on a Few Great Ideas." *Berea College Magazine*, Spring 2007.

Ellis, William, Hank Everman, and Richard Sears. *Madison County: 200 Years in Retrospect*. Richmond, Ky.: Madison County Historical Society, 1985.

Engels, Friedrich. *The Condition of the Working Class in England*. Oxford, U.K.: Oxford University Press, 1993.

Engler, Mark, and Paul Engler. *This Is an Uprising: How Nonviolent Revolt Is Shaping the Twenty-First Century*. New York: Nation, 2016.

Estep, Bill. "'Not Enough Jobs.' Nine of the 30 Poorest Counties in U.S. Are in Eastern Kentucky." *Lexington Herald Leader*, December 3, 2017.

Etehad, Melissa, and Kyle Kim. "The U.S. Spends More on Healthcare than Any Other Country—but Not with Better Health Outcomes." *Los Angeles Times*, July 18, 2017.

Evans, Ben. *Nerve: How a Small Kentucky Town Led the Fight to Safely Dismantle the World's Chemical Weapons*, 2015.

Fairlie, Simon. "A Short History of Enclosure in Britain." *The Land* 7 (2009): 16–31.

Fels, Thomas Weston. *Buying the Farm: Peace and War on a Sixties Commune*. Amherst: University of Massachusetts Press, 2012.

Fields, Scott. "The Fat of the Land: Do Agricultural Subsidies Foster Poor Health?" *Environmental Health Perspectives* 112, no. 14 (October 2004): A820–23.

Filip, Iulia. "Nearsightedness and the Indoor Life." *Atlantic*, May 2, 2014.

Finn, Patrick. *Literacy with an Attitude: Educating Working-Class Children in Their Own Self-Interest*. 2nd ed. Albany: State University of New York Press, 2009.

Finnegan, William. "Leasing the Rain: The World Is Running out of Fresh Water, and the Fight to Control It Has Begun." *New Yorker*, April 8, 2002.

Fisher, Stephen, ed. *Fighting Back in Appalachia: Traditions of Resistance and Change*. Philadelphia: Temple University Press, 1993.

Frost, Robert. *The Poetry of Robert Frost: The Collected Poems*. New York: Macmillan, 2002.

Fung, Archon, and Erik Olin Wright. *Deepening Democracy: Institutional Innovations in Empowered Participatory Governance*. New York: Verso, 2003.

Gandhi, Mohandas K. *An Autobiography: The Story of My Experiments with Truth*. Boston: Beacon, 1993.

Gartrell, Nanette, Henny Bos, and Naomi Goldberg. "Adolescents of the U.S. National Longitudinal Lesbian Family Study: Sexual Orientation, Sexual Behavior, and Sexual Risk Exposure." *Archives of Sexual Behavior* 40, no. 6 (December 2011): 1199–1209.

Gaventa, John. *Power and Powerlessness: Quiescence and Rebellion in an Appalachian Valley*. Urbana: University of Illinois Press, 1982.

Gilbert, Ben. "Why Tesla Motors Can't Sell Cars in Most of the United States." *Engadget*, July 17, 2014. https://tinyurl.com/y6gxzuwj.

Glass, Jennifer, and Philip Levchak. "Red States, Blue States, and Divorce: Understanding the Impact of Conservative Protestantism on Regional Variation in Divorce Rates." *American Journal of Sociology* 119, no. 4 (January 1, 2014): 1002–46.

Gould, Rebecca. *At Home in Nature: Modern Homesteading and Spiritual Practice in America*. Berkeley: University of California Press, 2005.

Green, Penelope. "Where Tiny Houses and Big Dreams Grow." *New York Times*, September 23, 2015.

Hacker, Jacob, and Paul Pierson. *Winner-Take-All Politics: How Washington Made the Rich Richer—and Turned Its Back on the Middle Class*. New York: Simon and Schuster, 2010.

Halperin, Rhoda. *The Livelihood of Kin: Making Ends Meet "The Kentucky Way."* Austin: University of Texas Press, 2013.

Hancock, LynNell. "Why Are Finland's Schools Successful?" *Smithsonian*, September 2011.

Hanisch, Carol. "The Personal Is Political." In *Notes from the Second Year: Women's Liberation*, edited by Shulamith Firestone and Anne Koedt. New York: Radical Feminism, 1970.

Hanlon, Chris. "22% of Americans Believe World Will End in Their Lifetime." *Daily Mail* (Canada), May 2, 2012.

Harkinson, Josh. "How the Nation's Only State-Owned Bank Became the Envy of Wall Street." *Mother Jones*, March 28, 2009.

Hart, Betty, and Todd Risley. "The Early Catastrophe: The 30 Million Word Gap by Age 3." *American Educator* 27, no. 1 (2003): 4–9.

Hatcher, Robert. "Appalachians and Little Tennessee River Geologic History, Occasional Paper No. 23." Knoxville, Tenn.: McClung Museum of Natural History and Culture, n.d. Accessed August 4, 2018.

Heath, Shirley Brice. *Ways with Words: Language, Life and Work in Communities and Classrooms*. New York: Cambridge University Press, 1983.

Herek, Gregory. "Facts About Homosexuality and Child Molestation." Accessed July 25, 2018. https://tinyurl.com/lxar.

Hirschman, Elizabeth. *Branding Masculinity: Tracing the Cultural Foundations of Brand Meaning*. New York: Routledge, 2016.

"Historical Census Browser." University of Virginia Library, n.d. https://mapserver.lib.virginia.edu/.

Hitchens, Christopher. "Where Aquarius Went." *New York Times*, December 19, 2004.

Hoffman, Jan. "A Dose of a Hallucinogen From a 'Magic Mushroom,' and Then Lasting Peace." *New York Times*, December 1, 2016.

Holsaert, Faith, Martha Prescod, Norman Noonan, Judy Richardson, Betty Garman Robinson, Jean Smith Young, and Dorothy Zellner. *Hands on the Freedom Plow: Personal Accounts by Women in SNCC*. Urbana: University of Illinois Press, 2010.

Howell, Joseph. *Hard Living on Clay Street: Portraits of Blue Collar Families*. Long Grove, Ill.: Waveland, 1991.

Hoyt, William. "An Evaluation of the Kentucky Education Reform Act." In *Kentucky Annual Economic Report*, 21. Lexington: University of Kentucky, 1999.

The International Bank for Reconstruction and Development. *World Development Report 2006: Equity and Development*. New York: World Bank and Oxford University Press, 2005.

Ironmonger, Duncan. "Counting Outputs, Capital Inputs and Caring Labor: Estimating Gross Household Product." *Feminist Economics* 2, no. 3 (1996): 37–64.

Isaacs, Stephen, and Steven Schroeder. "Class—the Ignored Determinant of the Nation's Health." *New England Journal of Medicine* 351, no. 11 (2004): 1137.

Jacob, Jeffrey. *New Pioneers: The Back-to-the-Land Movement and the Search for a Sustainable Future*. University Park: Penn State University Press, 1997.

Jefferson, Thomas. *Notes on the State of Virginia*. Chapel Hill: University of North Carolina Press, 2011.

Jha, Prabhat, Chinthanie Ramasundarahettige, Victoria Landsman, Brian Rostron, Michael Thun, Robert Anderson, Tim McAfee, and Richard Peto. "21st-Century Hazards of Smoking and Benefits of Cessation in the United States." *New England Journal of Medicine* 368, no. 4 (January 23, 2013): 341–50.

Johnson, David. *The Lavender Scare: The Cold War Persecution of Gays and Lesbians in the Federal Government*. Chicago: University of Chicago Press, 2009.

Johnson, Sally. "Excesses Blamed for Demise of the Commune Movement." *New York Times*, August 3, 1998.

Johnson, Stephen. "Want Less Car Accidents? Remove Traffic Signals and Road Signs." *Big Think*, August 31, 2017.

Jones, Maldwyn. "Scotch-Irish." In *Harvard Encyclopedia of American Ethnic Groups*, edited by Stephan Thernstrom. Cambridge, Mass.: Belknap, 1980.

Jordan, Tim. "Washington Monthly Ranks Berea No. 1 Twice; As Best National Liberal Arts College and Best Bang for the Buck." *Berea College*, August 29, 2017.

Joseph, Lawrence. *Apocalypse 2012: A Scientific Investigation into Civilization's End*. New York: Morgan Road, 2007.

Kains, Maurice. *Five Acres and Independence: A Practical Guide to the Selection and Management of the Small Farm*. New York: Greenberg, 1945.

Kates, Joanne. "Yuppies Have Shed Their Hippie Eating Habits." *Globe and Mail* (Canada), July 24, 1985.

Kelly, Marjorie. *The Divine Right of Capital: Dethroning the Corporate Aristocracy*. Oakland, Calif.: Berrett-Koehler, 2001.

———. *Owning Our Future: The Emerging Ownership Revolution*. Oakland, Calif.: Berrett-Koehler, 2012.

Kentucky Historical Society. "Index for Old Kentucky Surveys and Grants," 1975.

Khazan, Olga. "Kentucky Is Home to the Greatest Declines in Life Expectancy." *Atlantic*, May 8, 2017.

Kincaid, Robert. *The Wilderness Road*. Indianapolis, Ind.: Bobbs-Merrill, 1947.

King, Martin Luther, Jr. "Letter from a Birmingham Jail." *Liberation* 8, no. 4 (1963).

Klein, Ezra. "Why an MRI Costs $1,080 in America and $280 in France." *Washington Post*, March 3, 2012.

Kolata, Gina. "A Surprising Secret to a Long Life: Stay in School." *New York Times*, January 3, 2007.

Kolbert, Elizabeth. *The Sixth Extinction: An Unnatural History*. New York: Henry Holt, 2014.

Kozol, Jonathan. *Savage Inequalities: Children in America's Schools*. New York: HarperCollins, 1991.

Kubey, Robert, and Mihaly Csikszentmihalyi. "Television Addiction Is No Mere Metaphor." *Scientific American*, 2002.

Kurtzleben, Danielle. "While Trump Touts Stock Market, Many Americans Are Left Out of the Conversation." *NPR*, March 1, 2017.

Lacey, Stephen. "Drift Is a New Startup Applying Peer-to-Peer Trading to Retail Electricity Markets." Green Tech Media, May 31, 2017.

Lapowsky, Issie. "Free Money: The Surprising Effects of a Basic Income Supplied by Government." *Wired*, November 12, 2017.

Lareau, Annette. *Unequal Childhoods: Class, Race, and Family Life*. Berkeley: University of California Press, 2003.

Latson, Jennifer. "The Invention That Spawned a Fashion Revolution." *Time*, August 12, 2015.

Lavigne, Yves. "A Real Tough Row to How: Is the Back-to-the-Land Movement Ploughed Under?" *Globe and Mail* (Canada). June 23, 1984.

Lemieux, Paul, Christopher Lutes, Judith Abbott, and Kenneth Aldous. "Emissions of Polychlorinated Dibenzo-p-Dioxins and Polychlorinated Dibenzofurans from the Open Burning of Household Waste in Barrels." *Environmental Science and Technology* 34, no. 3 (February 1, 2000): 377–84.

Lewis, Helen Matthews, Linda Johnson, and Donald Askins. *Colonialism in Modern America: The Appalachian Case*. Boone, N.C.: Appalachian State University, 1978.

Lewis, Michael. *Liar's Poker: Rising Through the Wreckage on Wall Street*. New York: W. W. Norton, 1989.

Lynch, John. "The Average American Watches so Much TV It's Almost a Full-Time Job." *Business Insider*, June 28, 2016.

MacKay, David. *Sustainable Energy: Without the Hot Air.* Cambridge, U.K.: UIT Cambridge, 2009.

MacKenzie, Debora. "More Education Is What Makes People Live Longer, Not More Money." *New Scientist,* April 18, 2018.

Madrick, Jeff. "Why Mainstream Economists Should Take Heed." *Feminist Economics* 3, no. 1 (1997): 143–49.

Manchester, William. *A World Lit Only by Fire: The Medieval Mind and the Renaissance—Portrait of an Age.* New York: Little, Brown, 2009.

Mann, Charles. *1491: New Revelations of the Americas Before Columbus.* 2nd ed. New York: Vintage, 2006.

Marçal, Katrine. *Who Cooked Adam Smith's Dinner?: A Story of Women and Economics.* New York: Pegasus, 2016.

Marshall, Robert. "The Dark Legacy of Carlos Castaneda." *Salon,* April 12, 2007. https://www.salon.com/2007/04/12/castaneda/.

Marx, Karl. *Capital: Volume 1.* New York: Penguin Classics, 1990.

Mayer, Jane. *Dark Money: The Hidden History of the Billionaires Behind the Rise of the Radical Right.* New York: Knopf Doubleday, 2016.

Mazzucato, Mariana. *The Entrepreneurial State: Debunking Public Vs. Private Sector Myths.* New York: Anthem, 2015.

McFarland, Melanie. "Master Deceivers: When Roger Ailes Met Richard Nixon." *Salon,* May 18, 2017.

McNeill, William. *Plagues and Peoples.* New York: Anchor, 1998.

Mendel-Reyes, Meta. *Reclaiming Democracy: The Sixties in Politics and Memory.* New York: Routledge, 2013.

"Mercedes Innovation: The Crumple Zone in 1952." Motor1.com, July 10, 2009.

Michaels, Marguerite. "Billy Graham: America Is Not God's Only Kingdom." *Parade,* February 1, 1981.

Milar, Katharine. "The Myth Buster." *Monitor on Psychology* 42, no. 2 (February 2011).

Miller, Timothy. *The Hippies and American Values.* Knoxville: University of Tennessee Press, 1991.

Minton, Henry. *Departing from Deviance: A History of Homosexual Rights and Emancipatory Science in America.* Chicago: University of Chicago Press, 2002.

Mitchell, Stacy. "How One State Escaped Wall Street's Rule and Created a Banking System That's 83% Locally Owned." Institute for Local Self-Reliance, September 1, 2015.

More, Thomas. *Utopia.* Ware, Hertfordshire, U.K.: Wordsworth, 1997.

Morford, Mark. "The Hippies Were Right!" *San Francisco Chronicle,* May 2, 2007.

Morgan, Robert. *Boone: A Biography.* Chapel Hill, N.C.: Algonquin, 2008.

Mosher, Dave, and Skye Gould. "How Likely Are Foreign Terrorists to Kill Americans? The Odds May Surprise You." *Business Insider,* January 31, 2017.

Moskowitz, Peter. "Chattanooga Was a Typical Postindustrial City. Then It Began Offering Municipal Broadband." *Nation,* June 3, 2016.

Motavalli, Jim. "Zero Factory Waste: Automakers Save Money, and Rake in Green PR." CBS News, August 18, 2011.

Mungo, Raymond. *Total Loss Farm: A Year in the Life.* New York: E. P. Dutton, 1970.

Nabhan, Gary Paul. *The Desert Smells Like Rain: A Naturalist in O'odham Country.* Tucson: University of Arizona Press, 2016.

National Center for Employee Ownership. "A Statistical Profile of Employee Ownership." Accessed February 20, 2019.

Negin, Elliott. "ExxonMobil Is Still Funding Climate Science Denier Groups." *Huffington Post,* July 13, 2016. https://tinyurl.com/y43acn6v.

Nembhard, Jessica Gordon. *Collective Courage: A History of African American Cooperative Economic Thought and Practice.* University Park: Penn State University Press, 2014.

Netting, Robert. *Smallholders, Householders: Farm Families and the Ecology of Intensive, Sustainable Agriculture.* Stanford, Calif.: Stanford University Press, 1993.

Nilsson, Jeff. "Why Did Henry Ford Double His Minimum Wage?" *Saturday Evening Post,* January 3, 2014.

Niman, Michael. *People of the Rainbow: A Nomadic Utopia.* Knoxville: University of Tennessee Press, 1997.

Norman, Gurney. "Divine Right's Trip: A Novel of the Counterculture." In *The Last Whole Earth Catalog,* edited by Stewart Brand. Menlo Park, Calif.: Portola Institute, 1971.

Ong, Walter. *Orality and Literacy: The Technologizing of the Word.* New York: Methuen, 1982.

Oreskes, Naomi, and Erik Conway. *Merchants of Doubt: How a Handful of Scientists Obscured the Truth on Issues from Tobacco Smoke to Global Warming.* New York: Bloomsbury, 2010.

Ostrom, Elinor. *Governing the Commons.* New York: Cambridge University Press, 2015.

Otto, Mary. *Teeth: The Story of Beauty, Inequality, and the Struggle for Oral Health in America.* New York: The New Press, 2017.

Patterson, Clint. "A Century of Forestry at Berea College." Berea, Ky.: Berea College Printing Services, 2013.

Pencavel, John. *Worker Participation: Lessons from Worker Co-Ops of the Pacific Northwest.* New York: Russell Sage, 2002.

Pérotin, Virginie. "What Do We Really Know about Worker Co-Operatives?" Cooperatives UK, n.d. https://tinyurl.com/yxkb6fdw.

"Perverts Called Government Peril; Gabrielson, G.O.P. Chief, Says They Are as Dangerous as Reds." *New York Times,* April 19, 1950.

The Pew Charitable Trusts. "Household Expenditures and Income," March 2016.

Piketty, Thomas. *Capital in the Twenty-First Century.* Cambridge, Mass.: Harvard University Press, 2014.

Popovic, Srdja. *Blueprint for Revolution: How to Use Rice Pudding, Lego Men, and Other Nonviolent Techniques to Galvanize Communities, Overthrow Dictators, or Simply Change the World.* New York: Random House, 2015.

Pratten, Clifford. "The Manufacture of Pins." *Journal of Economic Literature* 18, no. 1 (1980): 93–96.

Price, Roberta. *Huerfano: A Memoir of Life in the Counterculture*. Amherst: University of Massachusetts Press, 2006.

"Quick Facts About Nonprofits." National Center for Charitable Statistics. Accessed August 14, 2017.

Raskin, Sam. "Nancy Pelosi to Leftist NYU Student: We're Capitalists, Deal with It." *NYU Local*, February 1, 2017.

Reece, Erik. "Cleveland Model Could Work in E. Ky. by Keeping Wealth in Workers' Hands." *Lexington Herald Leader*, March 16, 2014.

Reece, Erik, and James Krupa. *The Embattled Wilderness: The Natural and Human History of Robinson Forest and the Fight for Its Future*. Athens: University of Georgia Press, 2013.

Reich, Robert. *Saving Capitalism: For the Many, Not the Few*. New York: Vintage, 2016.

Renner, Jeff. "Daniel Boone's Station Camp." Accessed August 1, 2018. https://tiny url.com/y66x9rqn.

Restakis, John. *Humanizing the Economy: Co-Operatives in the Age of Capital*. Gabriola Island, Canada: New Society, 2010.

Reynolds, David. *Taking the High Road: Communities Organize for Economic Change*. Armonk, N.Y.: M. E. Sharpe, 2002.

"Richard W. Sears (1863–1914)." Sears Archives, March 21, 2012. http://www.searsarchives .com/people/richardsears.htm.

Ridley, Matt. *The Evolution of Everything: How New Ideas Emerge*. New York: HarperCollins, 2015.

Roach, Mary. *Bonk: The Curious Coupling of Science and Sex*. New York: W.W. Norton, 2009.

Robb, Amanda. "Pizzagate: Anatomy of a Fake News Scandal." *Rolling Stone*, November 16, 2017.

Roberts, Rachel. "Russia Targeted Key States with Anti-Clinton Fake News, Trump-Russia Hearings Chairman Reveals." *Independent*, March 30, 2017.

Rock, V. J., A. Malarcher, J. W. Kahende, K. Asman, C. Huston, and R. Caraballo. "Cigarette Smoking Among Adults—United States, 2006." *Morbidity and Mortality Weekly Report / Centers for Disease Control* 56, no. 44 (November 9, 2007): 1157–61.

Rubin, Lillian. *Worlds of Pain: Life in The Working-Class Family*. New York: Basic Books, 1976.

Ryan, Jake, and Charles Sackrey. *Strangers in Paradise: Academics from the Working Class*. Lanham, Md.: University Press of America, 1996.

Ryen, Dag. "Cherokee." In *The Kentucky Encyclopedia*, edited by John E. Kleber. Lexington: University Press of Kentucky, 1992.

Salstrom, Paul. "Newer Appalachia as One of America's Last Frontiers." In *Appalachia in the Making: The Mountain South in the Nineteenth Century*, edited by Mary Beth Pudup, Dwight Billings, and Altina Waller. Chapel Hill: University of North Carolina Press, 2000.

———. "The Neonatives: Back-to-the-Land in Appalachia's 1970's." *Appalachian Journal* 30, no. 4 (2003): 308–23.

Sayer, Andrew, and Richard Walker. *The New Social Economy: Reworking the Division of Labor.* Hoboken, N.J.: Wiley, 1992.

Schiavo, Anthony, and Claudio Salvucci. *Iroquois Wars I: Extracts from the Jesuit Relations and Primary Sources from 1535 to 1650.* Pennsauken Township, N.J.: Arx, 2003.

Schlanger, Zoë. "It's Not Just Volkswagen. Every Diesel Car Company Is Emitting More Pollution than Tests Show." *Quartz,* May 18, 2017. https://tinyurl.com/y459c9sm.

Schnurer, Eric. "When Government Competes Against the Private Sector, Everybody Wins." *Atlantic,* March 11, 2015.

Schor, Juliet. "The (Even More) Overworked American." In *Take Back Your Time: Fighting Overwork and Time Poverty in America,* edited by John De Graaf. San Francisco: Berrett-Koehler, 2003.

———. *The Overworked American: The Unexpected Decline of Leisure.* New York: Basic Books, 1993.

Schoutens, A., E. Laurent, and J. R. Poortmans. "Effects of Inactivity and Exercise on Bone." *Sports Medicine* 7, no. 2 (February 1989): 71–81.

Scott, James. *Two Cheers for Anarchism: Six Easy Pieces on Autonomy, Dignity, and Meaningful Work and Play.* Princeton, N.J.: Princeton University Press, 2012.

Seaton, Carter Taylor. *Hippie Homesteaders: Arts, Crafts, Music and Living on the Land in West Virginia.* Morgantown: West Virginia University Press, 2014.

Selin, Noelle. "One of the Biggest Consequences of the Volkswagen Diesel Scandal." *Fortune,* September 30, 2015.

Shapiro, Henry. *Appalachia on Our Mind: The Southern Mountains and Mountaineers in the American Consciousness, 1870–1920.* Chapel Hill: University of North Carolina Press, 1986.

Sharp, Gene. *Waging Nonviolent Struggle: 20th Century Practice and 21st Century Potential.* Manchester, N.H.: Extending Horizons, 2005.

Sherman, Gabriel. *The Loudest Voice in the Room: How the Brilliant, Bombastic Roger Ailes Built Fox News—and Divided a Country.* New York: Random House, 2014.

Sieber, R. Timothy. "The Politics of Middle-Class Success in an Inner-City Public School." *Journal of Education* (1982): 30–47.

Silver-Greenberg, Jessica, and Robert Gebeloff. "Arbitration Everywhere, Stacking the Deck of Justice." *New York Times,* October 31, 2015.

Singh, Gitanjali, Renata Micha, Shahab Khatibzadeh, Stephen Lim, Majid Ezzati, and Dariush Mozaffarian. "Estimated Global, Regional, and National Disease Burdens Related to Sugar-Sweetened Beverage Consumption in 2010." *Circulation* 132, no. 8 (2015): 639–66.

Slonecker, Blake. *A New Dawn for the New Left: Liberation News Service, Montague Farm, and the Long Sixties.* New York: Palgrave Macmillan, 2012.

Smith, Adam. *The Wealth of Nations*. New York: Bantam Dell, 2003.

Smith, Brendan. "The Case against Spanking." *Moniter on Psychology* 43, no. 4 (April 2012): 60.

Smith, Laura. "Zoos Drive Animals Crazy." *Slate*, June 20, 2014.

Smith, Mark. "Show, Don't Tell: How Video Is Swamping the Internet." *BBC News*, March 11, 2016.

Smith, Stephen. "Radio: The Internet of the 1930s." *American RadioWorks*, November 10, 2014.

Spence, Robert. "Annual Report . . . Rockcastle and Southern Madison Counties." Berea, Ky.: Berea College Special Collections, 1956.

Stevens, Heidi. "'Dr. Spock's Baby and Child Care' Empowered, Encouraged Parents." *Chicago Tribune*, January 6, 2012.

Stewart, Emily. "Study: Conservatives Amplified Russian Trolls 30 Times More Often than Liberals in 2016." *Vox*, February 24, 2018.

Stiglitz, Joseph. *The Price of Inequality: How Today's Divided Society Endangers Our Future*. New York: W. W. Norton, 2012.

Stinson, Elizabeth. "Check Out Fox News' Insane $30M Election Day Studio." *Wired*, November 8, 2016.

Tarrow, Sidney. *Power in Movement: Social Movements and Contentious Politics*. New York: Cambridge University Press, 1998.

Tate, Curtis. "Another Ailes Legacy: Helping Underdog McConnell Win His 1st Senate Race." *McClatchy DC Bureau*, May 18, 2017.

Thompson, Daniella. "Berkeley Landmarks: Theta Xi Chapter House." Berkeley Architectural Heritage Association, n.d. Accessed July 3, 2018.

Thompson, Edward Palmer. *Whigs and Hunters: The Origin of the Black Act*. New York: Pantheon, 1975.

Thoreau, Henry David. *Walden: Or, Life in the Woods*. New York: T.Y. Crowell, 1899.

Turman-Deal, Jinny. "'We Were an Oddity': A Look at the Back-to-the-Land Movement in Appalachia." *West Virginia History* 4, no. 1 (2010): 1–32.

US Census Bureau. "Bicentennial Edition: Historical Statistics of the United States, Colonial Times to 1970," September 1975.

US Census Bureau. "CPS Historical Time Series Tables." Accessed March 4, 2019. https://tinyurl.com/y66bc8lh.

US Census Bureau. "Census Explorer." Accessed August 5, 2018. https://www.census.gov/censusexplorer/censusexplorer.html.

US Census Bureau. "Median and Average Sales Prices of New Homes Sold in United States," n.d. https://tinyurl.com/mgajjr9.

US Department of Commerce. "2015 Characteristics of New Housing," 2015.

Veblen, Thorstein. *The Theory of the Leisure Class: An Economic Study of Institutions*. New York: B. W. Huebsch, 1912.

Virginia General Assembly. Special Grant of Land (1778). https://tinyurl.com/yypjca60.

Wallis, Jim. "From a Shoebox to a Movement." *Sojourners*, November 1, 2011.

Watts, Michael. "1968 and All That . . ." *Progress in Human Geography* 25, no. 2 (2001): 157–88.

Weis, Lois. *Working Class Without Work: High School Students in a De-Industrializing Economy*. New York: Routledge, 1990.

Weisman, Alan. *The World Without Us*. New York: Macmillan, 2007.

White, Gillian. "Escaping Poverty Requires Almost 20 Years with Nearly Nothing Going Wrong." *Atlantic*, April 27, 2017.

Williams, Florence. "This Is Your Brain on Nature." *National Geographic,* December 8, 2015.

Willis, Paul. *Learning to Labor: How Working Class Kids Get Working Class Jobs*. New York: Columbia University Press, 1977.

Wolf, Eric. *Peasants*. Englewood Cliffs, N.J.: Prentice-Hall, 1966.

Wolf, Maryanne. *Proust and the Squid: The Story and Science of the Reading Brain*. New York: Harper Collins, 2007.

Wolff, Richard. *Democracy at Work: A Cure for Capitalism*. Chicago: Haymarket, 2012.

Wolff, Richard, and David Barsamian. *Occupy the Economy: Challenging Capitalism*. San Francisco: City Lights, 2012.

Woodcock, George, and Ivan Avakumović. *Peter Kropotkin: From Prince to Rebel*. Montreal: Black Rose, 1990.

Wright, Erik Olin. *Class Counts: Comparative Studies in Class Analysis*. New York: Cambridge University Press, 1997.

Yong, Ed. *I Contain Multitudes: The Microbes Within Us and a Grander View of Life*. New York: HarperCollins, 2016.

Younge, Gary. "Trump Fears Terrorists, but More Americans Are Shot Dead by Toddlers." *Guardian*, February 8, 2017.

Zhang, Benjamin. "Ranked: The 20 Best Airlines in the World." *Business Insider*, June 20, 2017.

Zirin, Dave. "Those Nonprofit Packers." *New Yorker*, January 25, 2011.

Index

Page numbers in *italics* refer to illustrations. Pseudonyms have been used for most interview subjects and some place names.

JASON G. STRANGE is an assistant professor of general studies and peace and social justice studies at Berea College, and the chair of the Department of Peace and Social Justice Studies.

The University of Illinois Press
is a founding member of the
Association of University Presses.

———————————————————

Composed in 10.5/13 Aldus LT Std
by Lisa Connery
at the University of Illinois Press
Cover designed by Dustin Hubbart
Cover illustration: A passive solar home.
Photo by Jason G. Strange.
Manufactured by Sheridan Books, Inc.

University of Illinois Press
1325 South Oak Street
Champaign, IL 61820-6903
www.press.uillinois.edu